MW00532915

Women and Indigenous Religions

Women and Indigenous Religions

SYLVIA MARCOS, EDITOR

Women and Religion in the World
Cheryl A. Kirk-Duggan, Lillian Ashcraft-Eason,
and Karen Jo Torjesen, Series Editors

 PRAEGER

AN IMPRINT OF ABC-CLIO, LLC
Santa Barbara, California • Denver, Colorado • Oxford, England

Library of Congress Cataloging-in-Publication Data

Women and indigenous religions / [edited by] Sylvia Marcos.
      p. cm. — (Women and religion in the world)
  Includes bibliographical references (p.   ) and index.
   ISBN 978-0-275-99157-9 (alk. paper) — ISBN 978-0-313-08273-3 (ebook)
1. Women and religion.   2. Women—Religious life.   3. Indigenous peoples—Religion.
I. Marcos, Sylvia.
  BL458.W5634   2010
  200.82'091724—dc22   2010006508

ISBN: 978-0-275-99157-9
EISBN: 978-0-313-08273-3

14 13 12 11 10   1 2 3 4 5

This book is also available on the World Wide Web as an eBook.
Visit www.abc-clio.com for details.

Praeger
An Imprint of ABC-CLIO, LLC

ABC-CLIO, LLC
130 Cremona Drive, P.O. Box 1911
Santa Barbara, California 93116-1911

This book is printed on acid-free paper ∞

Manufactured in the United States of America

Contents

Introduction: Perspectives of Indigenous Religious
Traditions from the Americas, Asia, and Australia   vii

PART I. WOMEN, FAMILY, AND ENVIRONMENT

1. Ngarrindjeri Women's Stories: Kungun and Yunnan   3
   Diane Bell

2. Feminine Rituality and the Spirit of the Water in Peru   21
   Frédérique Apffel-Marglin

PART II. SOCIOECONOMICS, POLITICS, AND AUTHORITY

3. Indigenous Spirituality, Gender, and the Politics
   of Justice: Voices from the First Summit of Indigenous
   Women of the Americas   45
   Sylvia Marcos

4. Authority and Ritual in the Caves of Tepoztlán, Mexico:
   Women Priestesses in Popular Religion   69
   Ana María Salazar Peralta

PART III. BODY, MIND, AND SPIRIT

5. Dressing up the Spirits: Costumes, Cross-Dressing, and
   Incarnation in Korea and Vietnam   93
   Laurel Kendall and Hien Thi Nguyen

6. Women and Sacred Medicines among the Khasis
   in the Highlands of Northeast India   115
   Darilyn Syiem

7. The Not-So-Subtle Body in Dais' Birth Imagery   127
Janet Chawla

Part IV. SEXUALITY, POWER, AND VULNERABILITY

8. Ritual Gendered Relationships: Kinship, Marriage, Mastery, and Machi Modes of Personhood   145
Ana Mariella Bacigalupo

9. Sexuality and Ritual: Indigenous Women Recreating Their Identities in Contemporary Mexico   177
Nuvia Balderrama Vara

Part V. WOMEN, WORLD VIEW, AND RELIGIOUS PRACTICE

10. Drawing the Connections: Mayan Women's Quest for a Gendered Spirituality   195
Morna Macleod

11. Decolonizing our Spirits: Cultural Knowledge and Indigenous Healing   217
Renee Linklater

Suggested Reading   233
About the Editor and Contributors   241
Index   245

Introduction: Perspectives of Indigenous Religious Traditions from the Americas, Asia, and Australia

Sylvia Marcos

The field of indigenous religions is commanding increased attention from scholars of religion in a variety of cultural contexts. It is of great significance that increasingly serious efforts are being made to understand indigenous religions as valid expressions of belief. In fact, such a turning point has become an ethical imperative. For centuries, indigenous religions have indeed been reduced to the "primitive," "primal," "native," and "animistic" (not to mention the terms "heathen," "superstitious," and "irrational"). An initial step toward recognizing other worldviews in their own terms and acknowledging the epistemic specificities of indigenous religious beliefs was reached in the work of some scholars such as Ninian Smart.[1] According to Jonathan Z. Smith[2] such categories as "primitive," "native," or "animistic" are part of the "history" of the study of religions. The first methodological problem in the study of indigenous religions is the construction of the category of religion itself by historians of religion, still under debate among scholars.

Not all religions function in the same way. Indigenous religions are indeed quite complex, vary from society to society, and have been affected considerably by change. Since naming, defining, and conceptualizing these traditions is and will remain problematic, it is better to regard any definition as a working definition.[3] Graham Harvey, in *Indigenous Religions*, makes the same point: "[Even if] it is possible to find considerable common ground that justifies the label [indigenous religions] . . . we will not forget that it remains an imprecise tool, a broad category and a wide generic term."[4]

Other scholars follow David Carrasco's proposal that "when dominated peoples choose and select from materials transmitted to them from the dominant and [also from] the indigenous cultures, their creative work is always incomplete and open-ended. I am emphasizing this point to encourage historians of religions to give *greater value to the creative possibilities of incomplete, open-ended contact zones and narratives*" [emphasis in the original].[5]

It is an interesting fact that the first use of the term "religion" to describe indigenous forms of worship is to be found in the writings of the Spanish friars who came to Mesoamerica. J. Z. Smith cites nobody less than the conquistador Hernán Cortés and the letters he wrote to the emperor in 1520, as well as the learned Jesuit Joseph de Acosta, who, between 1590 and 1604, wrote a *Historia Natural y Moral de las Indias*.[6] Although the conquerors and the friars denounced the natives' practices that they encountered as "pagan," they were nonetheless able to recognize a religion—or religions—in the complex social organizations and highly elaborated rituals that they met in the New World. It remains that, in most contacts with the inhabitants of Asia, Africa, or the Americas, the European colonizers first refused to grant the status of religion to the native's practices and beliefs.

The relevance of studying indigenous religions is heightened by the exciting challenge they offer to prevalent—Western—academic concepts of and approaches to religion. It is important to advance some analyses and propose insights on methodological approaches to multicultural religious categories. Ethnographers and anthropologists can contribute further with what has been called an "engaged and embattled dialogical anthropology."[7]

Indigenous religious traditions are mainly oral traditions. Texts, even if they exist, are not at the core of their belief structure. If we try to systematize the religions that are transmitted through oral traditions with the methods used for systematizing religions rooted in textual traditions, we will distort and misinterpret them. Historical and textual methods presuppose a fixed narrative as a basis for analysis. Oral traditions are fluid, flexible, and malleable. The subtle shifting and changing of words, metaphors, and meanings easily slip through the "text" cast by historical and textual analysis. New methods are needed to capture a tradition that is in continuous change.

Some classical or typical characteristics of oral transmission within indigenous religions are: the use of redundancy as a means for the re-membering of traditions, the metaphoric use of parallelism, the formulaic structure of songs and stories, the power of words and utterances that call reality into being, and the indissociability of myth and history. For a deeper development of how these processes shape indigenous religious traditions, please refer to my book *Taken from the Lips,* in the bibliography.

Narratives and stories need to be kept in their integrity because they are the "method" for transmission. We can find these aforementioned characteristics exemplified in several of the chapters of this book, especially with the stories from Australia, Peru, and Mexico. As an unwritten code of regulations, tradition is the transmission of beliefs, rules, customs, and rituals by word of mouth, and has nonetheless a regulating power that is often more persuasive than written law and texts.

It is especially in religions that depend on oral performance and rituality for their permanence and transmission that women play a prominent role. They preside over rituals, preserve but also re-create traditions.

I consider that to approach respectfully and rigorously indigenous religious traditions in Asia, Australia, and in the Americas, we must propose a shift in methodology for their study. First of all, careful ethnographic methods are crucial for the study of indigenous religions. Some of the particularities of these traditions that will become evident in the analysis of the materials selected to form this volume are the concepts of nature and of the Divine, in which a merging of transcendence and immanence occurs. Another trait common to most indigenous religions is a belief in a bidirectional flow of spiritual forces between the realm of the deities and human existence.

Metaphors are the selected vehicles for conveying hermetic meanings, and beliefs are articulated implicitly rather than explicitly. Besides, the utterance of certain words is considered efficient and powerful in itself.

In the chapters on Shamanism in South Korea and Vietnam as well as on autochthonous religious practices and healing in Meghalaya (Northeast India), we find that the same definition is pertinent. On the other hand, Catholicism—as a colonizing enterprise—has permeated deeply into the indigenous traditions in the Americas. There is hardly any possibility of separating pure indigenous traditions from Catholic rites, images, and symbols. In the Americas, we prefer to delve deeper into those epistemic characteristics of the native religions that set them radically apart from the Christian paradigm. These indigenous traditions or forms of "spirituality," as they are called by the indigenous people themselves, are alive today, and remain discernible, especially through those characteristics aforementioned.[8]

The description of the transformations of indigenous religions that do not occur through conversion, hybridization, or commodification, but through their own internal metamorphoses and migrations, that is, through their own processes, is our main purpose in this volume in the series Women and Religion in the World.

NOTES

1. Smart, Ninian, *Worldviews: Cross-Cultural Explorations of Human Beliefs,* New York: Scribner's, 1983, pp. 2–3.

2. Smith, Jonathan Z., "Religion, Religions, Religious," in Mark C. Taylor (ed), *Critical Terms for Religious Studies,* Chicago, IL: University of Chicago Press, 1998, pp. 269–84.

3. Olupona, J., "Beyond Primitivism: Indigenous Religious Traditions and Modernity," in *Religious Studies News,* Bulletin of the American Academy of Religion, Nov. 1996, p. 16.

4. Harvey, Graham, "Introduction," in Graham Harvey (ed), *Indigenous Religions,* London, New York: Cassell, 2000, p. 7.

5. Carrasco, David, "Jaguar Christians in the Contact Zone," in Jacob Olupona (ed), *Beyond Primitivism, Indigenous Religious Traditions and Modernity,* New York, London: Routledge, 2004, pp. 128–38.

6. J. Z. Smith, op.cit., pp. 269–70.

7. Mannheim, Karl and Tedlock, Dennis, 1995, cited in Kenneth Morrison, "The Cosmos as Intersubjective: Native American Other-Than-Human Persons," in Graham Harvey (ed), op.cit., p. 24.

8. Marcos, Sylvia, *Taken from the Lips: Gender and Eros in Mesoamerican Religions,* Leiden: Brill Academic Publishers, 2006, pp. 109–19.

PART I

Women, Family, and Environment

CHAPTER 1

Ngarrindjeri Women's Stories: Kungun and Yunnan

Diane Bell

There is a whole ritual in weaving, from where we actually start, the centre part of the piece, you're creating loops to weave into, then you move into the circle. You keep going round and round creating the loops and once the children do those stages they're talking, actually having a conversation, just like our Old People. It's sharing time. And that's where our stories are told.

—Aunty Ellen Trevorrow 2007

ALL WE NEED IS IN OUR STORIES

How are stories told? Who gets to tell them? Who gets to listen? What happens when the spoken word is written down and may reach a wider audience, an audience not necessarily bound by the cultural rules of the storyteller? Ngarrindjeri take their stories seriously. Stories sustain and structure the Ngarrindjeri social world; explain the mysterious; provide a secure haven in an otherwise hostile world; bring order to and confer significance on relationships amongst the living; hold hope for future generations; and open up communication with those who have passed on. Stories of cultural life recall the creation of the land, of the seas, rivers, lakes, and lagoons. They tell of the differentiation of species and of languages. They spell out the proper uses of flora and fauna. These are stories of human frailty and triumph, of deception and duty, of rights, responsibilities and obligations, of magical beings, creative heroes and destructive forces. Everything has a story, but not everyone knows every story. Nor does everyone have the right to hear every story, or having heard it, to repeat the words.[1]

In many diverse ways—some highly visible, some almost invisible—Ngarrindjeri women and men care for country. This care is all part of being proud of Ngarrindjeri culture, past, present, and future. Knowing the stories, passing on the stories, and being a storyteller are ways that Ngarrindjeri care for country. This is what Ngarrindjeri *miminar* (women) had to say:

> We have to keep our culture alive.
> We want access to our special places, our lands and our waters.
> We need to be able to protect our places, our *ngatji* [totems], our Old People and restore damaged sites.
> We want respect for our land and our water and we want to pass down knowledge.

Respect is a core Ngarrindjeri value: respect for country, stories, the Elders, the Old People who have passed away. The respect system sets out the proper way of behaving: it specifies who may know what, when, and in what detail. The code is strictly followed and constantly reinforced. Of their growing up, older *miminar* say: "We listened to our Elders. We didn't question them. We wouldn't have dared. We waited to be told." Younger people demonstrate their respect for their Elders in their daily behavior. They defer to their Elders and never address them by a first name without prefacing it with the appropriate kin term. Violating the respect system brings shame. In this way "shame" reinforces the respect system. "Shame is an aspect of your *miwi* [inner spirit] telling you things, letting you know what's right and wrong."

The stories of the Old People guide younger generations; the recounting brings sorrow and joy. The stories told here are ones that are owned; that highlight key aspects of caring for country; that emphasize how *ngatji* (totems), *ruwi* (country), *miwi* (inner spirit), weaving, bush tucker and medicine, care for children and care for country are interwoven in Ngarrindjeri identity. The women are concerned that the stories are kept alive. "If we Elders die, then who passes on our culture, heritage, and stories? We need to look after our Elders with proper health care and housing and we need culturally appropriate ways of recording our stories of the past and present. We need to be telling those stories to young people," Aunty Margaret Dodd insisted. "Telling stories helps me know where I fit into things and who I'm allowed to boss around and who can boss me around," said Aunty Eileen McHughes.

Younger women are aware that there is much to learn of Ngarrindjeri *ruwi* and culture from their Elders. They asked:

What was it like for Mum and Dad when they were growing up?

Tell me the good and the bad.

How are our families related?

What bush tucker did you eat?

Here are three stories, told by Ngarrindjeri Elders, explaining how they care for country.

AUNTY LEILA'S STORY

The story of the funeral for Aunty Leila Rankine (1932–1993) is one that is told over and over. Aunty Maggie Jacobs (1920–2003), defender of her culture, storyteller, and singer extraordinaire, speaks with respect and authority of the day her sister-in-law's ashes were scattered on the Coorong.

While working with the Ngarrindjeri women on the application to secure protection for their sacred places on Kumarangk (Hindmarsh Island) under the *Aboriginal and Torres Strait Islander Heritage Protection Act 1984,* and while they were explaining to me how *ngatji*— variously translated as friend, totem, countryman, protector—bring messages, I asked for more details about *ngatji*. This is how Aunty Maggie told the story to Aunty Veronica Brodie, Leila's younger sister, and me in 1996.

I'll tell you about *ngatji,* that totem. You know it was Leila's wish to come down and have one last look at all the countryside before she died. Well, the pelican is her *ngatji*. We brought Leila from Camp Coorong to Raukkan, and we had a bit of a service for Leila there. And when we went to go off, to leave Raukkan, and we came down to the ferry and, you know that little jetty at the Raukkan, there's always hundreds of pelicans, you know, they're always sitting there. *Una?* [Isn't it?] We started to come across but there were no pelicans. You see them in the water swimming, see them sitting, four of them sitting there. But that day there wasn't a pelican to be seen. We come along to the ferry and just before we pulled into the ferry, one pelican was sitting there, and he just looked in and we had the window open, and he, only one pelican, he just looked in to Leila and he went like this with his wings. [Aunty Maggie folds her arms in and out across her chest.] You know, three or four times, and Veronica said to her sister, "Leila, look, he's saying goodbye to you." And that is exactly what he was doing, you know, he was saying goodbye. And Leila said, "Yeah."

Then, after she died, and we were having a service at Pelican Point, one pelican flew over, flew right over us, the group that was on the bank there. And Lizzie Rigney said, she said, "Oh look," she said, you know, "There's Aunty Leila, or old Granny Koomi [Leila and Veronica's mother]

or somebody like that" because that's their *ngatji*. Anyway, after we finished the service and we got to the ranger boat to come down to Ngarlung
and then all of a sudden there was another pelican. You usually see them
in the dozens you know, but this time there was only one pelican, *Una?*
[Isn't it?], other than the one that flew over us when we started off, there
was one pelican, and when we got in the boat, the ranger boat. The pelican flew low on the water, like this, right in front of us. [Aunty Maggie
swoops with her arms.] It skimmed.

One pelican flew right in front of us, took us right over to where we
were. When we got off at Ngarlung the women were singing the hymn,
"God be with you." I carried Leila's ashes. Veronica and I went to walk up
and we found it a bit hard, you know, because the sand was a bit heavy.
And Tom [Trevorrow] said, "No, it's not the place; it's down further." There
was only a few of us, those that were pretty close to Leila, and we started
off again. And this one pelican, just the one pelican again, he was just
almost touching the water and he flew right up, right to where we buried
Leila, to where we put Leila's ashes, then he disappeared, see. All right,
then that was all right. You know, Roslyn Milera, Leila's care person, she
couldn't get over it. But we know what happens. *Una,* Veronica? That's the
ngatji, you see. Our animals tell us everything.

By coming home to be buried, Aunty Leila made a statement about
whose country it was and who should care for it. Future generations are
being taught how to read the story, the significance of the single pelican leading the way; to remark on the spiritual associations with country; to watch
the behavior of *ngori* (pelican) and other *ngatji*; to see themselves as part of
this world. When the Old People were returned to their country in 2006, and
the pelicans led the way to the reburial site on the Coorong, Aunty Leila's
story was recalled.

The only way Aunty Leila could be buried on her country was to have
her ashes scattered. There are no official cemeteries in the sand dunes of
the Coorong. The site to which her kin were led by the pelican was a favorite
Wilson [Veronica and Leila's father line] lookout, with full oversight of the
spiritual breeding grounds of *ngatji,* and far enough back from the edge so
that erosion would not disturb the place. Uncle George Trevorrow explained:
"She said this is where the meeting of the fresh and salt waters began. So
that's why we brought Aunty Leila here. That was her wish and we carried it
out. Aunty Leila is here."

Aunty Leila Rankine is remembered as a storyteller, poet, speech-maker,
and fighter for the rights of her people. Her poems tell of her feelings for her
country and the importance of her spiritual ties to the area. In her poem,
"The Coorong" she wrote:

Oh the spirit of the long ago
And guardian of the past
As I stand beside your waters
My soul knows peace at last.

—*Leila Rankine (c. 1980)*

With the lack of water in the Murray-Darling system to flush the river, lakes and Coorong, and increased salinity—the Southern Coorong is now saltier than the Dead Sea—the *ngori* [pelican] breeding grounds are shrinking. This *ngatji* is no longer thriving in its own *ruwi*. The stress on the *ngatji* echoes the stressed *ruwi* and stressed people.

AUNTY ELLEN'S STORY

Aunty Ellen Trevorrow is a cultural weaver. "It's a meditation," she says. Her work has been exhibited at home and abroad. The getting of the rushes (*Cyperus gymnocaulos*), the preparation, the working, and the teaching are core activities that connect Aunty Ellen to her *ruwi*. At various times over the last decade Aunty Ellen has told her story of growing up on the river, of moving to the Coorong, and has shared her feelings about the country. She worries about the well-being of the land. She grieves the damage done to her country. "When I went across to Kumarangk [Hindmarsh Island] for the first time," Aunty Ellen explains, "I was with my Elders and I felt it in my tummy, all stirred up, and I cried. And that's when I believed what my Elders were saying about the island being sacred women's business. When I went home that night and told Tom, he said that it was my *miwi* speaking to me, so it's true."

Here is Aunty Ellen Trevorrow's story.

I was born at Raukkan, Point McLeay, and then I was taken with my grandmother to live at *Murrunggung* [Brinkley], that's just this side of Wellington, so we were at the tail end of the River. I grew up there until the age of 11. Everything was so plentiful. It was a beautiful area and it still is today but then my grandmother would take us fishing. We'd fish, up and down. She'd spin. We'd fish for some nice *pondi* [Murray Cods] and row them up to Wellington and sell them. We'd go down to where Lake Alexandrina and the River meet, to where we call "Leeches." My grandmother would fish there and she would also go up and collect the *thukabi ngartheri* [turtle eggs] to take back. We experienced a lot of the Lake there and the River and where the River and Lake meet. That was my lifestyle with my grandmothers, right up to the age of 11. It was a beautiful area to us but when I go back up around the river area now, the river is going in a bad way. The fish, the birds, it's all in a bad way.

Basket weaving was all around me as a child, but it wasn't my mother or grandmother who taught me. They said I needed to have an education, a white education. The welfare department would take children away if they didn't go to school. So I missed out on a lot as a child, but in my late forties my mother started to pass on important cultural information to me because we were running Camp Coorong. I was taught weaving by Aunty Dorrie Kartinyeri [née Gollan], around 1980 at a workshop that was arranged by the South Australian Museum with Steve Hemming and Aunty Dorrie. She was an Elder and I always thanked her for teaching me weaving. I enjoyed weaving, because I reminisced on my life, my childhood and my grandmother, my family and the basket weaving. From then on, I was teaching the basket weaving and my first class was a Year Nine at Meningie. I've been teaching ever since and working toward exhibitions.

The rushes like fresh water and a lot of considerate farmers leave them so we have supplies. I move around and just thin out the good places. I'm finding it very hard down our end close to the Coorong because there was a lot there, but the salt water table is taking over. We need fresh water. Sometimes along the roadside, because it's not on the farmer's property, but just where the water runs off the road, the rushes are growing very nice, and you'll see someone picking them. But I move around in a cycle. I pick and move and let the other lot grow. They grow very quick. Later I can return when the young ones have come up again. You can see where I've been.

My Nanna Brown made baskets to sell or to make trade for some clothing or something for us. After the age of 11, I moved to Bonney Reserve with my mum. I did my schooling at Meningie and straight from school I went into a family with my husband Tom Trevorrow. He was working for a fisherman at the time and we would eat a lot of fish. My life is based from *Murrunggung* to Meningie and that's where I still am today, here with my family, weaving. It's cultural weaving because I use the same rushes that my Old People used—it's the three-pronged type of fresh water rushes. There's a lot of different types of rushes, but this is one that was used because it lasts a long time. Weaving is not just something I do to make money. I don't sell a lot. I work toward exhibitions. I love teaching. I love sharing the basket weaving.

Aunty Ellen Trevorrow, eldest daughter of Mrs. Daisy Rankine, is named after Nanna Ellen Brown, the daughter of Margaret "Pinkie" Mack whose stories and songs were recorded by anthropologists Ronald and Catherine Berndt in the early 1940s (Berndt, C. 1994a; Berndt et al. 1993). Pinkie Mack's mother, Louisa Karpany could remember the early white explorers who came into her country. Aunty Ellen makes these connections for the next generation: "Every time we go past *Murrunggung*, I tell the same story. Luke gets sick of it. *Una?* But if there is a new face in the car, I tell it again. I share with the nieces and nephews. 'This is where Nanna collected rushes,' I tell them. 'It's an honor to pick rushes where Nanna picked them.'"

Ngarrindjeri weaving is visible in the early European record of settlement in South Australia. In 1833, explorer Charles Sturt (1833, p. 155) described the circular mats on which women sat. In the 1840s, artist George French Angas (1844, 1847) drew them. In the 1870s, the Rev. George Taplin (1873, p. 43) wrote of women's weaving and mentioned they had mats to sell. In a 1915 photograph of "Queen" Louisa Karpany, there are baskets of the design now made by her great, great granddaughter Aunty Ellen Trevorrow. In a 1927 newspaper article about Granny Ethel Wympie Watson, we read of how the "gift of a beautifully made basket made in green and red rushes indicated that this primitive [sic] art is still being practiced" and of how the reporter talked with Granny Ethel Wympie Watson about the old times "of corroborees we had both witnessed and of the subsequent lavish suppers provided by my mother. 'Those were the days,' said Ethel furtively wiping away a tear." (E.S.A. 1927). Baskets such as these are on display at Camp Coorong and Ngarrindjeri *miminar* continue to demonstrate their skills and knowledge with their weaving.

Aunty Ellen Trevorrow:

The thing is now, is today, I'm a weaver. The rushes are a part of our culture that the land provides for us. The land is already salting up, and pesticides are ruining our rushes. We have to travel a long way today to collect our freshwater rushes for weaving. To go and collect the rushes where my grandmother collected her rushes, there's nothing there. There isn't any. It's a really big change in our environment and it's very important to look after it. We've got to look after it, especially for our children. If you look at us now, what are we leaving behind for our children? What are we leaving behind?

The River is in a bad way. Now there's talk about a weir down the end, there past Wellington at Pomanda Island. What's our direction? It's very important for us to look after what we've got because we're leaving something behind. Like I said with the rushes, I'm looking all the time; I'm coming right over to Strathalbyn, to collect rushes. That's saying enough just for the rushes, let alone the fish and the birds we caught around our area. There were nice size fishes.

When I first moved to the Coorong, I thought, "Hey, look at this!" The environment was so good because where I had been living, the land was cleared. And then to go down to the Coorong, down at Bonney Reserve, there was lots of everything. There was a big difference, but now there are big changes. What I mean, I moved here when I was 11, I spent my life there on the River, it was beautiful, there was lots of everything. On the Coorong, there was lots of everything, but what do we have now?

What is our direction?

Where are we going?

What are we leaving behind?

There's our young ones, our children and their children.

We're all of an age. I'm talking of ages about what I've experienced. We have to put things right for our young ones. It's most important. I feel really bad when I hear us arguing about one bit of water. What about looking after the whole river?

Uncle Tom and Aunty Ellen Trevorrow bring their knowledge of their country and their concerns to their work at Camp Coorong (Hemming 1993). They say: "We teach our Ngarrindjeri basket-weaving techniques. We tell of our stories relating to the land, waters, trees, plants, birds and animals— people call them our Dreaming stories. They are our way of life, our survival teaching stories."

AUNTY EILEEN'S STORY

Aunty Eileen McHughes had many opportunities for hearing stories from her Elders and learning about the country first hand while living with her extended family at the Three Mile Camp at Tailem Bend and holidaying at the One Mile Camp at Meningie. The eldest of eight siblings, Aunty Eileen traces her family line through her father to Old Kropinyeri who died in 1875; through her mother's father's line to Old Gollan (1817–1877); and through her mother's mother's line to Adeline Sumner (1890–1932), born on the Coorong. These are important Ngarrindjeri lineages. Her mother died when the youngest child was only five and Eileen became the one who told the stories. "This was before television," Eileen's younger sister, Vicki Hartman, says, "Eileen shared with us. We'd sit around *yunnan*. She'd tell us about the *mulyawongk* hole at Tailem Bend and not to swim until the dandelions had died off—otherwise you'd get sick and turn yellow."

Here Aunty Eileen McHughes tells of the *mingka* bird, the messenger of death. It is a story that many Ngarrindjeri know, but Aunty Eileen is one of the few people who has seen the bird.

Down at the One Mile Camp at Meningie, I guess I was about 11 or 12. I remember Aunty Marj Koolmatrie and Bill, Aunty Tingie and Nulla [Richards], Jean Gollan [Neville Gollan's mother], Granny Rosie from

Kingston way, Aunty Pud and Uncle Mervyn, Uncle [George] Walker and his wife, George Johnston and Aunty Thora Lampard [mother of George and Tom Trevorrow] were all there. It was getting towards evening and all us kids we were playing outside, running through the bushes and scaring each other, when we heard this noise. We knew it was a bird, but we didn't know what kind of bird it was. The Old People just gathered us up and popped us inside. They even covered the windows up. It was a *mingka* bird. The next day we knew something had happened because they had begun crying, and it wasn't crying like we cry. It was wailing and it went on all day and half the next.

Then, when I was about 12, it was when we had moved up to Tailem Bend, and I was going down to the River for a swim. I walked past the trees going down and something caught my eye. I felt a little bit scared but I was nosey and wanted to know. I went back and parted the leaves and there was this little bird. The face looked almost human, it had actual, real eyelashes. People really think I'm weird now [in telling the story]. Dad came looking for me. When we walked back up the cliff, I told Dad about the bird and showed him. He said it was a *mingka* bird. Previously, I thought the *mingka* bird was a mopoke, but it's not. It's different. It's a grey bird. The one I saw was about the size of a Murray Magpie. When I close my eyes I can still see it. When you go up to a bird it usually flies away. I know not many people have seen it but I'm sure about what I saw.

They told me when it cries like a baby, a baby dies. When it cries like a woman, a woman dies, and when it is a deeper sort of cry is when a man dies.

We were taking a break from the workshop, sitting outside in the weak winter sun and Aunty Eileen began talking her *ngatji*. The tiger snake is Aunty Eileen and Aunty Vicki's *ngatji* on their father's side. They tell stories of a tiger snake, attracted by the music from the vibrations of an old wind up player, coming up from the river. "It was at the Three Mile Camp. We had a big tarp on the ground and the women were washing and yarning. The snake came right up to the tub." Eileen has many stories about snakes. "Grandfather Mike told us about one of his uncles putting a rag in a snake's mouth, pulling out the fangs and stitching up the lips." Then there was a brown snake that chased one of the grandchildren at Camp Coorong. "Just over there," says Aunty Eileen pointing beyond where we are sitting. And there are stories of putting a snake under your shirt to keep it warm. Aunty Eileen explains: "I was taught the tiger snake was my *ngatji* on my father's side and the huntsman spider is our *ngatji* on our mother's side. We were taught to have respect, not to harm our *ngatji*."

The Ngarrindjeri *miminar*'s stories provide a framework for thinking about the future. This is what they had to say:

Our *ngatji* need protection. We can't just get up and move. This is our place.
    There are special places where we can show our kids Ngarrindjeri *ruwi* and keep our culture alive, teach them about bush tucker and bush medicine. There are places with long uninterrupted histories of Ngarrindjeri care, places where we can fish on the Coorong, the ocean. Places like Bonney Reserve, *Warnung* (Hack's Point), Raukkan. Places where we collect rushes.
    We'd like to visit the Three Mile Camp at Tailem Bend, the One Mile Camp at Meningie and tell younger ones about what life was like there.
    It is good to visit the Granites, the 42 Mile, Boundary Bluff, but transportation can be a problem.

Aunty Eileen recalls being taken on the back of a truck from Tailem Bend to the Lakes to fish. Some would be cooked and eaten there and some would be taken home. The women are sad that today they can't get to some of their places. In some places, developments and subdivisions along the river and lakes have restricted Ngarrindjeri access to favorite camping sites and resources.

We used to go to Leeches for turtle eggs.
    Where can we go to gather bush tucker?
    Where can we gather pelican feathers to make feather flowers?
    Where can we gather swan eggs?
    We want access to our traditional food, to the material resources we need for events like for NAIDOC [National Aboriginal and Islander Day Observance Committee] Day and cultural events.

Aunty Ellen and her granddaughter, Ellie Wilson, talk about times they have been collecting cockles. "It was February this year [2007]. We crossed the Coorong, near Hack's Point, that's the narrowest part, and walked to the ocean side where we got cockles. We returned at Parnka Point and Tom met us in the car. Tanya led the way across the Coorong. She's in front, guiding us across, and Hank is leading the group through the water. I was waiting on the shore with the others. We had a girl who couldn't do the walk and Tanya came back and helped us across." Ellie talks about dancing for cockles to bring them up and demonstrates by swirling. When asked where she learned the cockle dance, Ellie says, "With my family." Aunty Ellen smiles, "They're always alongside us. I've got photos of Luke and Joe doing the same thing."

THE KUMARANGK STORY

The dedication of Ngarrindjeri *miminar* [women] to caring for country came to national attention with the struggle to protect sacred places in the Kumarangk (Hindmarsh Island), Goolwa, and Murray Mouth areas. Telling the story is painful.[2] The legal history is tortuous, the ethnographic facts contested, the media reporting uneven. The reality for the Ngarrindjeri is that their personal lives have become public property and the knowledge of their Old People has been challenged and treated with disrespect. Healing is needed but it will take time and resolve along the lines of the February 13, 2008, Apology to Australia's Indigenous People by Prime Minister Kevin Rudd (2008) to write "this new page in the history of our great continent."

Perhaps, at some future date, it may be possible to write this "new page" without reference to the various legal proceedings that probed the authenticity of the claim by the Ngarrindjeri women who brought two applications under the Aboriginal and Torres Strait Islander Heritage Protection Act, 1984 (Heritage Act). Perhaps not, as some legal narratives have wider circulation than others.[3] Here is an outline of key moments in matters Hindmarsh.[4]

1994: The first Heritage application. The proposal to build a bridge from the mainland at Goolwa across the channel to Kumarangk to service a marina on the island was opposed by a number of groups (environmentalists, local residents, unionists). However, it was the Ngarrindjeri women, who believed that the building of the bridge across those waters would desecrate their sacred places, and the men who were supporting them, who took decisive legal action and fought until they exhausted all legal remedies available to them. A 25-year ban, the maximum possible under the Heritage Act, was placed on development of the site. The ban was short-lived. It was set aside on technical grounds: Robert Tickner, then minister of Aboriginal Affairs had not read all the documents, but rather had respected the restrictions placed on two appendices to the report of Cheryl Saunders (1994). Aunty Doreen Kartinyeri had reluctantly agreed to write down part of the sacred story she knew and have it placed in a sealed envelope labeled "TO BE READ BY WOMEN ONLY."

1995: The Royal Commission. The restriction was not honored for long. The so-called secret envelopes were brandished in federal Parliament in March 1995 by Ian McLachlan, then minister for the environment and member for Barker, a district that takes in Goolwa and Hindmarsh Island (see Fergie 1994, 1996). A group of Ngarrindjeri women spoke out saying they did not know the story about "women's business" (Wilson 1998). The Royal Commission heard from these women but Aunty Dodo, as the late Doreen Kartinyeri is fondly known, refused to appear before the Royal

Commission and in her absence, she and the other applicants were found to have fabricated beliefs to thwart development on Kumarangk (Stevens 1995).

At the time, Aunty Ellen Trevorrow said, "I believe in my Elders and I love them for what they're doing and I'm sorry that all of this has happened this way for my Elders because it's drained us all."

1996: *The second Heritage application*. As soon as the findings of the Royal Commission were known, a second application was lodged but the Mathews Report (1996) was set aside in mid-1996 when the High Court ruled that the appointment by the commonwealth government of Justice Jane Mathews, a federal court judge, as the person to report on the Heritage application was ineffective.[5]

Victor Wilson of Murray Bridge paid tribute to the women in his 1996 song that was first sung at Amelia Park, Goolwa, the site of many protests and the site of the Ngarrindjeri Embassy.

> *My clan woman sister,*
> *We owe so much to you,*
> *You're our mother, our aunty, our grandmother too,*
> *You're a stateswoman, freedom fighter, defender of our*
> *   land.*
> *My clan woman sister, we stand in awe of you.*

1997–1998: *Hindmarsh Island Bridge Act 1997*. This piece of commonwealth legislation said that sacred sites could be protected anywhere but on Hindmarsh Island. The Ngarrindjeri High Court challenge to this legislation brought in the High Court by Doreen Kartinyeri and Neville Gollan failed because the court held that the government could pass laws and the government could amend laws.[6] From this perspective, the new law was not discriminatory, simply an amendment of an existing law. The outcome for the Ngarrindjeri applicants was that Australian law had failed to protect places sacred to women. The Ngarrindjeri applicants had not had their day in court.

1997–2001: *The Compensation Case*.[7] Federal court Judge von Doussa heard from all parties to the dispute: those who knew the story and believed that Kumarangk was sacred to women; those who contested the existence and content of the knowledge; anthropologists, historians, and museum men; a federal minister; and a law professor. There was rigorous cross-examination. The hearings ran from December 1999 to March 2001 and produced thousands of pages of transcript and hundreds of exhibits.

Judge von Doussa found Doreen Kartinyeri to be a credible witness: "I am not prepared to find that her evidence about the circumstances in which she received the restricted women's knowledge from Auntie Rose, and about the knowledge itself, is a lie" (von Doussa 2001, para 310). Aunty Dodo used to say, "What was my intent? Why would I have lied about my culture? No one ever asked me that." It seems that it is easier to construct the women as liars than to come to terms with their passionate commitment to care for their country.

How to explain the finding of fabrication in 1995? In his Reasons for Decision delivered on August 21, 2001, von Doussa (para 12) wrote:

> The evidence received by the Court on this topic is significantly different to that which was before the Royal Commission. Upon the evidence before this Court I am not satisfied that the restricted women's knowledge was fabricated or that it was not part of genuine Aboriginal tradition.

This vindication of the Ngarrindjeri offered some comfort to those who had been labeled liars but came too late to stop the bridge. It was built and opened to traffic on March 4, 2001. As foretold, women became ill.

In the course of the Royal Commission, the term "secret women's business" became the brunt of sexist, racist, and deeply offensive jokes. The Ngarrindjeri fight for their *ruwi*,[8] their country, became an inquiry into women's *ruwar*, their bodies. The relationship between body and land is marked in the language—*ruwar* is the plural of *ruwi*—and is evident in Ngarrindjeri beliefs and practices about their *ngatji* as their friend, country-man and totem. As we heard in Aunty Maggie's story of the scattering of Aunty Leila's ashes, *ngori* (pelican) led the way. Her *ngatji* brings her *ruwar* home to her *ruwi* on the Coorong.

A number of women at the forefront of the struggle have passed away. "I really miss her," Aunty Ellen said at Aunty Veronica's funeral on May 11, 2007. "She was such a support for us all." Aunty Veronica was a respected Elder, a trailblazer in the formation of many community initiatives and organizations. In her book, *My Side of the Bridge,* Aunty Veronica wrote: "It's been a long-drawn-out process and a lot of hurts have been brought out with it, and a healing process needs to start now among the women"(Brodie 2007, p.143). For her, the Old People are still on the island and "the spirits still walk the island. You cannot take away the fact that the Ngarrindjeri women's business did take place on Hindmarsh Island" (p. 144).

Now there is a generation of young women who have come to maturity during and since the struggle to protect Ngarrindjeri places on Kumarangk. Any discussion that takes up the issue of the safety and integrity of women's bodies is likely to evoke bitter memories of the struggle to protect their sacred places on Kumarangk. The stories are being kept alive. The Ngarrindjeri Regional Authority (NRA) is the indigenous governance body with whom all future developers will have to deal. The tragedy of Kumarangk must never be repeated.

A STORY OF PRACTICAL RECONCILIATION

In September 2002, an excavation that was part of the Goolwa wharf redevelopment project desecrated the burial site of a Ngarrindjeri mother and child (Hemming and Trevorrow 2005). Ngarrindjeri knew their Old People had been buried on the site. They had said so during the struggle to protect Kumarangk. The site was listed by the South Australian Department of Aboriginal Affairs and Reconciliation. But the approach of members of the Alexandrina Council had been that the site was part of the colonial history of the river. Goolwa was a river port to be redeveloped: this was where the wooden boats festival was celebrated. In their view, Ngarrindjeri interests had been washed away. It seemed that little had changed since the bridge— only meters away from the redevelopment—had been built. The Ngarrindjeri could have taken legal action against the Council. Instead, after a month of intense negotiations, they chose to lead by example; to bring members of the Alexandrina Council into their world of caring for country, stories, and Old People by negotiating an agreement.

The Kungun Ngarrindjeri Yunnan (Listen to Ngarrindjeri Talking) agreement signed on October 8, 2002, by the Alexandrina Council and the Ngarrindjeri was a step toward rebuilding trust. In the letter of apology the Alexandrina Council wrote:

> To the Ngarrindjeri people, the traditional owners of the land and waters within the region, the Alexandrina Council expresses sorrow and sincere regret for the suffering and injustice that you have experienced since colonization and we share with you our feelings of shame and sorrow at the mistreatment your people have suffered . . .
>
> We are shamed to acknowledge that there is still racism within our communities. We accept that our words must match our actions and we pledge to you that we will work to remove racism and ignorance.
>
> (Bell 2008: 22)

By saying sorry for the wrong that was done, acknowledging the Ngarrindjeri as the traditional owners of the land and showing respect for their culture, the Alexandrina Council has engaged in what the Ngarrindjeri leadership terms an act of "practical reconciliation." But the story does not end there. The Old People whose grave had been desecrated had to be laid to rest according to Ngarrindjeri law. On October 17, 2002, with proper ceremony and support of the local council and state government, the Ngarrindjeri reburied the woman and child. In so doing, Ngarrindjeri Old People became part of the renegotiated landscape of a major rural town (Hemming and Trevorrow 2005, p. 255).

FUTURE STORIES

Ngarrindjeri *miminar's* stories offer insights concerning their priorities and cautions regarding how best to proceed. They need access to their places to gather materials, to be at peace in the home of their forebears, to be able to teach their children and grannies (grandchildren). They need to be able to share the stories of their places under conditions of their own making. They have a contribution to make on issues such as the increased salinity of the waterways and its impact on their *ngatji*, many of which are now endangered or displaced. "It is," as Aunty Ellen teaches the next generation, "an honor to pick rushes where Nanna picked them." "We were," Aunty Eileen emphasizes, "taught to have respect, not to harm our *ngatji*."

NOTES

I gratefully acknowledge the permission of the Ngarrindjeri storytellers to republish their words which first appeared in *Listen to Ngarrindjeri Women Speaking* (Spinifex Press, 2008). This book was based on four workshops I conducted with Ngarrindjeri women at Camp Coorong (South Australia) between June and October 2007 where issues of "ownership" of stories and protocols regarding who may tell what stories and under what conditions were negotiated. Thanks to Spinifex Press, Adelaide, Australia, for permission to publish materials from *Listen to Ngarrindjeri Women Speaking*, Diane Bell (ed.), 2008.

1. See Bell 1998, p. 45. The poetics and politics of Ngarrindjeri storytelling have been explored at some length, particularly in the context of Kumarangk (Hindmarsh Island), but also with reference to exhibits and publications regarding Ngarrindjeri culture (see Bell 2001; Clarke 1995, 1996; Department of Education 1990; Hemming et al. 1989; Mattingley and Hampton 1988; Pearson 1998; Simons 2003).

2. The case pitted women who claimed they did not know the story of the sacred places against those who knew the story (Brodie 2007; Wilson 1998). The authenticity of the story was further contested in the media (Brunton 1999; Kenny 1996; Simons 2003), by anthropologists (Bell 1998, 2001, 2008; Fergie 1994, 1996; Hemming 1996; von Doussa 2001), in the courts (Mead 1995; Stevens 1995; von Doussa 2001), parliament (Saunders 1994; Mathews 1996), and the museum (von Doussa 2001).

3. The "Lies. Lies. Lies." headline of the Adelaide *Advertiser* of December 22, 1995, has wide currency. Reporting of the von Doussa decision was more muted.

4. See Fergie 1994, 1996; Saunders 1994 re the first Heritage application; Hemming 1996; Mead 1995; Stevens 1995 re the Royal Commission; Bell 1998; Simons 2003 re the second Heritage application.

5. *Dorothy Anne Wilson and Ors v. Minister for Aboriginal Affairs,* High Court of Australia, September 6, 1996, challenged the ability of a Chapter III judge to report to the federal minister under the Heritage Act. It was not that the court thought Justice Mathews was not impartial but that there could be an appearance that the judge, appointed by the minister, would be acting as his agent.

6. *Kartinyeri v. Commonwealth* ('*Hindmarsh Island Bridge* case') (1998) 195 CLR 337.

7. The Chapmans sued the Commonwealth and others for compensation for delays in building the bridge. Their appeal against the decision of 2001 was dropped in 2002. Judge von Doussa's findings stand uncontested. See *Thomas Lincoln Chapman and Ors v. Luminis Pty Ltd,* 088 127 085 and Ors, Federal Court of Australia, No. SG 33 OF 1997.

8. Also spelled *ruwe*; *ngatji* also spelled *ngartji*.

REFERENCES

Angas, George French. (1844). *Original Sketches for South Australia.* Illustrated. London: T. McLean.

Angas, George French. (1847). *Savage Life and Scenes in Australia and New Zealand: Being an Artist's Impression of Countries and People at the Antipodes.* London: Smith Elder and Co.

Bell, Diane. (1998). *Ngarrindjerri Wurruwarrin: A World That Is, Was, and Will Be.* Melbourne: Spinifex Press.

Bell, Diane. (2001). The Word of a Woman: Ngarrindjeri Stories and a Bridge to Hindmarsh Island. In Peggy Brock (Ed.), *Words and Silences: Aboriginal Women, Politics and Land* (pp. 117–138). Sydney: Allen and Unwin.

Bell, Diane. (2007). For Aborigines? Rights and reality. In Neil Gillespie (Ed.), *Reflections: 40 Years on From the 1967 Referendum* (pp. 97–107). Adelaide: Aboriginal Legal Rights Movement.

Bell, Diane. (Ed.) (2008). *Listen to Ngarrindjeri Women Speaking: Kungun Ngarrindjeri Miminar Yunnan.* Melbourne: Spinifex Press.

Berndt, Catherine H. (1994). Pinkie Mack. In David Horton (Ed.), *The Encyclopaedia of Aboriginal Australia: Aboriginal and Torres Strait Islander History, Society and Culture* (pp. 639–640). Canberra: Aboriginal Studies Press.

Berndt, Ronald M., and Catherine H. Berndt with John Stanton. (1993). *A World That Was: The Yaraldi of the Murray River and the Lakes, South Australia.* Melbourne: Melbourne University Press at the Miegunyah Press.

Brodie, Veronica. (2007). *My Side of the Bridge: The Life Story of Veronica Brodie as Told to Mary-Anne Gale.* Kent Town, South Australia: Wakefield Press.

Brunton, Ron. (1999). Hindmarsh Island and the Hoaxing of Australian Anthropology. *Quadrant*, May, pp. 11–17.

Clarke, Philip. (1995). Myth as History? The *Ngurunderi* Dreaming of the Lower Murray, South Australia. *Records of the South Australian Museum,* 28 (2) pp. 143–156.

Clarke, Philip. (1996). Response to Secret Women's Business: The Hindmarsh Island Affair. *Journal of Australian Studies,* 50/51, pp. 141–149.

Department of Education. (1990). The Ngarrindjeri People: Aboriginal People of the River Murray, Lakes and Coorong. *Aboriginal Studies,* 8–12. Adelaide: Department of Education.

E.S.A. (1927). A Dusky Ruler. *Register,* May 11.

Fergie, Deane. (1994). *To All the Mothers That Were, to All the Mothers That Are, to All the Mothers That Will Be: An Anthropological Assessment of the Threat of Injury and Desecration to Aboriginal Tradition by the Proposed Hindmarsh Island Bridge Construction. A Report to the Aboriginal Legal Rights Movement Inc. in Relation to Section 10 of the Aboriginal and Torres Strait Islander Heritage Protection Act 1984.*

Fergie, Deane. (1996). Secret Envelopes and Inferential Tautologies. *Journal of Australian Studies,* 48, pp. 13–24.

Hemming, Steven J. (1993). Camp Coorong: Combining Race Relations and Cultural Education. *Social Alternatives,* 12 (11) pp. 37–40.

Hemming, Steven J. (1996). Inventing Ethnography. In Richard Nile and Lyndall Ryan (Eds.), *Secret Women's Business: The Hindmarsh Affair,* special issue, *Journal of Australian Studies,* 48, pp. 25–39. St Lucia, UQP.

Hemming, Steven J. (1997). Not the Slightest Shred of Evidence: A Reply to Philip Clarke's Response to Secret Women's Business. *Journal of Australian Studies,* 5 (3) pp. 130–145.

Hemming, Steven J. and Philip G. Jones with Philip A. Clarke. (1989). *Ngurunderi: An Aboriginal Dreaming.* Adelaide: South Australian Museum.

Hemming, Stephen J., and Tom Trevorrow. (2005). *Kungun Ngarrindjeri Yunnan*: Archaeology, Colonialism and Re-claiming the Future. In Claire Smith and H. Martin Wobst (Eds.), *Indigenous Archaeologies: Decolonising Theory and Practice Routledge,* pp. 243–261. New York: Routledge.

Kenny, Chris. (1996). *Women's Business.* Potts Point, NSW: Duffy and Snellgrove.

Mathews, Jane. (1996). *Commonwealth Hindmarsh Island Report Pursuant to Section 10 (4) of the Aboriginal and Torres Strait Islander Heritage Protection Act 1984.* Canberra: Australian Government Printer.

Mattingley, Christobel, and Ken Hampton. (Eds.) (1988). *Survival in Our Own Land: Aboriginal Experiences in South Australia since 1836, Told by Nungas and Others.* Adelaide: Wakefield Press.

Mead, Greg. (1995). *A Royal Omission.* South Australia: the author.

Pearson, Christopher. (1998). A Twist in the Tale: Yarns and Symbols. *Australian Financial Review,* August 17.

Rankine, Leila. (c.1980). *Poems*. Adelaide: self-published.

Rudd, Kevin. (2008). Apology to Australia's Indigenous Peoples. Votes and Proceedings. *Hansard*. p. 1. House of Representatives. Commonwealth of Australia, Wednesday, February 13.

Saunders, Cheryl. (1994). *Report to the Minister for Aboriginal and Torres Strait Islander Affairs on the Significant Aboriginal Area in the Vicinity of Goolwa and Hindmarsh (Kumarangk) Island*. Adelaide: South Australian Government Printer.

Simons, Margaret. (2003). *The Meeting of the Waters: The Hindmarsh Island Affair*. Sydney: Hachette.

Stevens, Iris. (1995). *Report of the Hindmarsh Island Bridge Royal Commission*. Adelaide: South Australian Government Printer.

Sturt, Charles. (1833). *Two Expeditions into the Interior of Southern Australia*, 2 vols. London: Smith, Elder and Co.

Taplin, George. (1873). The Narrinyeri. Reprinted in J. D. Woods (Ed.), *The Native Tribes of South Australia* (pp. 1–156). Adelaide: E. S. Wigg & Son.

Trevorrow, Ellen. (2007). Workshop at Camp Coorong, South Australia.

von Doussa, John. (2001). Reasons for Decision. Thomas Lincoln Chapman and Ors v Luminis Pty Ltd, 088 127 085 and ors, Federal Court of Australian, No. SG 33 OF 1997.

Wilson, Dulcie. (1998). *The Cost of Crossing Bridges*. Mitcham, Victoria: Small Poppy Publishing.

CHAPTER 2

Feminine Rituality and the Spirit of the Water in Peru

Frédérique Apffel-Marglin

For Marcela Machaca, a native Andean woman from the community of Quispillacta in the high Andes and an agronomist (one who studies soil management, land cultivation, and crop production), the festival of Yarqa Aspiy in her community is carried out together with the water and the other beings of the other-than-human world. For her and others in her community water is not a "natural resource"; it is alive, a being that sings and speaks, a being whose birthday is celebrated. Water is one of many beings in her world. Although university instruction taught her to identify water as a natural resource, she refused this knowledge.

Natural resources did not always exist. The idea of nature as inert and there for the taking, a prerequisite for the emergence of the specific notion of natural resources, came into being at more or less the same time as modernity did, in 16th- and 17th-century Europe. This event was a momentous one; momentous because it became a worldwide phenomenon, diffused through modern education. The products of modernity may have penetrated into the most remote corners of the world, but its adherents, its believers, are overwhelmingly those who have received a modern education. The more ardent the belief, the higher the degree received, in general. Yet, some two-thirds of the world population is comprised of indigenous, peasant, and other traditional peoples whose cosmovisions are not that of modernity, and for whom the phrase "natural resources" is alien.[1] Among this social majority, the other-than-human world has not died. It has not become an inert material mechanism, lying around for our exclusive use, but continues to be alive with spirits, powers, deities of all kinds with whom people reciprocate and converse, spirits and deities with whom one must share the bounties of this world.

Assuming that such a consciousness is a magical or more simply, a metaphorical mode of thought representing a prescientific archaic stage in human evolution is a perspective taken from within the paradigm of modernity. It is one that shares modernity's basic assumptions about the nature of reality.

This chapter approaches the issue of humans speaking with the water from a standpoint that does not take the assumptions made by modernity about the world for granted. This is no simple enterprise since I am a thorough product of modern education. Being an anthropologist does not ensure my ability to step outside its basic framework. Anthropologists have commonly interpreted natives' beliefs in spirits as a metaphorical form of thought. My approach begins by listening to the voice of an Andean native woman from the indigenous community of Quispillacta in the central Peruvian Andes, Marcela Machaca.[2] Her voice is highly unusual. She is the first generation in her family and community, to go to university. What is unusual here is that her long years of study failed to convert her to the modernist worldview. This was not due to her inability to comprehend her course of study; quite to the contrary, since she was at the top of her class.

Listening to her voice is intended to make us transition into the world of her community by making us aware of our (that is our modern) taken-for-granted assumptions. Her life story will allow us to empathize and hopefully understand why she ultimately rejected what was taught to her. By the end of her story, we may be ready to let her be our guide in the second part of the essay. The second part is a description of the festival of the water in her community based mostly on Marcela Machaca's and her siblings' own published writings. In this part we are plunged in the very nonmodern world of the inhabitants of the high Andean community of Quispillacta. Here again we are invited to not stand on the sidelines as detached observers but rather to enter vicariously into the world of Yarqa Aspiy, the festival of the water in Quispillacta, feel its pulse, hear its songs.

The third part of the chapter is in my own voice. There I recapture how natural resources came into being. I recognize how and why we forgot that natural resources were invented at a certain time and place. I explore why the spirits disappeared, why they died. It is a complicated story that I briefly summarize. Remembering is the first step we need to take to realize that the world bequeathed to us by the advent of the scientific revolution is not the world as it really is but rather the world as it was invented for certain purposes by certain people. I am not thereby inviting us on a road to discover what the world really is but rather to make us aware that such a journey is impossible. Remembering is the first step in realizing that there are choices that kill the spirits and with them the waters, soils, animal and plant species, the air, our souls, among others, and that there are choices that nurture these instead.

With this effort, hopefully we will once again learn to nurture the spirits of the water, the soil, the minerals, the air, the plants, the animals, and everything that accompanies us in this world. We need to reverse the dying of the waters, of the soils, of the species, of the air, of everything, for the sake of the world, for the sake of our souls.

A NATIVE ANDEAN WOMAN'S TRAVAILS WITH MODERN EDUCATION

In 1975, when I was a little girl and had finished elementary school, my parents and all their children migrated to the city of Ayacucho. We were five related families of one ayllu [this is a local kin group that also comprises all the other local non-human beings, houses and other human-made things] with 10 children entering high school in the city. This was a time when development had come to our community in a big way. Various development projects, originating from the Agrarian Faculty of the University of Ayacucho through its extension programs as well as from a Swiss development project (COTESU) reached Quispillacta in the 1960 and 1970s. They brought chemical fertilizers, pesticides, improved pasture land, and so on. These professionals of agronomy trained many community members to become promoters of scientific agriculture in our community. My father became one of these promoters. My father gave my own chacra [cultivated field] to be used as an experimental plot by the agronomists. I remember clearly as a child that I did not plant in it what we normally ate such as corn, beans, and Andean root crops. Rather we used urea, a lot of agrochemicals and we planted hybrid seeds in the chacra. In our pastures where we fertilized our native grass species with chemicals, the grass grew tremendously tall. Now, conversing with my father, we tell each other what a mad venture this all was.

What struck me then was the attitude of the professionals who came to teach these technologies and these practices, which were said to have universal validity. These professionals possessed the solutions and the families of Quispillacta, who were pressured to abandon their own ways of doing things, had to adopt the professionals solutions. One of the professional agronomists in charge of a project later became the dean of the Agrarian Faculty where I studied and where I defended my thesis. All the professionals were arrogant and aloof; they knew it all and bossed the promoters around telling them what to do with the other Quispillactinos. These memories of my father as an agricultural promoter in projects of rural development have impacted me deeply and stayed with me.

In those years, my father used to tell us children: "you have to study to become agronomists. You must go to the University and become professional agronomists." However, I think that what my father had in mind was not for us to acquire the arrogant attitude of professional agronomists. Rather, he wanted us to learn how to improve our potatoes, our crops. He wanted us to help our community, not become arrogant professionals, not look down on the native people. Later, I better understood his motives for having his children become professional agronomists. It was because one is the target of a great deal of scorn. There is a great deal of aggression aimed at native life, and for the migrants to the city, such as we were, the aggression is very strong and one way to not be victimized was to become a professional agronomist.

So I began my university studies in a technical institute that trained professionals in agronomy and animal husbandry. I had set for myself the clear goal of finding ways of somehow supporting our community. I spent five years in this institute but when I graduated I had not found what I was looking for, namely a way of relating to our own way of life, the life of the chacra. I only learned technical questions, formulas such as how much fertilizer is needed, how many seeds, how many inputs, and the like. Therefore, I left the Institute disappointed. Then I was admitted to the Agrarian Faculty at the University in Ayacucho. My sister Magdalena and I entered the Faculty of Agronomy at the same time. We got our degrees after five years of study. I graduated first in my class and got a prize for being the best student. I mention this, so that my subsequent choices are not viewed as stemming from a lack of ability in agronomy. In spite of this, I did not succeed in satisfying what I was looking for in the University. I was not able to find answers to the questions I had put to myself when I entered the University . . .

As a member of my community [comunera] I have my own experience of living in the community, and the knowledge I lived with is for me extremely valid and important. For example, let us take the case of a sign, a plant whose state tells me that in that year, there will be a lot of rain and this knowledge will enable me to have good crops. One does not find reference to this type of sign in any course; nowhere in the University do they teach that such a sign-plant can teach you how to cultivate crops. Quite the contrary, they teach you to see things separately: the plants separately, the soil separately—not even the whole plant but parts of plants, segmented, very separate. Whereas, in the community, plants are sacred, and we focus on a more holistic approach.

During the first two years of University study, I learned basic science, such as the carbon cycle, photosynthesis and the like. It was not possible to talk about the native communities' practices, such as the signs. Nowhere was Andean agriculture or the native farmers mentioned; rather the talk was of a lovely agriculture system with tractors, pesticides, and about when a plant does not grow properly one has to use hormones, accelerators, inhibitors, all these things. Whenever one wants to, one can accelerate the harvest, just when one desires it, wills it.

After graduating, the work of writing a thesis and its subject matter remained. My sister and I decided to reject all the research methodologies we were taught and to do it in our own way, even including Quechua words. This would have nothing to do with the technical type of work required of an agronomist. When we presented our proposed thesis project, they wanted us to transfer into the department of anthropology & sociology. Our professors were very disappointed. Because we had been such good students, they expected us to become efficient agents of development. They used to point us out as examples for other students. After that, they never again used us as examples to other students. However, since we had been such exemplary students, our proposal was finally accepted. They were curious to see how we would carry out the project . . .

For the thesis work, my sister and I went back to our community to collect knowledge, testimonies in Quechua as well as in Spanish. I did my work based on Quispillactinos' testimonies. The time for the thesis defense arrived. There was a great deal of anticipation: how would we defend an indefensible thing, without graphs, statistics, without a scientific method? Defending something that existed, that was alive, I was not afraid. I defended with a great deal of cheek [frescura], in the Andean manner. The dean of the Faculty of Agronomy was there and so was Professor Valladolid. Fortunately, by the time I finished the thesis, several of the faculty had attended the PRATEC course on Andean Culture and Agriculture and the topic was being discussed. The faculty was divided between a pro-Andean agriculture faction (led by Prof. Julio Valladolid) and a pro-science faction. At the end, the dean asked why I distanced myself from my peers, from my professors who loved me so much, and became something that was no longer an example for others at the University. He said: "you have shown the knowledge of your community; we know that you have been a brilliant student; of what use is this going to be to you?" What I understood him to say to me is the following: how will the knowledge imparted to you at the University serve you to carry out cultural affirmation? Since the necessity for cultural affirmation was the conclusion of my thesis. I answered him in what I thought was a diplomatic fashion, namely that the knowledge of the University would not be of use in my work of cultural affirmation. He took my answer as a total rejection. With this "no" my professors concluded that all that they had taught me was thrown overboard. One of my professors got very angry. He said that this type of student should no longer be admitted in the University and that we did not deserve the degree. This created great difficulties when our younger brother Gualberto wanted to start his studies there. We had to fight for him. This professor had done his studies in the US and said "how is it possible

*that at the end of the twentieth century you talk about native knowledge
and about ritual?" He wanted to take away my degree. He said that I was
ruining the reputation of the professional agronomists of Ayacucho, who
were highly valued in the professional market and putting in jeopardy their
market value. How could I throw away everything the faculty of agronomy
taught? I understood clearly that the training at the university is to make us
into efficient agents of development.*

*We had returned to our community after 1987, during the period of vio-
lence [due to Shining Path and the Army] and were carrying out work for our
thesis. From the projects of development that started in the 1960s, nothing
remained. Many irrigation channels, reservoirs and other things are left as
witnesses to these projects of development. My sister Magdalena and I also
tried then to find out why there were so many development efforts and why
they did not work. We began working with our own relatives. One of the first
things we did was to document how these development efforts in the community had eroded the soils, the seeds, life in general, and the whole of the
culture. A central activity of ours became acting for the return of traditional
seeds, the return to the community's own wisdom, and centrally, a return to
the practice of rituals. Eventually we and our other siblings as well as some
friends from Quispillacta created the non governmental organization Asociacion Bartolome Aripaylla (ABA). All of us in ABA have done the PRATEC
course. Magdalena and I were the first; the others followed. We carry out this
work now within ABA.*

The narrative illustrates that science—in this case the science of
agronomy—and its various applications in the form of rural development
schemes, scorns Andean ritual agriculture for being backward, obsolete,
and inefficacious. None of the 24 faculties of agronomy in Peruvian universities teach Andean agriculture. A remarkable fact since the Andes are one
of a handful of world centers where agriculture first emerged and is recognized as one of the regions of the world with the highest level of biodiversity
in cultivars (Kloppenburg 1988). Marcela, her sister Magdalena, and her
brother Gualberto's refusal to entertain the suggestion to shift into departments of social sciences such as anthropology or sociology is emphatic.
They are agriculturalists, and agriculture—along with animal husbandry
and herding—are the principal activities of native Andeans. Their hope in
entering the university was not only to escape the scorn meted out by professionals and other university-educated folks toward the peasantry but also
to acquire a knowledge they could use to make improvements in agriculture
and animal husbandry in their communities. This latter goal could not be
attained in departments of anthropology or sociology.

Why the insistence on the part of ABA on rituals? Much of the activity of ABA consists in revitalizing collective rituals in Quispillacta. Are we

here dealing with a version of the well-known centuries old tension, if not contradiction, between religion and science inaugurated by Galileo's trial? Marcela Machaca in the foregoing words has spoken eloquently of the close connection between development efforts and science, of development as applied science. She has also repeatedly associated native wisdom and knowledge with ritual activities. It may be useful, before delving in greater depth into the specifics of rituals in Quispillacta, to situate native rituals vis-à-vis established religions in the Andean context. Marcela's brother, Gualberto Machaca Mendieta, points out that since 1916 there has been a law in Peru protecting freedom of religion. However, he maintains that the law is a dead letter and that all the official religions delegitimize Andean spiritual practices (G. Machaca 1998, p. 75)

Andean spirituality has been the object of tenacious persecution, first on the part of the Catholic religion during the colonial period and in the last several decades on the part of Evangelical sects, which have intensified the persecution. By their exclusionist attitude, Evangelical sects label Andean spirituality "mundane" and call the Andean deities "evil spirits" and the like.

Thus, various forms of Christianity have in the past, and some continue, to persecute Andean spirituality. In particular, many Christians view the belief in the existence of spirits or deities that inhabit the world as blasphemous. Below, we will discuss the origins and implications of the similarity of attitudes toward Andean ritual agriculture on the part of both developmentalists with their reliance on science and various forms of Christianity.

What characterizes Andean practices is that all the inhabitants of the Pacha—and this includes the rocks, the waters, the sun, the moon, the stars as well as the plants, the animals and the people—are alive and communicate or converse with the human inhabitants through a multiplicity of signs. Marcela mentioned a plant-sign; signs can also be animals—their cry, the number of eggs or offspring in a given season—the brilliance or lack thereof of the stars, the shape and color of the clouds, the quality of the winds, and so forth. During certain moments of the agricultural cycle seeds, crops, flowers, the soil, irrigation canals, water sources, and the like are the recipients of offerings as well as the protecting mountain deities (Apus).

One of the development schemes in Quispillacta had to do with improving irrigation in the lower parts where every comunero has an irrigated chacra. Many of the ancient earthen canals were lined with cement. The result is that the water does not reach as far as it used to. In the words of Modesto Cisnero of Quispillacta:

Before, our grandparents had only earthen irrigation channels, but the water reached to the place called Puchquyaku, but now that these are lined with cement the water does not even reach the Soqa chapel, that is

only half as far; it does not even reach far enough for the animals to drink;
instead of more water, there is less.

Before it was a fiesta to bring the water, drinking lots of good chicha
[fermented corn water] at the spring and burying the offering there. Like
that, the water traveled happily and quickly. Now we are ashamed of doing
these things. Pressured by the Evangelical religion, now they drink colored
water instead of chicha, and we clean the channels without enthusiasm;
so with what strength will the water travel? The water too will be lazy. We
have forgotten the Wamanis [sacred ones]; we no longer bring offerings to
the water, neither to the frost or the hail. Because of that they will have
become wild just like when we do not take care of our animals they get
emaciated and die; just like that the Wamanis are lost and forgotten, and
the frost and the hail also. (quoted in Gualberto Machaca 1998, p. 86)

Besides lining the existing irrigation channels with cement, a development project also created a small reservoir and cement-lined channels leading from and to it in a certain location of the irrigated part of the community.
I visited the community with Magdalena and Lorenzo Nuñez of ABA in May
of 1999. The reservoir had only recently been cleared of an overgrowth of
water plants in it. It had not yet been used by anyone, nor had the channels
leading into and from it. Instead, the Quispillactinos had dug earthen channels that bypassed the reservoir. The official (as opposed to the traditional)
leadership of the community wants to convince everyone to use the reservoir
and the new canals. They fear that a rejection of this small project might
close the door to further projects. ABA's response has been to support the
enactment of the traditional festival of Yarqa Aspiy, the annual cleaning of
the irrigation channels. This festival has been enacted in full force in the
last few years. It is a major communal event, mobilizing all 1,200 families
(some 5,000 persons) in Quispillacta. Marcela and Magdalena told me that
now everyone participates, including the official leadership as well as those
belonging to Evangelical sects. The only concession the former make to their
religious affiliation is that instead of drinking chicha they drink sodas.

In ABA's office in Ayacucho, I asked Marcela why ABA promotes rituals.
This is what she told me:

*Everything that has to do with agriculture relates to the feelings of the people.
The most important thing is those feelings. Agriculture deteriorates because
this relationship of affinity with nature is being broken; with the soil, the
trees, the water, a relationship of exploitation begins to emerge. This is beginning to happen in Quispillacta. It has its origin in modern agricultural
practices, which separate productive activity from social activity. It begins in
the 40s and 50s but really comes in force in the 60s. What is most important
is to recover those feelings. The evangelicals openly promote individualism.*

The festivals are communal and create solidarity and reciprocity. The evangelicals say that these are mundane festivals; any rituals that have to do with nature they call mundane. They call the Apus and other sacred being demons and evil spirits. Evangelical religion is a more radical form of Catholicism; they are fundamentalists. Evangelism entered in Quispillacta between the 60s and 70s with members of the Swiss development project COTESU that comes in through the Peruvian government. And, with them also came bilingual programs Spanish/Quechua as an evangelizing project. They captured the allegiance of some leaders. Those who promulgated evangelism and those who promulgated development were the same persons. It created a great deal of conflict in the community and it has caused great damage to the communal rituals.

The conflict became worse in the 80's with the dirty war which began on May 18 1980, Sendero Luminoso or Shining Path burnt the electoral urns in Chuschi (the district head and on the other side of the stream from the town of Quispillacta; this event was the first act of violence in Peru on the part of Shining Path). There was an enormous amount of violence on the part of Sendero and the military. Both sides used the community as a shield. Sendero gathered all the maestros [shamans] of the community, some eight of them, and shot them dead. Only one survived, pretending to be dead. This one is my uncle. Sendero went to get them in their houses and told them to come and bring along their ritual bundles. They gathered all the people in the main square to force them to witness the shooting. Before shooting them, they told their victims to throw their ritual bundles in the fire. My uncle's bundle did not burn. For everybody, the question of ritual is difficult to eliminate and a major danger. It poses a serious obstacle to their actions. The function of the healers (shamans) is to harmonize the health of the community with that of nature. It goes much further than simply the health of an individual.

Yarqa Aspiy: Quispillactinos Converse with the Spirit of the Water

Yarqa Aspiy takes place on September 7, inaugurating the planting season.[3] All the families of the territory of Quispillacta gather in the town the day before. Very early the morning of the seventh, around 5 AM, all the traditional authorities—husband-wife pairs—as well as the elected official authorities gather in the municipal building and there they talk about the water, how the water nurtures all the people, and how the people in return must nurture the water. This mutual nurturance between the people and the water is enacted on a grand scale during the festival. Cleaning the irrigation channels is nurturing (*criar*) the water by enabling it to travel. When the water is able to travel, it is then able to reach all the community's fields and thus make the crops grow and nurture the community. The men do the arduous work of cleaning the channels and the women cook the food that enables the men to work. Some of the women become the running water, running fast and freely at one point. At the end, all the young men and women together—in pairs—dance along the channels, spiraling like water eddies. Women sing the "passion of the water," becoming its voice. Some folks are in charge of making everyone happy, the water as well as the *runas* (the humans), by performing funny skits. Without laughter, the water and the people would become sad and tired; the water would not reach the fields and nurturance would not happen. After the cleaning is done, everyone feasts.

THE FESTIVAL OF YARQA ASPIY

During the month of September, irrigation water becomes the most beloved, pampered being as well as the central deity . . . For certain anthropologists, the festival of Yarqa Aspiy is . . . "a cultural presence that has not yet vanished but is in a slow process of disappearance" (Condori, 1987). However, this is not true. Yarqa Aspiy is more than a festive communal activity, it is all of Andean life in a dense form, making visible the relationships between all the members of the Andean world. Humans, water, seeds, stars, etc. all participate in the festival in order to fully re-initiate life and make it bloom after a period of rest. (Marcela Machaca 1998, 61)

The previous three months, beginning in June—the very cold winter months in the High Andes—is the period of almost no agricultural activities. The cattle have been brought down from the highest puna region to the lower quechua region and people dedicate themselves to bartering products from one ecological level to another, to building and fixing their houses, and to weddings. Yarqa Aspiy marks the beginning of large-scale agricultural activity. This is how Marcela has written about this festival:

Humans do *ayni* with the water: humans prepare the path of the water and the water makes it possible to plant. The water is both a living being and one who gives life (Grillo, 1991) and because of that it requires care and love; one of this mode of caring or nurturing is to prepare the path so that it may travel without complaints and help to plant the corn. Don Julian Nunez, from the barrio of Puncupata, says the following about the festival: "Yarqa Aspiy is work, getting tired in the cleaning of the channels and above all it is joy" . . . We can then define Yarqa Aspiy as the festival of work and joy; joy being the abundance of food served by the Alvaceres/Alvaceras, Hatun Alcalde/Alcaleza and the Regidores/Regidoras.

Yarqa Aspiy is first of all the cleaning of the irrigation channels, the ones that are very old and have always been there; they are from the grandparents of our grandparents, as Don Alfonso Galindo of the barrio of Pampamarca told us. These canals continue today to be maintained by the comuneros through communal work done by the comuneros of all the 12 barrios of the community. The cleaning begins early in the morning and lasts till about 3 in the afternoon; each work party cleans about two kilometers of canal. All the comuneros arrive early in the morning and gather in the plaza of the town of Quispillacta. From there they go in many work groups to their assigned segment of canal which belongs to their barrio, carrying their hoes and shovels and most of all with great enthusiasm and joy so as to make the work seem lesser and lighter. One comes to the communal work with one's best clothes or with new clothes. All decorate their hats with the wild matawayta flowers brought from the high mountains by the Sallqa Alcalde . . . All participate in the cleaning: youths, children, adults and even elders In this world-view, water is nurtured just like another person and like a person it also has its saint's day on the 7th of September of each agricultural year which marks the beginning of the corn planting in the quechua zone. (pp. 60–63)

Yarqa in the Quechua language means canal and *aspiy* means cleaning and/or making a furrow. The authorities in charge of Yarqa Aspiy are the ones chosen on January 1 for the duration of the year. They are the ones who are in charge of all the rituals of the community as well as of various communal tasks for any given year. The authorities are always husband-wife pairs. Bachelors are ineligible as are widows and widowers or divorced or separated persons. To be chosen as an authority is spoken of as *pasar un cargo,* which can be translated as "taking on a responsibility for a (year's) time." These cargos are rotational and everyone in the community is expected to fill this responsibility at least once in a lifetime.

There also exists what are called the "official, elected authorities." These are individuals—as opposed to husband-wife pairs—and typically male. Their election fulfills a requirement of the state, which does not recognize the traditional authorities. They are in charge mostly of the relationship between the community and the exterior: the state and its various institutions such as public health and development projects, and this includes the university's extension program, as well as foreign projects.

AUTHORITIES AND THEIR RESPONSIBILITIES

The traditional authorities are collectively referred to as the *varayoqs* and they are as follows:

The Hatun Alcalde and the Mama Alcaleza. This husband-wife pair have passed through all the other cargos and are called father and mother by all. They are in charge of both feeding and teaching the seven Alva-ceres/Alvaceras couples who work for them during the whole year. The feeding is not daily, but takes place during festival times. They teach them how to be good *chacareros* (nurturers of the *chacra*). The Mama Alcaleza also teaches the Alvaceras how to be good cooks, how to wash clothes, spin, and take care of the children. The Alvaceras/Alvaceres are supposed to present themselves in the house of the Hatun Alcalde/Alcaleza around 4 AM when there is work to do. If they fail in this or in any other duties, they receive the lash (five for the men, three for the women). This way they learn how to become responsible, moral, *comuneros*. During their year of tenure, the Alvaceres/Alvaceras thus learn also how to become elder authorities, how "to shepherd" the community as it is said.

Two pairs of Regidores and Regidoras. These are two couples that already have several children and have passed one or preferably two other cargos. They work with the Hatun Alcalde/Alcaleza. They also have the responsibil-ity of feeding and teaching the seven Alvaceres/Alvaceras couples that work for them for the whole year of the cargo.

The Campo Alcalde and Alcaleza. This is a mature couple in charge of looking after the *chacras* from planting until harvesting. They are responsible for seeing that no animals enter the fields while crops are in them.

The Sallqa Alcalde and Mama Sallqa Alcaleza are responsible for the herds of the community. They must count the animals twice a year, are in charge of the festival of branding the cattle, see to the health of the cattle, take care of their illnesses, and appoint the shepherds. They also are in charge of visiting all the households in the community and see to their cleanliness and orderli-ness. When this is found wanting, they give out five lashes to men and three to women in punishment.

Fourteen couples of Alvaceres and Alvaceras. These are recently married couples that generally do not yet have children. Seven of these couples work for the Hatun Alcalde and Alcaleza and seven for the two couples of Regidores/Regidoras. They choose whom they would work with: the Hatun Alcalde/Alcaleza or the two Regidores/Regidoras couples.

Six couples of Ministros/Ministras who work for the Campo Alcalde/Al-caleza are also recently married couples.

OFFERINGS AND ASKING PERMISSION

It falls to the Sallqa Alcalde and his wife to gather a species of wildflower from the puna zone located above 4,800 meters altitude. It is an arduous task. It takes two days by horse to reach the place where those flowers grow. They must gather flowers to adorn the hats of every comunero (some 5,000 persons) during the festival. The task takes one whole week to accomplish. These flowers are extremely important. Without them, the festival would be sad. According to Lorenzo, these flowers are the spirits of the water and they embody the spirit of the mountain deity where they were gathered.

The night before the festival, the Campo Alcalde and Alcaleza prepare the *pago* (the offering) for the water, gathering sacred coca leaves, fruits, white and red carnations, liquor, and many other things. They meet with their Ministros and the two *waqrapukus*. The latter blow on curled horn trumpets. They all meet around 10 PM and after having set out the various items in the offering on a *mesa* (altar), they hold a vigil. In this vigil, they ask permission of the water to start the communal work. Then, just before the light of dawn, the Campo Alcalde and whoever wants to accompany him, walk in darkness upstream where the river water feeds the irrigation channels. There, they offer the pago to the source of water, after which they bury it nearby, under a rock.

Meanwhile, in the predawn, all the authorities go to the church to ask permission of God and the saints, carrying three crosses, which they take to the municipal building. There the senior authorities kneel in front of the elected official authorities and ask their permission to carry out the cleaning of the irrigation channels. They all converse about how the water nurtures the community and how the community must nurture the water in return, in mutuality, in ayni. The conversation also bears on how everyone must behave during the festival, how not to become excessively drunk. A little drunkenness is a good thing, though; a sign of joy, the feeling at the heart of the festival.

By that time all the comuneros have arrived, the men carrying their hoes and shovels for the work of cleaning the canals; the women carrying pots, pans, and all manner of cooking utensils; they all crowd the plaza. At that moment, all the authorities, traditional and elected, place their hats on the table in the municipal building and the Alvaceres/Alvaceras of the Sallqa Alcalde/Alcaleza place the flowers brought from the high mountains on all the hats in the form of a cross. They distribute the remaining flowers to all the people outside who place them on their own hats. The moment is extremely sacred.

Thus sacralized by the matawayta flowers, everyone walks to a small chapel higher up, close to the irrigated fields. There one of the crosses brought from the church is left and all the official elected authorities kneel in front of the traditional elder authorities (*varayoqs*) asking them permission for the festival as the latter had asked their permission earlier. The voices of the Mama Alcaleza and the two Regidoras can be heard singing the "passion of the water" to the sound of the waqrapukus' horns; here is a small snippet to give a flavor of the songs:

Crystalline water, dark water
Don't carry me away
Don't push me.
Muddy river, blood-red river
Where will you reach?
Where do you have to reach?
You have to reach all the way.
Do what you have to do.
Where you are going,
There I go too.
Where the muddy river goes
There goes the crystalline river,
There I go with you.[4]

At the moment when some men carry the other two crosses to some of the barrios, the Mama Alcaleza steals away, running toward her house. When the Alvaceras realize that she has left, they all run after her. They are the water flowing, running in the channels; the energy with which they run is the energy of the water running when it is released in the cleansed channels. Meanwhile the *compadres* (godfathers) of all the elder authorities offer bowls of *chicha* (fermented corn water) to all the authorities.

The moment has arrived; fortified, all the men go to the irrigation channels to clean them. The women go to prepare the food that has been brought from the chacras of the parents and relatives of the Alvaceras. These parents and their relatives are the parents-in-law of the Alvaceres (husbands of the Alvaceras) and are their *awras* (in-laws).

When the work of cleaning the channel is done in the mid-afternoon, everyone gathers in a cleared field near the irrigated lands to feast.

THE ANTICS OF THE *INVISIONES*

A group of men impersonate various characters and perform accompanied by musicians. While the men work, they walk from work group to work group, entertaining people even while they feast after the work is done. I was fortunate to see a video that Magdalena made of Yarqa Aspiy and I confess that I laughed so hard at the antics of one of these groups that tears were running down my face. The topics of those skits refer to historical events that have deeply affected the community.

A pair of men impersonating a Catholic priest and his sacristan parody the mass and perform mock weddings and baptisms. In the video that I saw, the priest, holding an upside down comic strip, chanted in mock solemn tones a hilarious imitation of the Latin mass while liberally sprinkling people with a bunch of twigs he kept dipping in a pot containing urine (as I was told), in mock benediction, shoving people to make them kneel. Meanwhile the sacristan wildly swung an incense holder with burning dung, smoking everyone out. I found their exaggerated gestures, tone of voice, clownish frocks, and other antics hilarious. I simply assumed that this parody was the people's revenge for the sordid and brutal history of "extirpation of idolatry." However, to my surprise, when I voiced this opinion, everyone present seemed bemused by my interpretation and insisted that there was no animosity whatsoever against the Catholic religion in this and that it was simply meant to make people laugh. I was told that people insist on having the priest marry them and baptize their children, and that the whole community comes out devoutly and in force to celebrate the community's saint's day, officiated by a Catholic priest.

Another skit is acted by a group of men dressed up as people from the lowlands (the Amazonian region), wearing feathers on their heads, headdresses and beads. These are called the *chunchos*. With them are another group of men whose faces are painted black and who hold wooden machetes. They mock fight with each other and the black faces appear to slice the throats and disembowel the chunchos. They are after their fat because it is said that the Catholic priests need this fat to smear on church bells so that they will sound better.[5]

After they eat all the food, and the *invisiones* have finished, the younger men and women hold hands and run along the cleared channels where the water is running fast, singing. At interval, they pause and form *muyunas* (eddies) echoing the movements of the water. Everyone returns to their barrios, the men playing guitars and the women singing along with the laughing, rippling water.

Remembering How the Spirits Died

As Gualberto Machaca points out, Andean spirituality has been the object of persecution on the part of both the Catholic Church and the Evangelical Protestant sects. From Marcela's two narratives, it becomes clear that developmentalists, both local and foreign, as well as the Maoist Shining Path are also bent on destroying Andean spirituality. For all of them, Andean spirituality is seen as a danger, an obstacle to their actions. The state, although legally committed to the freedom of religious expression, ends up joining most of these religious groups in its official support of the developmentalists, particularly the local ones in the state universities.

From these narratives and the description of Yarqa Aspiy, Andean spirituality means essentially ritual agriculture, ritual animal husbandry, and the activities on the part of the shamans of healing through harmonizing humans with the nonhuman world. The world is alive and populated with sacred beings such as plants, water in its many forms (river, lakes, springs, rain, frost, hail, etc.), the earth, the stars, and other heavenly bodies, the mountains, and so on. Among these are also found the Christian God, Jesus Christ, Mary, and many saints. However, as a shaman explained to me during a ritual I participated in, after he had recited a very Catholic sounding prayer, God is the sun, Mary is Pachamama (the earth), and Jesus is the moon. Although such explanations diverge greatly among shamans and other native Andean persons, what they all share is that these Christian figures are not located in a supernatural realm beyond the Pacha.

Andean ritual activity could be characterized as the mutuality between the human collectivity and the other-than-human collectivity; very specifically, the doing of ayni between and among these two collectivities. The other-than-human world is sacred and it nurtures humans, and humans in reciprocity nurture all the beings of the Pacha as well as know how to let themselves be nurtured by them. This is a process that requires humans to act collectively, in solidarity and in mutuality among themselves, for only thus can the nurturing of the human collectivity by the beings of the Pacha be received and reciprocated. In other words, Yarqa Aspiy shows us that the precise orchestration of human action can only be understood in terms of efficacious reciprocating action toward in this case, the water, whose birthday it is.

The language of nurturance [*crianza*] captures what Marcela underlines as being the most important thing, namely the feelings humans have for the beings of the Pacha. The state's and developmentalists' language of "the management of natural resources" is eminently inappropriate in such a context. That is a language reflecting an ontological rift between the human collectivity and the nonhuman one; a language that captures the hierarchical and nonreciprocal nature of relations between these two collectivities. This language conceives of the nonhuman world as nonsentient, nonintelligent, and not alive. The nonhuman world has become profane, inert, mechanical "nature." And, this "nature" defines negatively what it is to have "culture." Culture is everything that nature is not. It is all that humans learn and create. By definition, nature does not learn, does not consciously create. Nature only repeats what has already been created, whereas true creativity is the exclusive domain of humanity (and, of course, the original creativity belongs to God alone for believers).

The term "natural resources" is inextricably associated with a view of the world bequeathed to us by the scientific revolution. Modern science emerged in its final form in the latter half of the 1600s in Western Europe as the most convincing response to the loss of certainty brought about by the explosion of new spiritual-cum-epistemological movements in the Renaissance as well as by the event of the Reformation and its aftermath. The response was at once epistemological and political and it was successful. The politico-religious events of the period of the Renaissance and Reformation—corresponding to the witch hunts—gave rise to a new cultural map of modernity. In this now globalized map, natural resources are taken for granted as part of something that has always been there and not something invented by a particular group of people at a particular time and place.

The use of magic by the oral female peasant healers and herbalists, the so-called witches, opened them to the allegation that they were practicing black magic; that they were dangerous persons. They did not restrict themselves only to those places and objects authorized by the church as being efficacious, that is as having inherent agency. From the point of view of the church, they were thus engaged in superstitious and potentially satanic practices, that is, in magic.

The 16th and 17th centuries were marked by the violence of the witch hunts and of the wars of religion. Catholics and Protestants each claimed to have the One Indivisible Truth and thus came into violent conflict. The 16th century saw no less than eight bloody civil wars in France between the Protestant Huguenots and the Catholics as well as major religious conflicts in England. The voice of the tolerant Renaissance Humanists and that of the more pluralistically inclined occult philosophers was drowned by the fury of both Protestants and Catholics as well as the raging fires of the witch hunts.

A NEW NONRELIGIOUS CERTAINTY

The Catholic priest Marin Mersenne, close associate of René Descartes and cofounder of the French Académie, paved the way for Descartes's dualist and mechanical philosophy by publishing in Paris his *Quaestiones celeberrimae in Genesim* in 1623. In this work, he devoted particular attention to the attack on Giorgi's occult philosophy as well as on that of the English occult philosopher Robert Fludd and his Rosicrucian movement, both profoundly influenced by Christian Cabalas as well as by the wise women (the so-called witches). The historian Frances Yates argues that Mersenne rejected the nondualist worldview thus appeasing the witch-hunters and strengthening Descartes' dualist, mechanical philosophy (Yates 1979, p. 174).

Stephen Toulmin in his book *Cosmopolis* gives us the context of Descartes's life.[6] Toulmin focuses mostly on the conflict between Protestants and Catholics and in particular on Henri IV's assassination and the Thirty Years War (the international war of religion from 1618 to 1648), both of which touched Descartes' life directly. It is, however, vital to include also the attack on occult Renaissance philosophy and the popular magic of the wise women and their successful erasure through the witch hunts as part of that context. Descartes' dualistic and mechanical philosophy was the antithesis of that of the wise women and the occult philosophers. It was clear by this time that a nondualistic, vitalistic philosophy was doomed, as the occult philosophers were being doomed along with the witches. With the defeat of occult philosophy and along with it, the cosmology of Europe's oral peasantry, there only remained the two Christian churches with their intractable insistence on possessing the one truth, locked in an irresolvable political and epistemological deadlock.

The success of the new mechanistic dualistic philosophy was in great part due to the fact that, unlike popular practices and occult philosophy, this philosophy did not challenge either Protestant or Catholic doctrines. It rather established itself in the epistemological space that they shared. In the maelstrom of the early 17th century, escaping the wrath of the inquisition and escaping from the deadlock between the two warring factions of Christianity were not only epistemological moves, but survival tactics. These moves were eminently political, and as argued by Toulmin, consciously undertaken to restore the fractured certainty and unity without which Europe could not imagine itself.

By the end of the 17th century, the end of the scientific revolution—canonically dated with Newton's publication of the *Principia Matematica* in 1687—it was no longer possible legitimately to hold that nature had agency and sacrality. So much so that Newton assiduously hid his real alchemical beliefs in which gravity was a sacred and intentional force of nature. By this time, Renaissance movements such as alchemy, hermeticism, cabala, vitalism, Neoplatonism, and elite and popular magic, had been energetically and violently repressed. Occult philosophers and wise women, the mostly female practitioners of popular magic, remain the most well-known victims of the inquisitions of both the Catholic and Protestant churches.[7]

The defeat of occult philosophy, popular magic, and other Renaissance movements by both Catholics and Protestants severely constrained the parameters within which science was to establish itself. In other words, the nondualist worldviews of Renaissance movements, as well as their pluralism, became nonoptions.

When the church encountered native societies of the Americas, it declared all their spirits as "demons" or "devils." This appellation recognized the agency of these beings of the other-than-human world but declared it to be an evil one. The church, however, seems to have implicitly recognized the potency and agency of most of the native sacred places by erecting churches or installing crosses in those places. In other words, the possibility of aspects of the nonhuman world having agency was never questioned by the church, only the specific nature of that agency and its church authorization was questioned. From the church's point of view, it transformed the malevolent local spirits into beneficent Catholic ones.

Today in Quispillacta, Marcela refers to the orientation of those comuneros who do keep the rituals as "Catholics." Indeed, as the description of Yarqa Aspiy makes clear, the festival is done in a Catholic idiom. The Evangelical sects—a variety of Protestantism—which have swamped the Andes in the last several decades, are, in contrast, totally opposed to the performance of such rituals and strictly forbid them to their adherents, threatening them with hell and damnation.

Of course, Europeans and their non-European emulators, have overwhelmingly called the creation of an inert, mechanistic and material nature a milestone on the road to progress. It has and continues to be used as a justification for the conversion of everyone in the world to this particular Eurocentric vision of things. The fact that this development is totally unprecedented and that no other peoples have evolved such views, should, it seems to me, be a source of self-questioning.

The new scientific language did not infringe on the domain of religion, a domain that especially since the advent of modernity, is concerned with the "supernatural," that is, what is beyond the visible world as well as in individuals' personal and private relation to that domain. In other words, it is a secular language. What Andean practices and languages do—from a Eurocentric perspective—is to confound fundamental separations such as those between the natural and the supernatural, between the natural and the cultural, between ritual/spirituality and technology/science, between the divine and the human, between the secular and the sacred, between the public and the private and probably more beside.

The dominance of Western Europe worldwide, initiated with the invasion by Spain of the Americas, and the concomitant spread of these ideas and practices have lent an air of evolutionary inevitability to modernity. This view has been fostered by the characterization of Western science as being of universal import. The universal truth of science should progressively enlighten the whole world, reaching into its furthermost corners. This view is forcefully articulated by one of Marcela's university professors who in anger exclaimed: "How is it possible that at the end of the 20th century you talk about campesino knowledge and ritual?" The underlying assumption here concerns an evolutionary-like inevitability for the spread of Western science and technology and for modernization in general. The forward march of modernization, spread by developmentalists and globalizers of all ilk, is perceived as a natural, inevitable process. Marcela told me how often she and the others in ABA have been called "backwardists," accused of wanting "to go backward." Thus history is conceived of as an inclined plane, a rectilinear process and all those resisting the inevitability of it are simply unrealistic dreamers and romantics, doomed to the dustbin of history.

CONCLUSION: NURTURING THE SPIRITS BACK TO LIFE

It is difficult to find appropriate words in modern English that adequately capture indigenous practices. Both the word "spirituality" and "ritual" in their current connotations somehow imply that such practices belong to a nonutiliatrian, nonmaterially efficacious domain. It is precisely such connotations that lead to the conviction that indigenous practices are inefficacious in the material world. Such a view is born out of the assumption that indigenous people practice their kind of agriculture and other utilitarian activities out of an irrational attachment to their customs and their traditions, since these are intertwined with what is perceived as "religious" or "spiritual" (in the accepted sense of the word) "beliefs." The word "wisdom" seems to me a better term because it conveys that the cognitive part is intimately intertwined with affective, moral, and spiritual dimensions.

The response to indigenous communal rituals such as Yarqa Aspiy is in the last instance based on the threat they pose, if taken seriously, to the legitimacy of the separation between religion, government, and science as well as the denied but implicit collusion between governments and science. And, for these purposes it does not matter whether the government is liberal, conservative, dictatorial, or socialist/communist.

For indigenous peoples, the world is not divided between a material reality and a nonmaterial reality. The beings of the Pacha, such as the human beings, the water in its many forms, the earth, the plants, the animals, the stars, the sun, the moon, and so forth, all share the same world. Some among them, on the model of the human authorities who take turns with the communal responsibilities, the cargos, have greater authority. These beings are concrete, tangible, experienceable, just like the water is during Yarqa Aspiy. When new beings are introduced into the Pacha, such as for example the Christian God, Jesus Christ, Mary, and saints, these also become identified with tangible beings. They lose their supernatural status. The deities or spirits are not "believed in," they are experienced; they are conversed with and reciprocated with. Indigenous people of the Andes do ayni with them, nurture them as they are nurtured by them, as is shown in the case of Yarqa Aspiy.

Respecting, nurturing the water means that its ways of traveling is intimately known. In the place where the water is deviated to enter the irrigation channels, the stream is surrounded by lush vegetation. In fact, the whole stream is thus surrounded. These plants are the water's companions, its familiars. The water and the plants have an affinity for each other and the ancient earthen channels are made lovingly, respectfully, so that the water will not feel abandoned by its companion plants and will travel happily. The native Andeans' actions are ever mindful of the respect due to the beings of the Pacha. The earth, the water, the sun, the seeds, and so on, all that is needed to provide the sustenance for life is respected.

NOTES

1. See Darell Addison Posey, ed., *Cultural and Spiritual Values of Biodiversity*, UNEP, 1999. See Posey, page 4 for a definition of tradition not as indicating antiquity but a certain manner of sharing and learning knowledge, a knowledge that as often as not is new.

2. Marcela spoke at the following events: The conference on "Decolonizing Knowledge: Indigenous Voices of the Americas" organized by Frédérique Apffel-Marglin and John Mohawk at Smith College, May 5–7, 1995. The conference on "Mutual Learning in Theory and Practice" organized by F. Apffel-Marglin and Kathryn Pyne Addelson, Shutesbury, Massachusetts, October 13–15, 1998. The symposium on "Mutual Learning: Decolonizing Communities" organized by F. Apffel-Marglin and Kathryn Pyne Addelson, Smith College, October 16, 1998.

3. This description is based mostly on Marcela Machaca's published account of Yarqa Aspiy in Machaca et al., *Kancha Chacra Sunqulla*, 1998: 1–69. I also visited Quispillacta in May 1999 and gathered clarifying information at that time.

4. This was sung for me by Marcela Machaca in ABA's office in Quechua and she translated it for me into Spanish as well.

5. For a graphic historical account of such practices executed on the boss's order by black slaves on indigenous Peruvian Amazonian slaves during the rubber boom in the early 20th century see Søren Hvalkof's essay: "Outrage in Rubber and Oil," *People, Plants and Justice: The Politics of Nature Conservation*, ed. Charles Zerner, New York, Columbia University Press, 2000: 83–116.

6. Stephen Toulmin, *Cosmopolis: The Hidden Agenda of Modernity*, Free Press, 1990.

7. See Carolyn Merchant, *The Death of Nature*, New York: HarperOne, 1990; Morris Berman, *The Reenchantment of the World*, Ithaca, NY: Cornell University Press, 1981.

REFERENCES

Apffel-Marglin, Frédérique. "Rhythms of Life" in *Time in India: Concepts and Practices*, Delhi: Manohar, 2007: 99–121.

Belmont, Nicole. "Superstition and Popular Religion in Western Societies" in M. Izard / P. Smith, eds., *Between Belief and Transgression: Structuralist*

Essays in Religion, History, and Myth, Chicago: Chicago University Press, 1982: 9–23.

Berman, Morris. *The Reenchantment of the World,* Ithaca, NY: Cornell University Press, 1981.

Burke, P. "Historians, Anthropologists, and Symbols" in E. Ohnuki-Tierney, ed., *Culture Through Time,* Stanford: Stanford University Press, 1990.

Clifford, James. *The Predicament of Culture: Twentieth-Century Ethnography, Literature, and Art,* Cambridge, MA: Harvard University Press, 1988.

Haraway, Donna. *Modest_Witness@SecondMillenium.FemaleMan_Meets_Onco Mouse: Feminism and Technoscience,* New York: Routledge, 1997.

Hvalkof, Søren. "Outrage in Rubber and Oil: Extractivism, Indigenous Peoples, and Justice in the Upper Amazon" in Charles Zerner, ed., *People, Plants, and Justice: The Politics of Nature Conservation,* New York: Columbia University Press, 2000: 83–116.

Kloppenburg, Jack Jr. *First the Seed: The Political Economy of Plant Biotechnology, 1492–2000,* Cambridge: Cambridge University Press, 1988.

Machaca, Marcela, Magdalena Machaca, Gualberto Machaca, and Juna Vilca Nunez, *Kancha Chacra Sunqulla: La cultura agrocéntrica en el ayllu Quispillacta,* Lima, Peru: PRATEC publication, 1998.

Merchant, Carolyn. *The Death of Nature: Women, Ecology, and the Scientific Revolution,* San Francisco: Harper & Row, 1983.

Noble, David. *The Religion of Technology: The Divinity of Man and the Spirit of Invention,* New York: Knopf, 1997.

Noble, David. *A World without Women: The Christian Clerical Culture of Western Science,* New York and Oxford: Oxford University Press, 1992.

Polanyi, Karl. *The Great Transformation,* Boston: Beacon Hill, 1957 [1944].

Posey, Darrell Addison, ed. *Cultural and Spiritual Values of Biodiversity,* Nairobi: United Nations Environmental Programme, 1999.

Scott, James. *Seeing Like a State: How Certain Schemes to Improve the Human Condition Have Failed,* New Haven and London: Yale University Press, 1998.

Uberoi, Jit Singh. *Science and Culture,* Delhi: Oxford University Press, 1978.

Valladolid, Julio. "Andean Peasant Agriculture: Nurturing a Diversity of Life in the Chacra" in F. Apffel-Marglin with PRATEC, *The Spirit of Regeneration: Andean Culture Confronting Western Notions of Development,* London: Zed Books and New York: St. Martin's Press, 1998.

Varela, F., E. Thompson, and E. Rosch. *The Embodied Mind: Cognitive Science and Human Experience,* Cambridge, MA: MIT Press, 1991.

Yates, Frances. *The Occult Philosophy in the Elizabethan Age,* London: Routledge, 1979.

PART II

Socioeconomics, Politics, and Authority

CHAPTER 3

Indigenous Spirituality, Gender, and the Politics of Justice: Voices from the First Summit of Indigenous Women of the Americas

Sylvia Marcos

The indigenous women's movement has started to propose its own "indigenous spirituality." The basic documents, final declarations, and collective proposals from the First Indigenous Women's Summit of the Americas, as well as at other key meetings, reveal an indigenous spiritual component that differs from the hegemonic influences of the largely Christian, mainly Catholic background of the women's respective countries. The principles of this indigenous spirituality also depart from the more recent influences of feminist and Latin American ecofeminist liberation theologies. The participants' discourses, live presentations, and addresses brought to light other expressions of their religious background.

Extracts from the book *Memoria, First Indigenous Women Summit of the Americas,* Fundacion Rigoberta Menchu TUM, IAP, 1era edicion, Mayo 2003, Mexico. Used with permission of Proyecto Andino de Tecnologias Campesina (PRATEC).

Drawing on several years of interactions and work with women in Mexico's indigenous worlds, my intention in this chapter is to systematize the principles that have begun to emerge from a distinctive cosmo-vision and cosmology. Religious references to an indigenous spirituality are inspired by ancestral traditions recreated today as the women struggle for social justice. The inspiration for their fight for social justice is often anchored in indigenous beliefs. These beliefs stem from ritual, liturgical, and collective worlds of worship that, though often hidden under Catholic Christian imagery, reflect a significant divergence from Christianity, revealing their epistemic particularity. Working, as some authors have suggested, from "cracks of epistemic differences," I characterize these groups as undertaking a "de-colonial" effort. These women are actively recapturing ancestral spiritualities in order to decolonize the religious universes they were forced to adopt during the historical colonial enterprise.

The First Indigenous Women's Summit of the Americas was a United Nations meeting that took place in December of 2002. It was promoted and organized by a collective of indigenous international leaders, such as Rigoberta Menchú, Myrna Cunningham, Calixta Gabriel, and other regional indigenous women leaders from communities in the Americas. They were joined by Pauline Tiongia, an elder from a Maori community in New Zealand. The meeting gathered around 400 indigenous women representing most countries and many indigenous communities.[1] In attendance were women from remote and isolated places such as the delta of the Orinoco River in Venezuela, where there are no roads, and the Amazon River basin. Prior to the summit, the organizers arranged a series of focus groups designed by the Centro de Estudios e Información de la Mujer Multiétnica (CEIMM) from the Universidad de las Regiones autonomas de la Costa Caribe Nicaraguense (URACCAN), Nicaragua's indigenous university. The focus groups' methodology aimed at bringing together indigenous women representative of the whole region to foster discussions on five main areas of interest: (1) Spirituality, Education, and Culture; (2) Gender from the Perspective of Indigenous Women; (3) Leadership, Empowerment, and Indigenous Women Participation; (4) Indigenous Development and Globalization; (5) Human Rights and Indigenous Rights. The selected women were invited to gather and participate in several of these preliminary focus groups around the region. During group interactions, they expressed their own thoughts, perspectives, and experiences concerning spirituality, gender, education, empowerment, development, and their relationships to international funding and cooperation agencies. The groups' discussions, which were transcribed and lightly edited, constituted the basic documents for the summit meeting.

The importance of research led and designed by the same subjects-objects of inquiry cannot be overemphasized. The asymmetrical power relations between urban women and indigenous peasant women are evident throughout the Latin American continent. It is urban women who have access to higher education, professional positions, and economic resources. Usually it is they whose voices, proposals, and projects for research find support. The summit selected its participants from a pool of indigenous women who are political leaders: senators, *regidoras*, congresswomen, heads of social organizations, leaders of political grassroots groups. All these women had many years of experience exercising political and social influence and leadership. The summit offered them a space where they could express their experiences and priorities in their own voices, without the mediations and interpretations of the area's hegemonic institutions. One of the main themes was "gender from the indigenous women's vision." This was and still is a debated issue that has sometimes created barriers between mainstream feminism and the indigenous women's movement. I had the privilege of being invited to be one of the few "nonindigenous" women participants at the meeting and also a consultant for their gender and empowerment documents. The organizers knew of my research on early Mesoamerican cosmology and activist work, and expressed the desire to hear the opinion of a feminist who has respect for indigenous cultures.

The theme of indigenous spirituality was transversal and intersected with every other issue addressed at the summit. It was so prominent that a study of the documents from the summit, voted by consensus, reveals the priorities of the contemporary struggles, concerns, and agendas of indigenous groups in the Americas. The documents set "indigenous spirituality" as an origin and a motor for the recreation of collectivities and for the emergence of a new pan-indigenous, collective subject in which women's leadership is emerging and potentially growing, defining the women as outspoken, strong, and clear agents for change.

The term "indigenous women" had no positive connotations as recently as a few years ago. It had never been used to name a self-constituted identity by the indigenous peoples themselves. Now it is the token for a collective subjectivity, a social actor that has been created by the indigenous women themselves through their political and spiritual practices. As workshop leader and consultant to indigenous women's organizations from several ethnic groups of Mexico and Latin America, I have witnessed their ties, their collective identification, and the strength of their spiritual and cosmological references.

THE MODERNITY OF ANCIENT SPIRITUALITY

The Latin American continent has long been known as a stronghold of Catholicism. Even today, the Vatican counts Latin America as one of the regions that boasts the greatest numbers of Catholics in the world.[2] Among indigenous social movements, claiming the right to develop and define their own spirituality is a novel attitude, yet one that is voiced with increasing intensity.[3] Beyond claiming a right to food and shelter, a decent livelihood, and ownership of their territory and its resources, the indigenous are turning an internal gaze toward their traditional culture. They are also daring to question the most ingrained sequels of Catholic colonization, rejecting the contempt and disdain with which their spirituality, beliefs, and practices are held by the Catholic majority. We will see an example of the mainstream Catholic perspective toward the indigenous peoples in the "Message of the Bishops to the Summit" below.

In spite of the conflicting perspectives held by scholars and others, the indigenous social movements are the most visible transformational force in the Latin American continent (Gil Olmos 2000a). The indigenous peoples no longer accept the image that was imposed on them from the exterior. They want to create their own identity; they do not want to be museum objects. It is not a question of reviving the past. Indigenous cultures are alive, and the only way for them to survive is to reinvent themselves, recreating a new identity while maintaining their differences (Gil Olmos 2000b). The work of anthropologist Kay Warren offers insights into the genealogy of the pan-indigenous collective subject. What Warren calls the "pan-Mayan collective identity" was forged out of the peoples' need to survive the aggressions of the state in Guatemala. As the distinct ethnic groups were threatened with cultural annihilation, their guides, true philosopher-leaders, formulated a collective identity drawn from their inherited oral, mythic, and religious traditions. As Warren explains, the bearers of cultural wisdom began to set forth an "assertion of a common past which has been suppressed and fragmented by European colonialism and the emergence of modern liberal states. In this view, cultural revitalization reunites the past with the present as a political force" (Warren and Jackson 2002, p. 11). Whatever the possible explanations for the genesis of this pan-indigenous collective social subject might be, it engenders a political collectivity, and one of its central claims is often based on its own self-defined "indigenous spirituality."

As for indigenous women, they, too, are claiming this ancestral wisdom, cosmo-vision, and spirituality. Theirs is a selective process. Issues within tradition that constrain or hamper their space as women are being contested. Meanwhile, those that have enhanced their position as women within their spiritual ancestral communities are held onto dearly, their survival supported and ensured by the community.

Addressing the Mexican Congress in March of 2002, Comandanta Esther, a Zapatista leader from the southern state of Chiapas, expressed the concern of indigenous women in this way: "I want to explain the situation of women as we live it in our communities . . . as girls they think we are not valuable . . . as women mistreated . . . also women have to carry water, walking two to three hours holding a vessel and a child in their arms" (Marcos 2005a, p. 103). After speaking of her daily sufferings under indigenous customary law, she added: "I am not telling you this so you pity us. We have struggled to change this and we will continue doing it" (p. 103). She was expressing the inevitable struggle for change that indigenous women face, but she was also demanding respect for their agency. They—those directly involved have to be the ones to lead the process of change. There is no need for pity and still less for instructions from outsiders on how to defend their rights as women. This would be another form of imposition, however well meant it might be. Comandanta Esther's discourse should convince those intellectuals removed from the daily life of indigenous peoples that culture is not monolithic, not static. "We want recognition for our way of dressing, of talking, of governing, of organizing, of praying, of working collectively, of respecting the earth, of understanding nature as something we are part of" (p. 103). In consonance with many indigenous women who have raised their voices in recent years, she wants both to transform and to preserve her culture. This is the background of the demands for social justice expressed by indigenous women, against which we must view the declarations and claims for "indigenous spirituality" that emerged from the First Indigenous Women's Summit of the Americas.

Among the thematic resolutions proposed and passed by consensus at the First Summit, the following are particularly emblematic:

We re-evaluate spirituality as the main axis of culture. (*Memoria*, p. 61)[4]

Revaloramos la espiritualidad como el eje principal de la cultura. (Memoria, p. 32)

The participants of the First Indigenous Women's Summit of the Americas resolve: that spirituality is an indivisible part of the community. It is a cosmic vision of life shared by everyone and wherein all beings are interrelated and complementary in their existence. Spirituality is a search for the equilibrium and harmony within ourselves as well as the other surrounding beings. (*Memoria*, p. 60)

Las participantes de la Primera Cumbre de Mujeres Indígenas de América consideramos: que la espiritualidad está ligada al sentido comunitario de la visión cósmica de la vida, donde los seres se interrelacionan y se complementan en su existencia. Que la espiritualidad es la búsqueda del equilibrio y la armonia con nosotros mismos y con los demás. (Memoria, p. 31)

We demand of different churches and religions to respect the beliefs and cultures of Indigenous peoples without imposing on us any religious practice that conflicts with our spirituality. (*Memoria*, p. 19)

Demandamos de las diferentes iglesias y religiones respetar las creencias y culturas de los Pueblos Indígenas sin imponernos ninguna prctica religiosa que contravenga nuestra espiritualidad. (Memoria, p. 19)

WHAT DOES INDIGENOUS SPIRITUALITY MEAN?

When I first approached the documents of the summit, I was surprised by the frequent use of the self-elected term "spirituality." Its meaning in this context is by no means self-evident and hence needs to be decoded. It has little to do with what the word usually means in the Christian traditions, in which I include all denominations. When the indigenous women use the word "spirituality," they give it a meaning that clearly sets it apart from Catholic and other Christian traditions that arrived in the Americas at the time of the conquest and the ensuing colonization:

> We indigenous Mexican women . . . take our decision to practice freely our spirituality that is different from a religion but in the same manner we respect every one else's beliefs. (Message from Indigenous Women to the Bishops, p. 1)
>
> *Las mujeres indígenas mexicanas . . . tomamos nuestras decisiones para ejercer libremente nuestra espiritualidad que es diferente a una religión y de igual manera se respeta la creencia de cada quien. (Message from Indigenous Women to the Bishop, p. 1)*

This stance is strongly influenced by an approach that espouses transnational sociopolitical practices. Indigenous movements and in particular the women in them are being increasingly exposed to a globalizing world. The presence of a Maori elder at the summit, as well as the frequent participation of Mexican indigenous women in indigenous peoples' meetings around the world, have favored new attitudes of openness, understanding, and coalition beyond their own traditional cultural boundaries. Through the lens of indigenous spirituality, we can glimpse the cosmo-vision that pervades the worlds of indigenous women.

THE BISHOPS' MESSAGE AT THE SUMMIT AND THE WOMEN'S RESPONSE

Reports about the summit's preparatory sessions, combined with the public status of its main organizer, indigenous Nobel Peace Prize laureate Rigoberta Menchú, attracted the attention of the Mexican bishops. They apparently feared that the indigenous worlds, which they regard as part of their domain, were getting out of control. Moreover, it was not only the indigenous peoples but the indigenous *women* who were taking the lead and gaining a public presence. There were also rumors about so-called reproductive rights being discussed on the summit's agenda. Catholic authorities spoke out against indigenous agitation. They felt pressed to send a message and a warning:

> The Summit touches on indigenous peoples' spirituality, education and culture from perspectives such as traditional knowledge, loss and reconstruction of collective and individual identities, and also from indigenous women's spirituality *from a perspective totally distant from the cultural and spiritual reality of the diverse ethnic groups that form our* [sic] *indigenous peoples.* (Bishop's Message, p. 2, emphasis added)
>
> *La Cumbre aborda la espiritualidad, la educación y la cultura de los pueblos indígenas desde conceptos de conocimiento tradicional, perdida y reconstrucción de identidad individual y colectiva, así como espiritualidad de la mujer indígena, desde una perspectiva completamente alejada de la realidad cultural y espiritual de las diferentes etnias que forman nuestros* [sic] *pueblos indígenas.* (Bishops's Mensaje, p. 2, emphasis added)

This patronizing and discriminatory message was sent to the summit by the Comision Episcopal de Indígenas, the Episcopal Commission for the Indigenous. This message is paternalistic throughout. Its tone is one of admonition of and condescension toward the indigenous subject. It assumes that rationality and truth are the exclusive domains of bishops, who seem to feel that it is their obligation to lead their immature indigenous women subjects, that is, to teach them, guide them, and scold them when the bishops think that the indigenous women are wrong. The reader gets the sense that, to the bishops, this collectivity of women is dangerously straying from the indigenous peoples as the bishops define them.

The indigenous women's response, *Mensaje de las Mujeres Indígenas Mexicanas a los Monseñores de la Comisión Episcopal de Indígenas,* emerged from a collective meeting. In this document, the 38 representatives of Mexican indigenous communities expressed their plight in the following words:[5]

> Now we can manifest openly our spirituality. Our ancestors were obliged to hide it . . . It is evident that evangelization was an imposition and that on top of our temples and ceremonial centers churches were built. (*Mensaje Mujeres Indígenas,* p. 1)
>
> *Ciertamente hoy podemos manifestar más plenamente nuestra espiritualidad, lo que no pudieron hacer nuestros antepasados porque lo hicieron a escondidas . . . Para nadie es oculto de la imposición de la evangelización y que sobre la espiritualidad y centros ceremoniales se fundaron las iglesias en nuestros Pueblos.* (*Mensaje Mujeres Indígenas,* p. 1)

We Mexican Indigenous women are adults and we take over our right to practice freely our spirituality that is different from a religion . . . we feel that we have the right to our religiosity as indigenous peoples. (*Mensaje Mujeres Indígenas*, pp. 1–2)

Las mujeres indígenas mexicanas somos mayores de edad y tomamos nuestras decisiones para ejercer libremente nuestra espiritualidad que es diferente a una religión . . . nos sentimos con derecho a ejercer . . . nuestra religiosidad como pueblos indígenas. (*Mensaje Mujeres Indígenas*, pp. 1–2)

We reconfirm the principles that inspire us to recover and strengthen reciprocity, complementarity, duality, to regain equilibrium. (*Mensaje Mujeres Indígenas*, p. 1)

Reconfirmamos nuestros principios que nos inspiran a recuperar y fortalecer . . . la reciprocidad, complementariedad, dualidad para recuperar el equilibrio. (*Mensaje Mujeres Indígenas*, p. 1)

Do not worry, we are analyzing them [the customary law practices that could hamper human rights], because we believe that the light of reason and justice also illuminates us, and certain things should not be permitted. (*Mensaje Mujeres Indígenas*, p. 1)

No se preocupen, las estamos analizando [los usos y costumbres que atentan contra la dignidad y los derechos humanos], porque también creemos que nos ilumina la luz de la razón y la justicia. (*Mensaje Mujeres Indígenas*, p. 1)

This last sentence makes a veiled reference to centuries of colonial and postcolonial oppression. First the colonizers, and then the modern state, both with the church's approval, denied the indigenous peoples the qualification of *gente de razón* ("people with the capacity of reason"). Even today, in some parts of Mexico, this qualification is reserved for whites and mestizos.

As a voluntary, "only listening" participant of this collectivity of 38 Mujeres Indígenas Mexicanas, I paid careful attention to all the discussions. These speakers of several indigenous languages groped for an adequate Spanish wording to convey the ideas sustaining their formal response to the monolingual bishops. At one point, when I was asked directly what I thought about the use of a particular term, I ventured an opinion. After they discussed it, they decided not to go with my suggestion. The significance here is that my opinion was treated not as authoritative, but as simply as worthy of consideration as any other. In their own classification, I was a "nonindigenous" supportive feminist. Fortunately, long gone were the days when an urban mestizo university woman could impose an idea or even a word.

The women's discussions were horizontally collective. The women present represented the majority of the Mexican ethnic communities. Their native languages included Nahuatl, Tzotzil, Tzeltal, Tojolabal, Chol, Zapotec, Mixe, Mazatec, Mixtec, and Purepecha, among others. The gathering was an expression of the new collective subject that is taking the lead in struggles for social justice. Notwithstanding traditional ethnic divides among them, all the women involved chose to emphasize their commonalities and identify themselves as Mexican indigenous women. Despite some language barriers, their discussions of ideas and words have stayed with me. They struggled with Spanish as they forged the language of their text. The editing of the document took all of us into the early hours of the next day. It was finally passed by consensus, in which my vote as "nonindigenous" counted as any other, as it should in a consensus-building process.

In addition to dealing with the constraints posed by the multiplicity of their languages, the women expressed the deeply pressing dilemma of having to deal with a religious institution that, in spite of its evangelical roots, has traditionally been misogynistic, as well as, for the most part, culturally and ethnically prejudiced against indigenous worlds. The insistence of the women on being *adults* ("*las mujeres indígenas mexicanas somos mayores de edad*") is a response to the assumption implicit in the Bishops' message, namely, that not only women but also indigenous peoples in general are minors and, as such, in need of strict guidance and reprimand. The ecclesiastical message also implies that they, the (male) bishops and archbishops, know better than the indigenous social activists themselves what it means to be "indigenous" in contemporary Mexico.

Considering the cautious reverence paid to Catholic authorities by most Mexicans—whether they are believers or not—the indigenous women's response is a significant expression of a newly gained spirit of autonomy and self-determination. The women's declaration, in both tone and content, also speaks of the erosion of the Church's dominion over indigenous worlds. These poor, unschooled women have shown themselves to be braver and less submissive than some feminist negotiators at a recent United Nations meeting with Vatican representatives.[6]

Decolonizing Epistemology

Several authors have argued that decolonizing efforts should be grounded at the epistemological level Mignolo 2007; Tlostanova 2007; Marcos 2005b). When speaking of the future of feminism, Judith Butler recommends a "privileging of epistemology" as an urgent next step in our commitments. She also reminds us that "there is no register for 'audibility'" referring to the difficulties of reaching out, understanding, and respecting "Other" subaltern epistemic worlds (Butler 2004).

The following analysis of some basic characteristics of indigenous spirituality is an invitation to understand it in its own terms. It is an effort toward widening the "register for audibility," so the voices and positions of the indigenous may bypass the opaque lenses of philosophical ethnocentricity. This

deepening of understanding will facilitate a less domineering and imposing relationship with women not only in society and politics but also in the
spiritual indigenous domains. As an indigenous woman from Moloj Mayib', a
political Mayan women's organization, complained regarding her encounter
with feminists:

> They question us very much, they insist that we should question our cul-
> ture . . . what we do not accept is their imposition, that they tell us what
> we have to do, when we have the power to decide by ourselves. (I do not
> mean) . . . that the feminist comes and shares tools with us and we are
> able to do it: that she could support me, that she can walk by my side . . .
> but she should not impose on me. This is what many feminist women
> have done, be imposing. (Maria Estela Jocón, *Memoria*, pp. 274–275)
>
> *Ellas insisten mucho en que tienes que cuestionar tu cultura. Lo que no*
> *nos gusta es la imposición, que te digan lo que tienes que hacer, cuando tu*
> *tienes el poder de decidir sobre ti. No es que la otra . . . eminista venga y me*
> *de las herramientas para hacerlo: que me puede ayudar, que puede cami-*
> *nar conmigo, . . . pero que no me imponga. Eso es lo que tal vez muchas*
> *mujeres feministas han hecho, imponer.* (Maria Estela Jocón, *Memoria*,
> pp. 274–275)

The opinion of this indigenous woman confirms Gayatri Spivak's observation of "the international feminist tendency to matronize the Southern
woman as belonging to gender oppressive second-class cultures" (Spivak,
p. 407).

A WORLD CONSTRUCTED BY FLUID DUAL OPPOSITIONS, BEYOND MUTUALLY EXCLUSIVE CATEGORIES

Duality is the centerpiece of spirituality understood as a cosmic vision of
life. Duality—not dualism—is a pervasive perception in indigenous thought
and spirituality. The pervasiveness of a perception without equivalent in
Western thought could, perhaps, in itself largely explain the persistent barrier to penetrating and comprehending indigenous worlds.

According to Mesoamerican worldviews, the dual unity of the feminine
and masculine is fundamental to the creation of the cosmos, as well as its
(re)generation, and sustenance. The fusion of feminine and masculine in
one bipolar principle is a recurring feature of almost every community today.
Mesoamerican divinities themselves are gendered: feminine and masculine.
There is no concept of a virile god (e.g., the image of a man with a white
beard as the Christian God has sometimes been represented) but rather a

mother/father dual protector-creator. In Nahua culture, this dual god/goddess is called Ometéotl, from *ome*, "two," and *teotl*, "god." Yet Ometeotl does not mean "two gods" but rather "god Two" or, better, "divinity of Duality." The name results from the fusion of Omecihuatl (*cihuatl* meaning woman or lady) and Ometecuhtli (*tecuhtli*, man or lord), that is, of the Lady and of the Lord of Duality.

The protecting Ometeotl has to be alternately placated and sustained. Like all divine beings, it was not conceived as *all* purely beneficial. Rather, it oscillated—like all other dualities—between opposite poles and thus could be supportive or destructive. In addition, a multiplicity of goddesses and gods entered into diverse relations of reciprocity with the people. Elsewhere, I have dealt more comprehensively with the gods and goddesses of the Mesoamerican cosmo-vision (Marcos 2006). Scholars recognize that the religiosity of the entire Mesoamerican region is pregnant with analogous symbolic meanings, rituals, and myths concerning the condition of the supernatural beings, the place of humans, and the cosmos. One of our most eminent ethnohistorians, Alfredo López Austin, refers to this commonality of perceptions, conceptions, and forms of action as the *núcleo duro,* the "hard core" of Mesoamerican cultures (López Austin 2001).

Duality, defined as a complementary duality of opposites, is the essential ordering force of the universe and is also reflected in the ordering of time. Time is marked by two calendars, one ritual-based and the other astronomical. The ritual calendar is linked to the human gestation cycle, that is, the time needed for a baby to be formed inside the mother's womb. The other is an agricultural calendar that prescribes the periods for seeding, sowing, and planting corn. Maize (corn) is conceived of as the earthly matter from which all beings in the universe are made (Marcos 2006). Human gestation and agricultural cycles are understood within this concept of time-duality, as are feminine and masculine, but dualities extend far beyond these spheres. For instance, life and death, above and below, light and dark, and beneficence and malevolence are considered dual aspects of the same reality. Neither pole invalidates the other. Both are in constant mutual interaction, flowing into one another. Mutually exclusive categories are not part of the epistemic background of this worldview, whose plasticity is still reflected in the way indigenous women deal with life and conflict. They seldom remain mired in a position that would deny the opposite. Their philosophical background allows them to resist impositions and at the same time to appropriate (modern) foreign elements into their spirituality. This fluidity and selectivity in adopting novel attitudes and values speaks of the ongoing reconfiguration of their world of reference.

The principle of fluid duality has held indigenous worlds together over the centuries. It has been both concealed and protected by its nonintelligibility to outsiders, and it has guarded this "subaltern Other" from inimical incursions into their native philosophical depths. The hard core of indigenous cultures has been a well-kept secret. Even today, among many native communities in the Americas, exposing this concealed background to outsiders is considered a betrayal to the community.[7] It is only recently that the unveiling has started to be done directly by the indigenous women themselves. From my position as an outsider, I felt pressed to seek permission of Nuvia, a Tepoztlán Nahua indigenous leader, regarding whether I could interview her about her beliefs, conception of duality, and ritual in the ceremonies of her village. She accepted but did not allow me to ask my questions without her explicit previous agreement. Presently, some indigenous women and men are becoming vocal carriers of their religious and philosophical heritage and have agreed to vocalize their heritage, to share it with the outside world.

The people incarnating living indigenous traditions have played almost no part in the formation of academic theories about their way of life. They were rarely consulted, but neither did they care to validate or invalidate the views of the so-called experts who had officially defined their worlds. Silence was their weapon of survival. Only recently have they learned to use, critically and autonomously, whatever knowledge has been collected about them. The women explained that they want to "systematize the oral traditions of our peoples through the elders' knowledge and practices" (*Memoria*, p. 62).

DUALITY AND GENDER

In the indigenous Mesoamerican world, gender is construed within the pervasive concept of duality (Marcos 1998, 2006). Gender, that is, the masculine/feminine duality, is the root metaphor for the whole cosmos. Everything is identified as either feminine or masculine, and this applies to natural phenomena such as rain, hail, lightening, and clouds; living beings: animals, plants and humans; and even to periods of time, such as days, months, and years (López Austin 1988). All of these entities have a feminine or masculine "breath" or "weight." It is evident, then, that this perception of gender corresponds to a duality of complementary opposites, a duality, in turn, which is the fabric of the cosmos. Duality is the linking and ordering force that creates a coherent reference for indigenous peoples, the knitting thread that weaves together all apparent disparities (Quezada 1997; Marcos 1993).

The documents from the summit foreground and help to explain the concept that duality is also a basic referent of indigenous spirituality:

> To speak of the gender concept presupposes the concept of duality emerging from the indigenous cosmovision . . . the whole universe is ruled by duality: the sky and earth, night and day, sadness and happiness, they

complement each other. The one cannot exist without the other. (*Summit Doc. Género, p. 6*)

Everything is ruled by the concept of duality, certainly, men and women. (*Memoria*, p. 231)

Hablar del concepto de género supone remitirse al concepto de dualidad manejado desde la cosmovisión indígena . . . ya que todo el universo se rige en términos de dualidad: el cielo y la tierra, la noche y el día, la tristeza y la felicidad, se complementan el uno al otro. (*Summit Doc. Genero, p. 6*)

Todo se rige en términos de Dualidad, indudablemente, el hombre y la mujer. (*Memoria*, p. 231)

Duality is something we live through, it is there . . . we learn of it within our spirituality and we live it in ceremonies, we live it when we see that in our families women and men, mother and father take the decisions. (Candida Jimenez, Mixe indigenous woman, *Summit Doc. Genero, p. 6*)

La dualidad es algo que se vive, que se da . . . nos la enseñan en la espiritualidad y lo vivimos en la ceremonia, lo vivimos cuando vemos familias en las que las mujeres y los hombres, el papa y la mama deciden. (Candida Jimenez, Mixe indigenous woman, *Summit Doc. Genero, p. 6*)

Yet, despite the reverential espousal of the ancestral concept of gender duality and complementarity, contemporary Indigenous women express some reticence and even rejection of some aspects of it. Their arguments are based on how it is lived today in many indigenous communities. For example, in the document of the summit dedicated to "Gender from the Vision of Indigenous Women," Maria Estela Jocón, a Mayan Guatemalan wise woman, remarks that duality today

is something we should question, it is a big question mark, because as theory it is present in our cosmovision and in our customary laws, as theory, but in practice you see many situations where only the man decides . . . mass media, schools, and many other issues have influenced this principle of Duality so it is a bit shaky now. (*Summit Doc, Genero*, p. 7)

La Dualidad hoy en día es cuestionante, es un signo de interrogación grandísimo, porque como teoría existe en nuestra cosmovisión y en nuestras costumbres, como teoría, pero en la practica se ven muchas situaciones donde solamente el hombre decide . . . los medios de comunicación, la escuela y muchos otros elementos han influido para que ese principio de la Dualidad esté un poquito tambaleante. (*Summit Doc. Genero,* p. 7)

Alma Lopez, a young indigenous self-identified feminist, who is a *regidora* in her community, believes that the concept of duality of complementary opposites has been lost:

The philosophical principles that I would recover from my culture would be equity, and complementarity between men and women, women and women, and between men and men. Today the controversial complementarity of Mayan culture, does not exist. (Duarte 2002, p. 278)

Los principios filosóficos que yo recuperaría de mi cultura son la equidad, la complementariedad entre hombres y mujeres, entre mujeres y mujeres, entre hombres y hombres . . . Actualmente esa famosa complementariedad de la cultura maya no existe. (Duarte 2002, p. 178)

However, beyond the reticence or even outright negations of the contemporaneous and lived practices of inherited philosophical principles, the indigenous women are still claiming them, still want to be inspired by them, and propose to reinscribe them in their contemporary struggles for gender justice. They deem it necessary not only to recapture their ancestral cultural roots and beliefs but also to think of them as a potent resource in their quest for gender justice and equity.

Today there are big differences between the condition of women in relation to that of men. This does not mean that it was always like this. In this case there is the possibility of returning to our roots and recovering the space that is due to women, based on indigenous cosmo-vision. (*Memoria,* p. 133)

En la actualidad existen grandes diferencias entre la situación de la mujer con relación a la del hombre, no significa que siempre fue así, en este caso existe la posibilidad de retomar las raíces y recuperar el espacio que le corresponde a la mujer basado en la cosmovisión indígena.(Memoria, p. 133)

The summit document dedicated to gender has the subtitle: *De los aportes de las mujeres indígenas al feminismo* (On the Indigenous Women's Contributions to Feminism). In this portion of the document, too, the women cast off their role as recipients of a feminism imposed on them by outside forces and instead proclaim that their feminist vision has contributions to offer to other feminist approaches. Among their contributions to feminism are the innovative concepts of parity, duality, and equilibrium. The first paragraph explains that

some key aspects from indigenous movements have to be emphasized. They are the concepts of duality, equilibrium and harmony with all the implications we have mentioned already. (*Summit Doc. Genero,* p. 31)

[hay que] puntualizar algunos visiones de equilibrio, dualidad y armonia, con todas las implicaciones anteriormente citadas. (*Summit Doc. Gener,* p. 31).

It also proposes

[t]o all indigenous peoples and women's movements a revision of cultural patterns . . . with the objective of propitiating gender relations based on equilibrium. (*Summit Doc. Genero,* p. 37)

[a] *todos los Pueblos Indígenas y movimientos de mujeres indígenas, revisión de los patrones culturales con capacidad autocrítica, con el fin de propiciar unas relaciones de género basadas en el equilibrio.* (*Doc. Genero,* p. 37)

Duality, equilibrium, and harmony are among the basic principles of their feminist practices. Indigenous women claim that the demands for equality by other feminist movements could better be interpreted within their spirituality and cosmo-vision as a search for equilibrium.

EQUILIBRIUM AS GENDER EQUITY

Equilibrium, as conceived in indigenous spirituality, is not the static repose of two equal weights or masses. Rather, it is a force that constantly modifies the relation between dual or opposite pairs. Like duality itself, equilibrium, or balance, permeates not only relations between men and women but also relations among deities, between deities and humans, and among elements of nature. The constant search for this balance was vital to the preservation of order in every area, from daily life to the activity of the cosmos. Equilibrium is as fundamental as duality itself.

Duality, thus, is not a binary ordering of "static poles." Balance in this view can best be understood as an agent that constantly modifies the terms of dualities and thereby bestows a singular quality on the complementary pairs of opposites that permeate all indigenous thought (as seen in the summit documents and declarations). Equilibrium is constantly reestablishing its own balance. It endows duality with a flexibility or plasticity that makes it flow, impeding stratification. There is not an exclusively feminine or exclusively masculine being. Rather, all beings possess feminine and masculine qualities in different nuances or combinations. Whether rocks, animals, plants, or people, all have an imperceptible feminine of masculine "load" or "charge." Frequently, entities possess both feminine and masculine capacities simultaneously in different gradations that perpetually change and shift (López Austin 1988).

The gender documents were direct transcriptions from the focus group discussions. The following rich and spontaneous evaluations of equilibrium express the indigenous manner of conceiving gender equity:

We understand the practice of gender perspective to be a respectful relationship . . . of balance, of equilibrium—what in the western world would be equity. (*Summit Doc. Genero,* p. 6)

*Se entiende así la practica de enfoque de género como una relación res-
petuosa, . . . de balance, de equilibrio-lo que en occidente sería de equidad.
(Summit Doc. Genero, p. 6)*

Equilibrium means taking care of life . . . when community values of
our environment and social community are respected, there is equilibrium. (*Memoria, p. 132*)

*El equilibrio es velar por la vida . . . Cuando los valores de la comunidad,
de nuestro medio social y de nuestro entorno son respetados hay equilibrio.
(Memoria, p. 132)*

Between one extreme and the other there is a center. The extremes and
their center are not absolute, but depend on a multiplicity of factors . . .
variable and not at all exact . . . [Duality] is equilibrium at its maximum
expression. (*Memoria, p. 231*)

*Entre extremo y extremo se encuentra el centro. Los extremos de la escala,
asi como su centro, no son cualidades absolutas, sino dependen de multitud
de factores . . . variables y en absoluto exactos . . . [la Dualidad] es el equilibrio, en su maxima expresión. (Memoria, p. 231)*

Indigenous women refer to equilibrium as the attainable ideal for the
whole cosmos, and as the best way to express their own views on gender
equity.

THE SPIRITUALITY OF IMMANENCE

In the fluid, dual universe of indigenous spiritualities, the domain of the
sacred is all-pervasive. There are strong continuities between the natural
and the supernatural worlds, whose sacred beings are closely interconnected
with humans who in turn propitiate this interdependence in all their activities. Enacting this principle, at the summit, every single activity started with
an embodied ritual. The women from Latin American indigenous communities woke up early in the morning. I was given a room on the second floor, directly above the room of Rigoberta Menchú. The sounds of the early morning
sacred ritual were a reminder that I was hosted, for those days, in an indigenous universe. The processions and chants were led by a couple of Mayan
ritual specialists: a woman and a man. We prayed and walked through the
gardens and premises of the hotel where we were hosted. A fancy four-star
hotel that had never witnessed anything like this was taken over by the indigenous world. Nothing ever started, at this United Nations protocol, without
rhythmic sounds and chants, offerings to the four corners of the world, of
"copal" (a sort of Mexican incense), fruits, flowers, and colored candles. The
sacred indigenous world was there present with us; we could feel it. It was
alive in the atmosphere and within each of the participants. It was also in the
flowers, candles, and fruits and in the rhythmic repetition of words.

In striking contrast with indigenous spirituality, the dominant tradition in Christian theology stresses "classical theism," defined as centered on a metaphysical concept of God as ontologically transcendent and independent from the world. This concept of God has met with increasing criticism, particularly among ecofeminist and process theologians (Keller 2002; Gevara 2001). In indigenous spirituality, the relationship to the supernatural world lies elsewhere:

> The cosmic vision of life is to be connected with the surroundings, and all the surroundings have life, so they become SACRED: we encounter earth, mountains, valleys, caves, plants, animals, stones, water, air, moon, sun, stars. Spirituality is born from this perspective and conception in which all beings that exist in Mother Nature have life and are interrelated. Spirituality is linked to a sense of COMMUNITY in which all beings are interrelated and complementary. (*Memoria*, p. 128)
>
> *La visión cósmica de la vida es estar conectado con el entorno y todo los que hay en el entorno tiene vida, por lo que adquiere un valor*
> *SAGRADO: Encontramos tierra, planicies, cuevas, plantas, animales, agua, aire, luna, sol, estrellas. La espiritualidad nace de esta visión y concepción en la que todos los seres que hay en la Madre Naturaleza tienen vida y se interrelacionan. La espiritualidad está ligada al sentido COMUNITARIO, donde los seres se interrelacionan y se complementan.* (*Memoria*, p. 128)

Ivone Gevara, a Brazilian ecofeminist theologian, recalls how an Aymara indigenous woman responded to her theological perspective: "With ecofeminism I am not ashamed anymore of expressing beliefs from my own culture. I do not need to emphasize that they have Christian elements for them to be considered good . . . they simply are valuable" (Gevara 2001, p. 21).

Ecofeminist theology promotes complex and novel positions centered on a respect for earth and reverence for nature. Many indigenous women perceive this feminist theology to be easier to understand and closer to the standpoint of their indigenous spirituality than Catholic theism. These bridges between Christian and indigenous spiritualities become more intelligible when we reflect on the main characteristics that shape indigenous spirituality's relationship to nature: its divine dimensions, the personification of deities in humans, the fluidity between the immanent and the transcendent, and the fusion with the supernatural that women can and should enact. There is no exclusive relationship to a transcendent being called God; there is no mistrust of the flesh and the body; there is sanctity in matter:

> We recover indigenous cosmovision as our "scientific heritage," recognizing the elders as ancestral carriers of wisdom. (*Memoria*, p. 60)

Retomamos la cosmovisión indígena o ciencia de los Pueblos indigenas,
reconociendo a los ancianos y ancianas como portadores de sabiduría ances-
tral . . . (Memoria, p. 31)

That the indigenous women of different cultures and civilizations of
Abya Yala do not forget that they are daughters of the land, of the sun, of
the wind and of fire and that their continuous relation with the cosmic
elements strengthen their political participation in favor of indigenous
women and indigenous peoples. (*Memoria,* p. 63)

Que las mujeres indígenas de las diferentes culturas y civilizaciones de
Abya Yala no se olviden que son hijas de la tierra del sol, del viento y del
fuego y que su relación continua con los elementos cosmogónicos fortalecerá
su participación política a favor de las Mujeres indígenas y de los Pueblos
indígenas. (Memoria, p. 34)

The woman's body, a fluid and permeable corporeality, is conflated with
Earth as a sacred place; they regard themselves as an integral part of this
sacred Earth. The spirit is not the opposite of matter and neither is the soul
of the flesh.

EMBODIED RELIGIOUS THOUGHT

According to dominant Western epistemic traditions, the very concept
of body is formed in opposition to mind. The body is defined as the place
of biological data, of the material, of the immanent. Since the 17th century,
the body has also been conceptualized as that which marks the boundaries
between the interior self and the external world (Bordo and Jaggar 1989,
p. 4). In Mesoamerican spiritual traditions, on the other hand, the body has
characteristics that vastly differ from those of the Western anatomical or
biological body. In the Mesoamerican view, exterior and interior are not separated by the hermetic barrier of skin. Between the outside and the inside,
permanent and continuous exchange occurs. To gain a keener understanding
of how the body is conceptualized in indigenous traditions, we must think of
it as a vortex, in whirling, spiral-like movement that fuses and expels, absorbs
and discards, and through this motion is in permanent contact with all elements in the cosmos.

A SPIRITUALITY OF COLLECTIVITY
AND THE INTERCONNECTEDNESS OF ALL BEINGS

For indigenous peoples, then, the world is not "out there," established
outside of and apart from them. It is within them and even "through" them.
Actions and their circumstances are much more interwoven than is the case

in Western thought, in which the "I" can be analytically abstracted from its surroundings. Further, the body's porosity reflects the essential porosity of the cosmos, a permeability of the entire "material" world that defines an order of existence characterized by a continuous interchange between the material and the immaterial. The cosmos literally emerges, in this conceptualization, as the complement of a permeable corporeality. It is from this very ample perspective that the controversial term "complementarity" should be revisited according to its usage by indigenous women. From their perspective, it is not only feminine and masculine that are said to be "complementary," but, as Comandanta Esther insisted in her address to the Mexican Congress, complementarity embraces everything in nature. She explained that earth is life, is nature, and we are all part of it. This simple phrase expresses the interconnectedness of all beings in the Mesoamerican cosmos (López Austin 1988). Beings are not separable from one another. This principle engenders a very particular form of human collectivity with little tendency to individuation. This sense of connectedness has been found consistently within contemporary indigenous medical systems and also in the first historical primary sources (López Austin 1988). The "I" cannot be abstracted from its surroundings. There is a permanent transit between the inside and the outside (Marcos 1998). Lenkesdorf (1999) interprets an expression of the Tojolabal language (a Mayan language of Chiapas): *"Lajan, lajan aytik."* The phrase literally means *"estamos parejos"* (we are all even) but should be understood as "we are all subjects." Lenkesdorf holds that this phrase conveys the "intersubjectivity" basic to Tojolabal Culture. According to the women at the Summit:

> [s]pirituality is born from this vision and concept according to which all beings that exist in Mother Nature are interrelated. Spirituality is linked to a communitarian sense for which all beings are interrelated and complement each other in their existence. (*Memoria*, p. 128)
>
> *La espiritualidad nace de esta visión y concepción en que todos los seres que hay en la Madre Naturaleza se interrelacionan. La espiritualidad esta ligada al sentido COMUNITARIO, donde los seres se interrelacionan y se complementan en su existencia. (Memoria, p. 128)*

Among the examples of several pervasive spiritual and cosmological references reproduced anew by the indigenous women of the Americas, this one seems to be at the core: the interconnectedness of everyone and everything in the universe. The intersubjective nature of men and women is interconnected with earth, sky, plants, and planets. This is how we must understand the defense of the earth "that gives us life, that is the nature that we are," as Comandanta Esther explained to the Mexican legislators (2001). The final documents of the summit of Indigenous women states:

Indigenous peoples' spirituality revives the value of nature and humans in this century. The loss of this interrelationship has caused a disequilibrium and disorder in the world. (*Memoria*, p. 134)

En la Espiritualidad de los pueblos indígenas se recupera el valor importante de la naturaleza y el ser humano . . . la pérdida de esta relación ha desatado una serie de desequilibrios en el mundo. (*Memoria*, p. 134)

A cosmic and conscious spirituality aids to re-establish equilibrium and harmony . . . as women we have the strength, the energy capable of changing the course for a better communal life. (*Memoria*, p. 135)

Una espiritualidad cósmica y consciente conduce al equilibrio, a la armonía . . . Como mujeresn tenemos la fuerza, la energía capaz de cambiar rumbos hacia una mejor vida comunitaria. (*Memoria*, p. 135)

Spirituality emerges from traditional wisdom, but the document also stresses that "we have to be conscious of the richness of the worldwide cultural diversities" (*Summit Doc. Género*, p. 31). Here again, we perceive a characteristic of openness, a "transnational" consciousness that has been influenced by women's movements and feminist practices.

Indigenous ethnicities are not self-enclosed but rather envision themselves in active interaction with a world of differences: national, binational, and transnational. The international indigenous movements are building bridges all over the world and gaining momentum. There is a growing transnational language of cultural rights espoused by the "indigenous" worldwide. They all acknowledge the damage that diverse colonialisms have done to their worldviews and have begun to echo each other concerning the value of recovering their own spiritualities and cosmologies.[8] In recent years, indigenous peoples have intensified their struggle to break free from the chains of colonialism and its oppressive spiritual legacy. Indigenous women's initiatives to recover their ancestral religious legacy constitute a decolonizing effort. Through a deconstruction of past captivities, they recreate a horizon of ancestrally inspired spirituality. They lay claim to an ethics of recovery while rejecting the violence and subjugation suffered by their ancestors within the religious and cultural domain. "We only come to ask for justice," the organized indigenous women have repeatedly declared. Yes, justice is their demand: material, social, and political justice. They also seek recognition of and respect for their cosmological beliefs as an integral part of their feminist vision.

NOTES

1. There are numerous definitions of the term, "indigenous." Here are some: According to Linita Manu'atu (2000), writing on Tongan and other Pacific

islands peoples: "Indigenous refers to the First Peoples who settled in Aotearoa (New Zealand), United States, Canada, and so on. Other terminologies are Tangata Whenua, First Nations or simply the People" (80). According to Kay Warren's writings on Guatemala, "indigenous . . . is itself, of course, a historical product of European colonialism that masks enormous variations in history, culture, community, and relations with those who are considered non-indigenous" (112). The UN ILO Convention, n.169, specifies:

> Indigenous communities, peoples, and nations are those groups who have a continuous history that originates from earlier stages to the presence of the invasion and colonization. Groups that develop in their territories or part of it, and consider themselves different to other sectors of the society that are now dominant. These groups are today subaltern sectors and they are decided to preserve, develop, and transmit to the future generations their ancestral territories and their ethnic identity. These characteristics are fundamental to their existential continuity as peoples, in relationship with their own cultural, social, institutional, and legal systems. ("Movimientos étnicos y legislación internacional" Doc. UN, ICN.41 Sub.2/1989/33 Add.3 paragraph 4, in *Rincones de Coyoacán*, 5. February–March, 1994. Convention n.169 of the ILO of United Nations)

2. During the last 20 years, the percentage of Catholics has been decreasing consistently. In Mexico now (2006), only roughly 82 percent of the population identifies as Catholic in contrast to 96.5 percent of two decades ago. The main domain of Catholic believers had been the impoverished and dispossessed of Mexico. Among them stand the 62 distinct indigenous peoples in the country.

3. This theme resounds around the world with other indigenous peoples. See the Maori claims in Linda Tuhiwai, *Decolonizing Methodologies, Research and Indigenous Peoples* (2003).

4. Quotations from the *Memoria,* the raw materials and transcriptions from focus groups, and documents from the summit vary in translation. Some of the documents are translated into English as part of the document, in which case the Spanish translation of a particular section has a different page number from the English. In some cases, the Spanish was not translated in the documents; this is particularly the case for the position statements, whereas the declarations and plans of actions are often in both Spanish and English in the documents. Unless otherwise noted, I am responsible for all translations.

5. The document was produced collectively after hours of proposals and debate. It was finally agreed on by a consensus vote, the only way to be truly "democratic" among indigenous peoples.

6. During several UN meetings of the reproductive rights network here in Mexico and in New York, I consistently noticed that many feminist activists, journalists, and academic researchers, though not necessarily Catholic believers, manifested a mix of fear and respectful reverence to the ritual garments and

other paraphernalia of church officials, which prevented them from effectively negotiating with the Vatican representatives, despite their deeply ingrained antireligious stand.

7. Inés Talamantes, a Native American Professor of Religious Studies who does ethnography on her own Mescalero Apache culture, once confided to me that she was forbidden by her community to reveal the deep meanings of their ceremonies.

8. See Kepa 2006; Tuhiwai 1999; Syiem 2005; Palomo et al. 2003; Manu'tu 2000; Champagne and Abu-Saad 2005; Villebrun 2005.

REFERENCES

Bordo, Susan R. and Alison M. Jaggar, eds. *Gender/Body/Knowledge*. New Brunswick, NJ: Rutgers University Press, 1989.

Butler, Judith. "Conversation between Gayatri Chakravorty Spivak and Judith Butler." Presentation at the Conference *Area Studies/Literary Fields/Multilinguism/Theory*. New York: New York University, 2004.

Champagne, Duane and Ismael Abu-Saad, eds. *Indigenous and Minority Education: International Perspectives on Empowerment*. Beer-Sheva, Israel: Negev Center for Bedouin Development, Ben-Gurion University of the Negev, 2005.

Duarte, Bastian and Angela Ixkic. "Conversación con Alma Lopez, Autoridad Guatemalteca: La Doble Mirada del Género y la Etnicidad." *Estudios Latinoamericanos*, nueva epoca 9, no. 18 (2002).

Esther, Comandanta. "Discurso ante la Cámara de Diputados." *Perfil de la Jornada*, March 29 (2001): iv.

Gevara, Ivone. "Epistemologia Ecofeminista." *Ecofeminismo: Tendencias e Debates*. Mandragora. Sao Bernardo do Campo: Universidade Metodista de Sao Paulo, 6 (2001): 18–27.

Gil Olmos, José. Interview with Alain Touraine, "Mexico en riesgo de caer en el caos y caciquismo." *La Jornada*, November 6 (2000a): 3.

Gil Olmos, Jose. Interview with Yvon Le Bot, "Moderno y creativo el movimiento de indígenas en América Latina." *La Jornada*, March 26 (2000b): 3.

Gonzalez, Hector, archbishop of Oaxaca; Sergio Obeso, archbishop of Jalapa, Veracruz; Lazaro Perez, bishop of Autlán, Jalisco; Rodrigo Aguilar, bishop of Matehuala, San Luis Potosí. *Mensaje a la Cumbre de Mujeres Indígenas de las Ameritas* Comisión Episcopal de Indígenas, Oaxaca, México, December (2002): Ms. 1–4.

Keller, Catherine. *From a Broken Web: Separation, Sexism, and Self*. Boston: Beacon Press, 2002, 1986.

Kepa, Mere. "The Coastal Blues and the Darker Picture of Development." Paper presented at the Conference, *To Live as Maori*, Maori Sector of the Association of University Staff, Hui Te Kupenga o Te Matauranga Marae, Massey University, Palmerston North, New Zealand, June 22–23, 2006.

Lenkesdorf, Carlos. *Los hombres verdaderos: Voces y testimonios tojolabales,* Mexico: Siglo XXI, 1999.

López Austin, Alfredo. *The Human Body and Ideology.* Salt Lake City: University of Utah Press, 1988.

López Austin, Alfredo. "El núcleo duro, la cosmovisión y la tradición mesoamericana." *Cosmovisión, Ritual e Identidad de los Pueblos Indígenas de México,* ed. Johanna Broda and Felix Baez-Jorge. Mexico: Fondo de Cultura Economica, 2001, 47–65.

Manu'atu, Linita. "Katoanga Fiaba: a Pedagogical Site for *Tongan* Students." *Educational Philosophy and Theory* 32, no. 1 (2000): 73–80.

Marcos, Sylvia. "The Borders Within: The Indigenous Women's Movement and Feminism in Mexico." *Dialogue and Difference: Feminisms Challenge Globalization,* ed. Sylvia Marcos and Marguerite Waller. New York: Palgrave, 2005a, 81–113.

Marcos, Sylvia. "La construcción del género en Mesoamérica: un reto Epistemológico." Paper presented at the 13th CICAES, Mexico, August 4, 1993.

Marcos, Sylvia. "Conversation on Feminist Imperialism and the Politics of Difference." *Dialogue and Difference: Feminisms Challenge Globalization.* New York: Palgrave, 2005b, 143–162.

Marcos, Sylvia. "Embodied Religious Thought: Gender Categories in Mesoamerica." *Religion* 28 (1998): 371–382.

Marcos, Sylvia. *Taken from the Lips: Gender and Eros in Mesoamerica.* Leiden: Brill, 2006.

Mignolo, Walter. "From Central Asia to the Caucasus and Anatolia: Transcultural Subjectivity and De-Colonial Thinking." *Postcolonial Studies* 10, no. 1 (2007): 111–120.

Mignolo, Walter D. and Madina Tlostanova. "Theorizing from the Borders: Shifting the Geo- and Body-Politics of Knowledge." *European Journal of Social Theory* 9, no. 1 (2006): 205–221.

Nash June. "The Mayan Quest for Pluricultural Autonomy in Mexico and Guatemala." *Indigenous Peoples and the Modern State,* ed. Duane Champagne, Karen Torjesen, and Susan Steiner. New York and Toronto: Altamira Press, 2005.

Palomo, Nellys, Eleanor Dictaan-Bang-oa, and Jack G. L. Medrana. "Conflict Resolution and Gender in Mexico: The Role of Women in Achieving Autonomy." *Tebtebba: Indigenous Peoples International Centre for Policy Research and Education.* Baguio City, Philippines, 2003.

Quezada, Noemí. *Sexualidad Amor y Erotismo: México prehispánico y México Colonial.* México: IIA-Universidad Nacional Autónoma de México y Plaza Valdez, 1997.

Shi, Shu-mei, Sylvia Marcos, Obioma Nnaemeka, and Marguerite Waller. "Conversation on Feminist Imperialism and the Politics of Difference." *Dialogue and Difference: Feminisms Challenge Globalization,* ed. Marguerite Waller and Sylvia Marcos. New York: Palgrave, 2005, 143–162.

Spivak, Gayatri. *A Critique of Postcolonial Reason*. Cambridge, MA: Harvard University Press, 1999.

Summit 2002. Documento "Género desde la Visión de las Mujeres Indígenas," Universidad de las Regiones Autonomas de la Costa Caribe Nicaragüense, URACCAN, Centro de estudios e Información de la mujer multietnica CEIMM, Documento Primera Cumbre Internacional de Mujeres Indígenas, 2002. Ms.1–43.

Summit 2002. *Mensaje de las Mujeres Indígenas Mexicanas a los Monseñores de la Comisión Espiscopal de Obispos*. Ms., Oaxca, Mexico, December 1–2, 2002.

Summit 2003. *Memoria de la Primera Cumbre de Mujeres Indígenas de América*, Mexico: Fundación Rigoberto Menchú Tum, 2003.

Syiem, Darilyn. "Religious Healing." Paper presented at the *10th International Women and Health Meeting*, New Delhi, India, September 15, 2005.

Tlostanova, Madina. "Why Cut the Feet in Order to Fit the Western Shoes? Non-European Soviet ex-Colonies and the Modern Colonial Gender System." Ms. Moscow, 2007.

Tuhiwai, Linda. S. *Decolonizing Methodologies: Research and Indigenous Peoples*. London and New York: Zed Books, 1993, and University of Otago Press, 2003.

Villebrun, Noeline. "Athabaskan Education: The Case of Denendeh Past, Present and Future." *Indigenous and Minority Education: International Perspectives on Empowerment,* ed., Duane Champagne and Ismael Abu-Saad. Negev Center for Regional Development, Ben Gurion University of the Negev, 2005.

Waller, Marguerite and Sylvia Marcos, eds. *Dialogue and Difference: Feminisms Challenge Globalization*. New York: Palgrave, 2005.

Warren, Kay, and Jean Jackson. *Indigenous Movements, Self-Representation and the State in Latin America*. Austin: University of Texas Press, 2002.

Warren, Kay, and Jean Jackson. *Indigenous Movements and Their Critics*. Princeton, NJ: Princeton University Press, 1998.

CHAPTER 4

Authority and Ritual in the Caves of Tepoztlán, Mexico: Women Priestesses in Popular Religion

Ana María Salazar Peralta

This work addresses two main objectives. First, it reflects upon the religious figures and symbolic production that lay groups with Mesoamerican indigenous roots have created in order to connect themselves to the sacred amid full-fledged globalization. Second, it considers the religious phenomenon of women's prominence within rain-invoking rituals.

The ethnographic research that we carried out in northern Morelos has allowed us to witness, over the years, an interesting repositioning of individual beliefs and the inertia of mass religious movements in Mexico. Particularly, among Tepoztlán's community of indigenous peoples, we find a significant religious syncretism.

I am interested in exploring the nature of women's participation within the gender order of popular religiosity, specifically among Tepoztlán's indigenous community. We maintain that religion has become one of the central axes in the collective identities of these modern traditional societies of central Mexico.

Cultural and religious practices, specifically *rituales de peticiones de lluvia* (rain-invoking rituals), exemplify the long-standing sociocultural dynamic of Tepoztlán's indigenous peoples. These rituals represent the sacred dimension of ancient culture and its significance for these modern traditional societies.

The central inquiry in the contemporary secular world is the following: What do nonbelievers, that is, intellectuals, believe in?[1] However, this question can also apply to other social segments whose local history links mystic-religious practices—expressions of the nature of sacred things, virtues, and powers—to the profane.[2] These practices highlight the complexity of sociocultural reality in a multiethnic and multicultural context, like the one we are investigating.

In today's world, we observe a range of modern conceptual frames that impose themselves on diverse cultural realities—realities defined by the individual cultures' ever globalizing codes of modernity. It is for that reason that we are interested in addressing the religious context of rituals and cultural practices linked to Mesoamerican cosmo-vision, the basis for contemporary popular Catholic religiosity among indigenous peoples.

Ancient history and Mesoamerican religion provide us with an extraordinary documentary source to interpret the popular religiosity based in Mesoamerican cosmo-vision. Therefore, as a point of departure, we will address the wide repertory of cultural practices associated with *the airs* and *the hills,* whose titular gods Tlaloc, Quetzalcoatl, and Ehecatl act as both deities and cultural mediators to provide rain, fertility, and sustenance.

Modern ethnography reveals an extensive register of Mesoamerican cultural practices; in light of that, we would like to understand the role that contemporary rain-invoking rituals plays in religious syncretism, insofar as the survival of indigenous cosmo-vision is concerned. Clearly, the cultural phenomenon of rain rituals has a long history that shapes and constitutes the Tepozteca identity.

The power structure that results from the asymmetrical relationship between popular religiosity and institutionalized religion arises from a process in which believers are continually negotiating their position in relation to religious leaders. Thus, believers go through the motions of creating symbolic capital, founded in both their faith and the legitimacy of their ritual practices.

The prominence of women in rain-invoking rituals does not simply invite us to examine the nature of this religious phenomenon, which is necessary to methodological positioning regarding gender order. This order is, in turn, determined by the manner in which Tepoztlán's indigenous peoples organize their ceremonial life and rituals.

In that sense, gender is a category of relational analysis that maps cultural practices, constructing social meanings of men and women. It permits a better, more in-depth understanding of the hard data of the research. Through gender we understand the cultural construction of sexual difference. Authors like Bourdieu, explaining the asymmetry between the genders, have suggested a sort of male-centric unconscious that would underlie all forms of patriarchal domination.[3]

Patriarchal domination is a result of historically determined cultural practices. Cristina Oehmichen tells us that social actors endowed with multiple resources and types of economic, cultural, and symbolic capital, fight to impose or modify the meanings attributed to masculinity and femininity.[4] They do not use symbols and practices to establish communication but rather to persuasively impose a sense of power. In this sense, culture does not just cover up or mask power relations; it also contributes to their reproduction and realization. Looking through a gendered lens, we can relationally approach the sum of all social spheres in order to understand the social institutions, representations, and ideologies that adhere to gender order, including social roles instituted in both popular Catholicism and Mesoamerican cosmo-vision.

In analyzing rain-invoking rituals, we must consider *sacred spaces* both historically and symbolically in order to correctly apply a *cultural interpretation* to the social subjects who constitute indigenous communities. For 21st-century Tepoztecas, sacred spaces are a fundamental component of collective memory. Their historic, symbolic basis comes from a particular indigenous worldview, which modern rituals now reflect.

It is worth noting that, today, the religious practices of Tepoztlán's indigenous peoples not only reproduce Mesoamerican precepts, but also incorporate external cultural concepts circulating in the globalizing electronic media. This fusion of beliefs could be explained as a textbook phase of global or globalized culture—a culture that does not yet exist. Gilberto Giménez has pointed out that:

> there is not a global culture, but a globalized culture in the sense that there is a growing interconnection between all cultures by virtue of communication technologies. We cannot speak about a global identity because there is no homogenous culture to sustain it, or common symbols to express it, or a collective memory to support it.[5]

In that sense, Tepoztlán's modern traditional societies are a synthesis of historic processes in which ancient and modern cultural symbols coexist, interconnect, and interact. Today, agrarian communities and indigenous peoples express this coexistence through ritual and popular religiosity. Calling upon Mesoamerican religious tradition, they maintain a close relationship between humans and nature.[6]

In these contexts, ritual or sacred spaces acquire symbolic value; as an example of how this happens, we can take the collective notion of community land, which the *axis mundi* represents, and which constructs one of the founding elements of Tepozteca identity. This example calls attention to the connection between otherness and normativity. Otherness, that is, the concept of communal space, is subject to normativity, such as, the idea of individual space contrasted with that of others: new neighbors and foreigners with whom inhabitants interact on various levels. Consequently, the land acquires *an ethic validation* from the community.

Land, therefore, is the result of a geographic space that a culture has transformed, manifesting religious thought. Tepoztlán's land consists of a mountain range of the same name: the Tepozteco, an *important ritual space* endowed with symbolic content;[7] consequently, the land transforms itself into sacred space, thus surpassing its simple utilitarian function.[8]

The land is also the place of residence for the cultural hero, Tepoztecatl: man-god-governor, alter ego of indigenous peoples, and core of the Tepozteca ethic. In his capacity as a god, because of his link with Quetzalcoatl, Petecatl, and Mayahuel, he is associated with the gods of fertility.

Among the various community spaces in Tepoztlán, rural areas have a collective identity that connects ceremonial life and rain-invoking rituals to both gods whom Tepoztecas have always venerated and people who faithfully maintain agrarian traditions by adapting to and resisting modernity through global cooperation.[9] The preservation of the agrarian way of life embodies the principles of indigenous Mesoamerican cosmo-vision. Thus, the contemporary conception of the cosmos is grounded in the cosmo-vision of Tepozteca ancestors. This ancestral cosmo-vision recalls a thought process structured around the agrarian cycle, particularly around the nascence of corn. Corn, the basis of agriculture and the core of rituals that facilitate links with the divine, operates as a founding notion of the mythic universe. In agrarian societies women are in charge of organizing the ceremonial life and the rituals, and this strengthens the primordial links with their ethnic territory.

These contemporary farming societies base their daily life upon agriculture and the continued cultivation of corn (together with beans, squash, and chilies). Their agrarian rituals bring about a harmonic equilibrium between humanity and the gods who will provide sustenance. This equilibrium results from human effort—ritual sacrifice and human labor—and the divine will that provides generosity of land, abundance of rain, and control of natural disasters. To achieve this equilibrium, people throughout the area worship the *yeyecatl-yeyecame* deities through festivities and ritual.

Hence, ritual is dedicated to fertility. Believers derive energy from the Mesoamerican pantheon, specifically from Tepoztecatl and the yeyecatl-yeyecame. They devote an intense, complex ritual to these deities, which we will illustrate with the case of *San Andrés de la Cal*, analyzing the tasks of *los tiemperos* or *los graniceros* (rainmakers or weather shaman).[10] These traditional specialists invoke the strength of the gods in order to bring about a good and abundant crop. The power of rainmakers is their ability to control and appease the rebuffs of the gods through ritual.

THE CULTURAL GEOGRAPHY OF
THE MUNICIPALITY OF TEPOZTLÁN

The Tepozteco mountain range has presented a challenge to human survival since the appearance of its first small villages.[11] Settlers there, vulnerable to landslides, erosion, and flooding, have had to precariously seize small parcels of cultivatable land. Populations located in the highlands confront cold and sudden frosts, capable of destroying an entire crop in one night alone. Very frequently, mountainous areas intercept rain-filled clouds, supplying hills and valleys with water, while leeward lands end up depleting. Under these conditions, water for drinking and watering crops becomes a fundamental element for social production and reproduction. Nature, unfortunately, has not provided favorable conditions for the existence and reproduction of Mesoamerican populations and, in particular, the inhabitants of the Central Altiplano (Mexican high plain).

Therefore, the residents of northern Morelos have developed an elaborate ideological system surrounding water, one of agrarian society's most basic needs. Where there is not a water system in place, women are often in charge of bringing water from the springs and other sources. Water shortage has always fostered technological creativity, and for millennia, Tepoztecas have developed strategies for efficiently conserving water resources in order to ensure human survival. Interestingly, Eric Wolf has noted that hundreds of place names in these towns and sites are related to the need for and lack of water.[12]

The mountainous region of the Tepozteco gives shelter and sustenance to a picturesque collection of indigenous towns. Over time, new settlements and neighborhoods have arisen, but they remain linked to the municipal organization of Tepoztlán's indigenous community, the seat of political and economic power.

In *Las Relaciones Geográficas* (*Geographic Relationships*), Acuña describes the Tepozteca seigniory as a dominion in the midst of crags and cliffs.[13] At the end of the 16th century, Tepoztlán was made up of seven towns subject to the nobility of Cuauhnahuac and Gustepec. The hills and mountains of the Tepozteco housed altars to the gods, and *the great devil* lived in Tlahuiltepetl, where believers performed sacrifices and made fire. Tepoztecatl also lived there.

The Tepoztecas have always maintained an ironclad belief in supernatural entities and deities. Tepoztecatl, their titular god, represents one of the 400 rabbits, the gods of *pulque* (fermented sap of the *agave,* a kind of cactus) and fertility. But he also represents a synthesis of the wind gods. In the various towns that comprise these modern traditional societies, there is still an extensive record of oral tradition and religious practice associated with *the airs* and *the rain*. For instance, a belief exists that bathing in a ravine can be motive for *a divine spell*, since *the airs* that harm people and make women pregnant live there.

We affirm that Mesoamerican cosmo-vision is the basis for contemporary indigenous religious practices and shapes a fundamental part of popular religiosity within these modern traditional societies. Throughout their long history, Mesoamerican communities have established two mythic-religious systems: popular beliefs and religious practices, which are manifested through an extensive range of cultural regional variations and temporal representatives of each creator society.[14] In contrast, we understand that worship of the hills is entirely related to Tepozteca ritual geography, which stems from Mesoamerican cosmo-vision. Ritual geography refers to a geographic landscape transformed or created by human groups, for example, temples, rock altars, carved stones, petroglyphs, and cave paintings, all channels for worship and ritual.

Tepoztlán's cultural geography encompasses hill worship and ritual.[15] Cultural geography refers to geographic space transformed and inhabited by different social groups. In this context, we are interested in emphasizing ritual geography in order to explain and interpret the nature of sacred space and the diversity of this space in the mountains of Tepoztlán.

Johanna Broda has stressed the importance of sacred spaces and hill worship in a Mesoamerican context.[16] She points out that sacred spaces are a symbolic representation of indigenous cosmo-vision; we can add that they are also the outcome of symbolic production on the part of indigenous communities. Druzo Maldonado, in turn, indicates that they result from the transformation of a profane space into a landscape that has acquired significance through ritual.[17] Finally, sacred spaces are geosymbols and places where the community carries out its religious ceremonies, establishing the crucial, identifying link between individuals and their native territory, their motherland.[18]

Studies on ancient Mesoamerican history offer us an extensive record of the repertory of religious practices and beliefs derived from the millennia-old indigenous cosmo-vision. Accordingly, these *modern traditional societies* continue to strengthen themselves by worshipping hills, caves, streams, rocky shelters, and springs; they perform rituals that reproduce indigenous Mesoamerican cosmo-vision and culture.

EHECATL, QUETZALCOATL, AND TLALOC

Tepoztlán's religious pantheon consists of Tepoztecatl, Ometochtli, and the yeyecatl-yeyecame, as well as a symbolic system of fertility and sustenance

gods: Ehecatl, Quetzalcoatl, and Tlaloc. The themes of fertility and sustenance dominate the festivities of the 18-month agricultural calendar and the
ritual pre-Hispanic calendar, both readapted to the modern agricultural calendar.[19] In the field of indigenous cosmo-vision, the importance surrounding
the presence of Tlaloc—god of rain and life and numen of the earth—is
associated with the gods of wind, sometimes represented by Ehecatl, sometimes by Quetzalcoatl. Quetzalcoatl emerges as one of the oldest and most
worshipped figures among the peoples of the Mesoamerican Altiplano.

Tlaloc's territory was the Tlalocan, depicted as a large cave or underground path, where the gods of rain, thunder, and lightning lived. The majority of Mesoamerican peoples were farmers, and the preeminence of the gods
Ehecatl, Quetzalcoatl, and Tlaloc was absolutely central to their life and
sustenance. They dedicated feasts and rituals to the gods. They believed that
the gods fed themselves and lived off sacrificial blood, while humans fed off
the land, plants, and animals.

> Tlaloc Tlamacazqui was the rain god. It was held that he offered rains in
> order to water the earth, rain that nourished all the grasses, trees, fruits,
> and sustenance. It was also held that he sent hail, lightning, rainstorms,
> and dangers of rivers and sea. *Tlaloc Tlamacazqui* means god who inhab-
> its the earthly paradise and who gives men the sustenance necessary for
> bodily life.[20]

Tlaloc personified the fundamental figure in the renewal of life and
nature.[21] Sacrifice assured the continuation of the lives of the gods.[22] Un-
derwater caves were perceived to be the entryways into the subterranean
reign. Some authors interpret these caves in the form of a tree or uterus.
Caves, hills, and their symbolic production are closely related; they create
a conceptual unity within indigenous Mesoamerican cosmo-vision, which
is linked with ancestors and origin, and gives legitimacy to ethnic-territorial
identity.[23]

> The thirteenth month was called *Tepeilhuitl*. In this month they held a
> feast to honor the eminent, cloud-shrouded mountains that run through-
> out New Spain. The people made statues of human figures for each one
> of them, using dough that was called *tzoal*, and they offered these statues
> out of respect for the mountains.[24]

Indigenous communities fervently worshipped mountains because of
their function as water catchers and providers, and storm controllers. They
considered mountains terrestrial deities who sent storms, hail, and disease.
But mountains also had beneficial properties, for example, making plants
grow, and their intervention determined agricultural success.

In the ancient world, during the Tepeilhuitl, or hill festival, people made miniature statues of the hills in gratitude for agricultural fertility and in memory of the dead.[25]

> *Tepeilhuitl.* To honor the mountains, they made snakes out of sticks or tree branches, and carved the head like a snake. They also made some pieces of wood as thick and long as a wrist; they called them *ecatotonti.* They covered both the snakes and the wooden pieces with the dough they call *tzoal.* They dressed these wooden pieces as mountains; on top they put their head, like the head of a person. They made these statues in memory of those who had drowned in the water or had died such a death that they weren't burned, but buried. After they had placed these statues on their altars with much ceremony, they offered them tamales and other foods, and also sang chants of praise and drank wine in their honor. Upon arrival to the party, in honor of the mountains, they sacrificed four women and one man. The first of the women was called *Tepóxoch;* the second called *Matlalcuae* the third called *Xochtécatl;* the fourth called *Mayáhuel;* and the man was called *Milnáhuatl.* They dressed these women and man with many papers full of *ulli,* and carried them in berths atop the shoulders of heavily costumed women. . . . Then, after having broken up the mountain statues to eat, they hung the statues' dressing papers in the *calpul.*[26]

Even during mid-20th-century festivals for Tepoztecatl, worshippers still made miniature depictions of the main hills, which served as a stage for the theatre piece *The Challenge Against the Tepozteco: Ecaliztli ihuicpan Tepoztecat.* The actors perform the play in the Nahuatl language in order to invoke the ancient gods.[27] Today, it is fascinating to observe how modern cultural practices, which inform the daily lives of indigenous peoples, originate from ancient history and parallel early beliefs and rituals.

Over the last few years, during our anthropological research in northern Morelos, I have been able to observe and record a series of rain-invoking rituals, as well as observe offerings in caves, rocky shelters, springs, watering holes, wells, and modern water faucets in San Andrés de la Cal.

It is important to point out that in 1993 a surprising archeological discovery occurred in one of the innumerable caves that dot the Tepozteco mountain range. A group of speleologists discovered the Chimalacatepec cave in San Juan Tlacotenco, a mountain town located in the north of the municipality. This cave has a long, wide entrance pitch with two chambers, in which scientists found numerous objects associated with rituals and gods. The archeological discovery consisted of three offerings, made up of more than 90 worship objects, among them: *cajetes* (glazed bowls), incense burners, and small figurines made of *chalchihuite* or green jade.[28]

The archeological evidence surrounding the hills of northern Morelos has stimulated research. Several local intellectuals took it upon themselves to video record not only the discovery of the speleologists but also the cave paintings found in the hills of Tepoztlán.[29] The majority of the paintings feature iconography associated with Tlaloc: serpents and lightning bolts, negative hands, and some other esthetic motifs that are difficult to recognize because of rock deterioration. Alive and intangible, rain-invoking rituals in Tepoztlán are a rich heritage; their relevance allows each town to have their own cave or group of caves, their own sacred spaces, and their own specialists. Each annual cycle, residents bring offerings and develop rituals connected to the agrarian cycle.

RAIN-INVOKING RITUALS

In Tepoztlán, hill worship belongs to a millennia-old tradition. Hernando Ruíz de Alarcón, charged by the Neo-Spanish Inquisition with traveling throughout the modern-day states of Morelos and Guerrero in search of superstitions, recorded his findings in the 17th century. During his travels, Ruíz de Alarcón found altars in

> mountaintops and high hills, with paths so marked it was as if they were for carriages. In those piles of rock they made sacrifices and said prayers; certain elderly people were responsible for the ministry of the sacrifices. They called them *tlamacazque* or priests. On the altars, there were idols of different makes and names. Their supreme god, lord of the world, was called *Tlalticpaque*, whom the *Tlamacazque* or *Tlamazcaqui*, the old priest, and the *Tlamaceuhqui*, the penitents, accompanied on the pilgrimage.[30]

Icpalican or Temaxcalitan, also named Acacueyecan, place of *saya* or *faldellín de caña* (a type of skirt or overskirt made of reeds), today known as San Andrés de la Cal, is a community located to the south of Tepoztlán.[31] Toward the end of the 16th century, this village appeared in *Las Relaciones Geográficas*. The records discuss a spring that flows out next to a particular spot in San Andrés:

> During the summertime, there is a little water in some of the crags, and in the rainy season, there is a greater amount. It runs about a fourth of a league down and then feeds into a cave between some limestone crags. They say that it plunges in there, but no one knows where it comes out. In the past, they would enter the cave to worship—they would lower themselves down with ropes and light the space with *ocote* pine torches. They

say worshippers found corncobs and other things, which they took out and exhibited for a tidy sum.[32]

Modern rain-invoking rituals in San Andrés de la Cal take place annually in mid-May; during these rituals, offerings are made to the wind and airs so that they'll bring rain. The Tlamazcaqui (the priest) is Doña Jovita Jiménez, an elderly woman, specialist and person in charge of continuing local tradition. The modern Tlamaceuhqui (the penitents) are the pilgrims who accompany Jovita; they continue the tradition described in the *Florentine Codex,* with the belief that the hills and mountains are like vessels, entities replete with water.

Hill worship and rain invocations reproduce the meaning and significance of water, land, corn, life, fertility, that which is female, that which is dark, and the serpent.

Modern worship of hills and caves in San Andrés de la Cal is a seasonal, ritual activity, headed by a specialist: la Tlamazcaqui, *la granicera, la tiempera,* or *la rayada* (one who has gained shamanic powers through surviving a lightening strike). Regionally, people use these titles to refer to male specialists, but San Andrés stands out because, there, these epithets are feminine.[33] The person in charge of conducting rituals and communicating with the yeyecatl-yeyecame is a woman. In Amatlán de Quetzalcoatl, weather forecasters were called *sabios* (sages); they were important figures with the ability to cross the hills until they reached the Xochiatlaco waterfall. These *sabios* remind us of the *weather-carriers* of Teotihuacan.

The municipal representative is in charge of organizing the people in order to assist Jovita with her tasks. The people meet in the town hall, where the ritual delegation finalizes details, and everyone begins to organize committees to solicit economic contributions from neighboring towns like Santa Catarina, which accompanies San Andrés on the requisite pilgrimage that precedes the offerings.

Doña Jovita will buy everything necessary for the offerings using community-donated funds. Several women go along with her to the market in Cuernavaca. They buy fruit there—the most fragrant of the season—as well as little toys (dolls that represent gender duality: feminine-masculine; as well as little snakes, animals, and toy soldiers). They buy the ingredients for green mole, a dish prepared with pumpkin seeds. They buy candies, *aguardiente* (a Mexican liquor), candles, bright and colorful tissue paper, as well as colored yarn and freshly cut flowers, mostly gladiolas. Then they add the pyrotechnic material: fireworks and gunpowder. Finally come the cigarettes, a necessary element for protection against bad airs.

With all these products on hand, the committee in charge of the offerings meets in the town hall, where they distribute the tasks of preparing tortillas and tamales, as well as blue corn *gorditas* (thick tortillas) in the shape of little figures: stars, snakes, and lightning bolts. They cook the mole and distribute it into several small jugs for transit.[34] They wrap the candies in the colorful tissue paper, along with the fruits, and decorate the bottles with pieces of colorful yarn. Then they place the offerings—food, drinks, fruit, toys, *pulque*, dolls, flowers, fireworks, gunpowder, all the necessary trappings—in large baskets. Everything is put together with a great deal of ingenuity and an extraordinary sense of esthetics. The municipal representative organizes the committee that will transport the prepared baskets to the altar of the small church.

The following morning, fireworks and ringing church bells awaken the community. A Catholic mass begins, officiated by the priest from Tepoztlán. In previous years, there were priests who refused to officiate mass because they considered this cultural practice to be a superstition. It is worth mentioning that, after the social conflict sparked by an attempt to build a golf club in Tepoztlán, there was a violent reaction against the bishop and the parish priest of Tepoztlán, the bishop's cousin, who supported the investors. The conflict provoked reactions of rejection and polarization among the population. Consequently, the bishop had to retract his statements and name another priest to replace his nephew. The substitute priest was Father Filiberto, experienced in indigenous ministry and sensitive to Tepozteca traditions. Upon Father Filiberto's return to his home parish in Totolopan, the ecclesiastical headquarters of Cuernavaca appointed Father Ignacio to Tepoztlán, another priest who is sensitive, tolerant, and in favor of preserving popular culture. These priests have gladly officiated the opening masses of rain-invoking rituals. When the mass concludes, the pilgrimage to the caves begins.

In recent times and owing to the advanced age of Doña Jovita, two groups have been formed to officiate the rituals: one group that advances to the high caves and another group that distributes offerings to the low caves, near Texcal. Felipe directs the former, Doña Jovita the latter. Felipe is a young man originally from San Andrés, a "captain of Mexicanidad" who has been learning from Doña Jovita so that when the moment arrives, he can replace her as Tlamazcaqui.[35] Alicia María Júarez Becerril, in her recent research on the topic, has detected a rivalry between the two Tlamazcaqui; essentially, Felipe's followers harshly criticize and slander Doña Jovita in their attempt to strip her of her power as Tlamazcaqui.[36]

As a possible explanation for this conflict, we can point to modern ideology about aging: Old age is the counter-discourse to youth, beauty, and power—characteristics that capitalism favors. Modern ideology opposes and implicitly looks down upon the experience, wisdom, and strength of spirit of the elderly, who once held a privileged status precisely because of these attributes. On the other hand, we can infer how *nativist* or *new Indian* followers

perceive the role of Tlamazcaqui. They uphold that the legitimate director of
the rituals must be a "captain of Mexicanidad" in order to cohere to the origin of ceremonial tradition. However, both explanations reveal an ideological
and political gender bias.

The established respect for the female Tlamazcaqui in San Andrés de la
Cal represents a transgression to patriarchal order, given that Tlamazcaqui in
other bordering communities are mainly men. However, knowledge of ritual
and ceremony is a form of cultural capital, a currency easily convertible in
politics, which, of course, can devolve into an arena for social conflict. Even
though the young "captain of Mexicanidad" has his followers, he does not
represent the collectivity. Doña Jovita has extensive experience and social
prestige that he cannot easily replace.

In order to carry out the rituals, an older man accompanies Doña Jovita.
He carries the baskets of offerings and prays with her, getting closer to the
gods. Let's recall what Alfredo López Austin says about the fundamental aspects of Mesoamerican religious tradition:

> Men were supposed to worship the gods and pay for godly assistance, be-
> cause gods were offended by lack of worship and unpaid debts. The treat-
> ment between gods and men was intense. The gods were loved, but also
> feared. Most importantly, men could communicate with them and influ-
> ence their will through pleas, prayers, offerings or insults and threats.[37]

The rituals begin in Tepepulco la Corona. Tepepulco is the most distant
cave on ritual land. Next comes Ayocatipac, known as the Elephant. Tepeco-
lihuiyan is the longest and largest cave; Oztocauiauha is the closest to Texcal;
Tlanancitepec is known as the New Window; Xochiocan is a crossroads; Xo-
chonpantla is a spring (an image of the virgin of Guadalupe can also be seen
here); and Xochitengo is another crossroads. At a specific site in Mexcono-
lapa, pilgrims set off fireworks and leave flowers to announce to the lords of
the caves that the faithful have come to ask for water.

The pilgrims begin to smoke cigarettes *so as not to catch a bad air*. Everyone is *sahumado* (encircled by burning incense), but especially those who
want to enter the caves. The basic belief is that the caves produce airs. These
airs are the *yeyecatl*, that help Tlaloc by sweeping the wind that brings rain
and water. Water is life. It is also a property guarded by the owners of the
caves, so if the pilgrims do not ask permission properly, the yeyecatl can send
a bad air.

Doña Jovita sweeps and picks up remnants from past offerings. The area
must be clean so that a new offering can be left. Afterward, she arranges the
colored paper like a tablecloth, designating the ritual space. Immediately following, the prayers begin in alternating Nahuatl and Spanish:

worker Lords, forgive those who do not know what they do,
   but we who are here respect the custom.
   All-powerful God, I come to ask you for a good rainy season,
   your child is here, amen.

Doña Jovita begins to put everything in place: the feminine-masculine dolls, the little animals, the candles, the flowers, the fruit, the candies, the tortillas, the little tamale figures, the *aguardiente,* the *pulque,* the cigarettes, the gunpowder, and so on.

They wanted to capture you, lords.
   here is this girl, this lovely girl is here
   so that she can do chores for you like a servant,
   for you worker lords.
   Take this girl away to work, to help you.
   Worker lords, come closer to this holy table,
   here are tortillas and food and drink.
   The gunpowder is for the worker lords who are going to work.
   Soldiers, come to work. We didn't bring you to rest . . .
   You lords, rest today . . .
   But afterwards, you are going to work all season like little soldiers . . .

Zochipizintle, zochipizintle (here Doña Jovita blows a whistles three times.)

Lords *ahuaquetezintle,* I came all the way here.
   Our Father, Most Holy Sacrament
   Our Father, Most Holy Trinity
   Our Father, Most Holy
   Our Father, Holy.
   You all are going to forgive us, not scare us . . .
   Lords, Holy temple, Holy cave
   Lords yeyecatl
   Lords yeyecame
   Worker lords,
   Lords of the airs,
   Worker lords of weather and storms
   We want and we ask you for a favor,
   We beg and implore you for rain aplenty . . .
   May God grant us water, without wind, without hail; well . . . that is what I would say; but if you all do not want it, you know, you provide . . .
   Worker lords, you should deserve what I brought you. What other people send you—people who work and earn but a cent, those who think and those who do not.

You must forgive them and excuse them, because they do not know what they do or say.

Forgive them for not cooperating with more strength.

May you have peace and happiness in your house, may you work contentedly and happily in your labors . . .

In the name of the father, the son, and the holy spirit, amen

Ave Maria Most Pure, Ave Maria Most Pure, may God our lord forgive us and aid us in what we ask. Thank you, lords.

Doña Jovita blows the whistle again and leaves the cave of Tepepulco. She and the other pilgrims follow these ritual prayers in every cave, using variations on the same theme.

After visiting the caves, crossroads, and ritual spaces, the pilgrims re-unite with all the townspeople and visitors around the patio of the town hall. Everyone is served green mole, white tamales, and tamarind juice. Then everything returns to normal, and the town waits for a good season and a good crop.

It is worth mentioning that Doña Jovita is also one of the local healers. Tepoztlán has always been a cradle of shamans and healers. This tradition has inspired knowledge surrounding the organization of ceremonial life, as well as Doña Jovita's expertise in herbs and healing. Doña Jovita's mother-in-law taught her about plants, cures, and treatments to fight common diseases. Considering her background, and with everyone gathered at the town hall, it was not strange that several people, both men and women, approached Doña Jovita to solicit consultations and treatments. They asked for services, advice, and tried to make appointments for treatment. This episode sheds light upon the community's recognition of the knowledge and abilities of the Tlamazcaqui.

FINAL CONSIDERATIONS

In summary, rain-invoking rituals mark a cyclical and seasonal activity that takes place at the beginning of the planting season. I am interested in recovering two important aspects of community life that rain rituals make visible, acting as social catalysts in the generation of social agency, social resistance, and reactivation of collective memory. One of these is the collective resistance that arose around the construction of the golf club, and the other is related to the climate change that is becoming more pronounced every dry season. Both cases have provoked significant anxiety and uncertainty, causing believers to appeal fervently to their gods.[38] The continuance of rain-invoking rituals also allows San Andrés and other indigenous communities in Tepoztlán to identify as *modern traditional societies*.[39] These societies, paradoxically, incorporate and coexist with both the elements of modern life and the cultural symbols of Mesoamerican cosmo-vision.

The yeyecatl-yeyecame—lords of weather, wind, rain, and fertility—are fundamental in the daily lives of Tepoztecas. They are closely linked with Tlaloc, Ehecatl, and Quetzalcoatl and are an apparition and representation of the *tlaloque*, Tlaloc's helpers. Known as fighters and tireless laborers, they are represented in rain rituals by the toy soldiers.

The small tamales figures directly allude to natural world representations of wind and rain deities: snakes, lightning bolts, and stars. Furthermore, the feminine-masculine dolls that are used during the offering refer to gender order; they represent the creator gods *Omecihuatl* and *Ometecutli*, a clear reference to the duality of the maker deities of weather and life.

The colors and gunpowder refer to rainbows and thunder, offshoots of rain. They allude to an intangible composition, made visible by a colorful lightning bolt that comes before the storm and rain. The scent of the fruit directly alludes to the characteristics, preferences, and telluric qualities of the gods.

Tepoztecas offer fruits of the earth and *pulque,* a sacred drink, to the gods. This action renews the presence of the *centzontotochtin* or four rabbits, apparitions of Tepuztecatl, Quetzalcoatl, Mayahuel, and Petecatl, gods of *pulque* and fertility. Hence, rain-invoking rituals are an example of popular religious syncretism. Over time, worshippers have incorporated rain rituals into their religious life, appropriating Catholic symbols. However, they have neither undermined Mesoamerican beliefs, nor the worship of terrestrial deities, that is, hills and caves.

I believe that these rituals continue because of the persistence of the agrarian way of life, which, aside from providing subsistence, allows indigenous peoples to organize their ceremonial life. The agrarian way of life also serves as a reservoir of knowledge about the nature and biodiversity of the land. Furthermore, it is the foundation that legitimates indigenous cosmovision, belief, and ritual, thus allowing social production and reproduction—but most importantly, the reproduction of rural ideology, popular religiosity and, in turn, Mesoamerican cosmo-vision. The cultural practice of rain-invoking rituals within agrarian society is a living example of a "long duration" tradition that constantly redefines itself according to the present.

Rain invocations are complex, dynamic processes in which millennia-old cultural symbols are imbued with modern cultural signs and codes. They allow us to recognize internal characteristics of social organization, including ceremonial life and ritual. Thus, the agrarian way of life becomes a backdrop for social production and reproduction, and stimulates persistence and continuity of Mesoamerican cosmo-vision.

Tepoztlán's agrarian tradition gives us a lens through which we can observe the complex structure and scope of each period of the life cycle. Work in the cornfield calls for family labor, while shortage of water requires the entire community to work and cooperate, reinforcing fundamental notions of collectivity and religious and spiritual solidarity.

Regarding the organization of ceremonial life, the work involved in rain-invoking rituals remains autonomous from *mayordomías* (a highly respected, traditional form of community leadership linked to a patron saint) and other traditional institutions. The *mayordomías* maintain their own sphere of responsibility, including caring for the chapel's cornfield and organizing the festival of the patron saint.

In terms of authority, the Tlamazcaqui is in charge of rain-invoking rituals. Her symbolic authority subordinates other forms of sociopolitical power. The municipal representative's authority, or constitutional civil authority, represents the town. Supposedly the "captains of Mexicanidad" are another "authority," but their influence is restricted to the people affiliated with the Mexicanidad dance group, not to the town as a whole.

In Julio Glockner's ethnography of Mexico's Sierra Nevada, where the Popocatepetl is located, rainmakers are known as the *teciuhtlazque*. These specialists set up a relationship with gods and ancestors in order to keep the tradition of rain invocations strongly rooted.[40] Sahagún refers to them as *hechiceros estorbadores de granizos,* or hail-deflecting sorcerers, named for their knowledge of spells to get rid of hail or set it off its course, far from the sown land. Their gift may come from one of several sources: *surviving a lightning strike,* the effect of *dreams, predestination,* or the induction of *visions* through consumption of hallucinogenic or psychoactive plants. These modern sorcerers use ritual and offering, or *huentle,* in order to persuade the primordial deities to help restore sacred order.

By contrast, in San Andrés de la Cal a woman directs the rainmakers—a woman who learned her vocation (practically speaking) not through the maternal line, but through gender sharing with her mother-in-law. Doña Jovita says that she gained her knowledge as a rainmaker and healer from her mother-in-law and husband. She remembers her mother-in-law as a simple woman who cared for her family, cured everyone in town, and who knew about plants and prayers. Today, Doña Jovita is the one who continues this tradition, caring for others and attending to the needs of the yeyecatl-yeyecame.

The singularity of women's leadership in rain-invoking rituals in San Andrés de la Cal evidences Tlamazcaqui Doña Jovita's preeminence and knowledge. It also highlights the societal recognition of women's power and empowerment within this indigenous community, and reminds us of women's political primacy in other historical moments. In the order of 17th- and 18th-century Nueva España, Tepoztlán was considered a República de Indios (Indian Republic).[41] In the 18th century, cacique Doña Juana María governed Tepoztlán, and it was she who launched a decades-long dispute to defend land and men's work from the abusive hands of Spanish and *criollo* (Mexican-born Spanish) governors.[42]

We observe then that gender has played a fundamental role in the social organization of these indigenous peoples. Therefore, within Tepozteca historical memory, the female condition has not always been one of patriarchal subjugation; rather, there has been acknowledgement and perhaps even balance between the genders—a dynamic balance that adapts to changing historical contexts. We can say that it is a dynamic equilibrium, intergender complementarity, depending on the changing historical contexts.

I believe that hill worship, in the context of sacred geography, is not simply a past social reality; on the contrary, it is a modern, thriving cultural phenomenon in which believers reclaim their ownership of the past, strengthening collective identities. For believers, the relevance of hill worship lies in controlling and neutralizing the chaos of modernity, providing balance in the face of an uncertain future.

Hill worship associated with rain invocations and major gods (Tlaloc, Ehecatl, Quetzalcoatl, Tepoztecatl, and the yeyecatl-yeyecame) is a modern religious practice that reestablishes not just the meaning of ritual discourse, but also of daily life. In Mesoamerican indigenous cosmo-vision, speech and words have profound ethic implications that give major symbolic value to religion as a social absolute of daily life. For that reason, in rain-invoking rituals the community transmits their words through an elderly woman, a woman with experience, wisdom, and strength of spirit, an expert on weather, and an authority on human pettiness, which ritual overtakes.

I believe that rain-invoking rituals do not merely correspond to Mesoamerican millenarianism [the belief that the world undergoes a major transformation every thousand years]. They also cannot be understood as a simple "nativist" practice, a folkloric tradition, or a New Age scheme. On the contrary, the complex rain-invoking ritual in San Andrés de la Cal embodies an enduring Mesoamerican religiosity that resignifies and reinterprets itself in light of the modern globalized world.

Therefore, in modern traditional societies, indigenous Mesoamerican cosmo-vision and religion continue to strongly influence the normative order of daily life. This ceremony symbolically expresses and redefines the fundamental link with nature and the fertility and generosity of the land. The land, along with human labor, generates sustenance, thereby strengthening the relationship between humans and nature. Rain-invoking rituals renew fundamental indigenous Mesoamerican beliefs about links to the land, represented by Mother Earth. These links express the idea of community as the container of ethnic-land identity.

The Tlamazacaqui, rainmakers, and weather shaman who preside over hill worship and rain-invoking rituals transmit and reproduce tradition and culture. Modern Tlamazacaqui redefine and modernize ritual and hill worship, feeding into Mesoamerica's abundant ethnographic inventory that continues paradoxically, to enrich itself in the midst of social contingencies, like global climate change and the predatory advance of capitalism.

Hill worship and rain-invoking rituals reveal how ritual—in both its meaning and function—concerns gender within a Tepozteca context. In this way, we find an opposite-complement dialectical relationship within gender order that crosscuts the political order regulated by modern society's normative ethics.

I maintain that the logic of ritual overrides and displaces patriarchal order. During ritual, the differentiation between women and men emphasizes women's power and influence. A female Tlamazcaqui mediates, demonstrating women's pedagogical ability to reproduce ritual normativity and social ethic. Ritual, therefore, is a social metaphor whose actors constantly search for gender balance and equity, not just in the past, but in the present and future as well. In this context women have a primordial importance not only because they are the majority of the population, but also because they are responsible for social transformations such as migration; women have taken the social roles of men. And finally because they are really committed to their cultural traditions.

In closing, I believe that Tepoztlán, and by extension the state of Morelos, offers an inexhaustible cultural inventory—customs, traditions, feelings, symbols, and beliefs passed down from generation to generation—that feeds into the greater national cultural heritage. Agrarian traditions and ways of life constantly evolve as they incorporate new modern, globalizing realities. The modern Tepozteca experience reminds us that traditions act as foundation for resisting/adapting to change, and protection from a complex and shifting world. Traditions manifest the values that define human existence, the past, and the ethnic-territorial identity of these modern societies. These values are solidarity with the collectivity, among those, the family, neighborhood, community, and the elderly. Specifically, communities view the elderly as a moral, organizing authority that the land has bestowed to protect and project themselves toward the third millennium.

NOTES

1. Umberto Eco and Carlo Maria Martini, *¿En qué creen los que no creen? Un diálogo sobre la ética en el fin del milenio* [What do nonbelievers believe in? A dialogue about ethics at the end of the millennium] (Madrid: Ediciones Temas de Hoy, S.A., 1997).

2. Emilio Durkheim, *Las formas elementales de la vida religiosa* [The fundamental elements of religious life] (México: Colofón, 2000), 41.

3. Pierre Bourdieu, *La domination masculine* (France: Collection Liber, Éditions du Seuil, 2000).

4. Cristina Oehmichen Bazán, *Identidad, género y relaciones interétnicas. Mazahuas en la ciudad de México* [Identity, gender, and interethnic relationships. Mazahuas in Mexico City] (Mexico City: UNAM, 2005), 68 and following.

5. Gilberto Giménez, "Territorio y Cultura," *Estudios sobre las culturas contempoáneas* [Land and culture, Studies on contemporary cultures, 2, no. 004] (December 1996): 505.

6. Ana María Salazar Peralta, "Las peticiones de lluvia en el norte de Morelos: signos culturales y significados en una moderna sociedad tradicional," *Revista Mexicana de Estudios Antropológicos* [Rain Invocations in the northern Morelos: Cultural symbols and meanings in traditional modern society, Mexican journal of anthropological studies] TXLIX (2006): 101–116.

7. Gilberto Giménez, "Cultura, identidad y metropolitanismo," *Revista Mexicana de Sociología* [Culture, identity, and metropolitanism, Mexican journal of sociology] 3 (2005).

8. Guy Mercier and Gilles Ritchot, "La dimensión moral de la geografía humana," *Diógenes* [The moral dimension of human geography, Diogenes] 166 (1997): 48–61.

9. Enrique Florescano, "La reconstrucción del pasado," *La Jornada Semanal,* domingo 23 enero [Reconstruction of the past, Weekly Journal, Sunday, June 23], 2000.

10. Julio Glockner, *Los volcanes Sagrados. Mitos y rituales en el Popocatepetl y la Iztaccihuatl* [Sacred volcanoes. Myths and rituals in the Popocatepetl and the Iztaccihuatl] (Mexico: Grijalbo, 1996).

11. The complex mountainous system of the Volcanic Transversal mountain range (also known in Mexico as the Sierra Nevada) spans Mexico from east to west; it is the spinal column of the Central Altiplano [Mexican high plain]. These mountains house the ecological corridor, Ajusco-Chichinautzin, in whose foothills are found the small mountain range, the Tepozteco.

12. Eric Wolf, *Pueblos y Culturas de Mesoamerica* [Peoples and cultures of Mesoamerica] (Mexico: Ediciones Era, S.A., 1979).

13. René Acuña, ed., *Relaciones Geograficas del siglo XVI: México* [Geographic relationships of the 16th century: Mexico] (Mexico, UNAM, 1986).

14. Alfredo López Austin, "La religión y la larga duración: Consideraciones para la interpretación del sistema mítico religioso mesoamericano" [Religion and the long term: Considerations for the interpretation of the Mesoamerican mythic religious system] (paper presented at the symposium *Languages of the Heavens and Rituals of the Earth: Interpreting Native American Religious Systems,* 47th International Conference of Americanists, New Orleans, USA, July 1991).

15. Pedro Armillas, *Pedro Armillas: Vida y Obra* [Pedro Armillas: Life and work] (Mexico: INAH, 1991).

16. Johanna Broda, "Cosmovisión y observación de la naturaleza: el ejemplo del culto a los cerros en Mesoamérica," *Arqueometría y Etnoastronomía en Mesoamerica* [Cosmovision and observation of nature: the example of hill worship, Mesoamerica, Arqueometry and Archeoastronomy], ed. Johanna Broda, Stanislaw Iwaniszewki, and Luprecia Maupamé (Mexico City: UNAM, 1991).

17. Druzo Maldonado Jiménez, *Deidades y espacio ritual en Cuauhnahuac y Huastepec. Tlahuicas y xochimilcas de Morelos (siglos XII–XVI)* [Dieties and ritual space in Cuauhnuac and Huastepec. Tlahuicas and Xochimilcas of Morelos (12th–16th century)] (Mexico City: UNAM, 2004).

18. Luís González and González, "Patriotismo y matriotismo, cara y cruz de México," El nacionalismo mexicano [Patriotism and matriotism, face and cross of Mexico, Mexican nationalism], ed. Cecilia Noriega Elio (México: Zamora, 1992): 480.

19. Fray Bernadino de Sahagún, *Códice Florentino: Historia General de las cosas de Nueva España* [Florentine Codex: General history of the things of New Spain], Tomo I, Josefina Quintana y Alfredo López Austin, estudio introductorio, paleografía y glosario, Conaculta (Mexico: Alianza Editorial Mexicana, 1989) Second Book: 77–179.

20. Fray Bernadino de Sahagún, *Códice Florentino: Historia General de las cosas de Nueva España* [Florentine codex: General history of the things of New Spain], Tomo I, Josefina Quintana y Alfredo López Austin, estudio introductorio, paleografía y glosario, Conaculta (Mexico: Alianza Editorial Mexicana, 1989) Volume 1, 38.

21. Paul Kirchhoff, *Principios estructurales en el México antiguo* [Structural principles in ancient Mexico], ed. Teresa Rojas (Mexico: Centro de Investigaciones y Estudios Superiores en Antropología Social, 1983), 3–27.

22. María el Carmen Anzures, "Tlaloc señor del monte y dueño de los animales," en *Historia de la Religión en Mesoamerica y Areas afines* [Lord Tlaloc of the mountain and owner of animals, in History of religion in Mesoamerica and neighboring areas], 2nd Symposium, (Mexico City: UNAM, 1990).

23. Johanna Broda, "El culto en la cueva de Chimalacatepec. Una interpretación," *Memoria del tercer Congreso Interno del Centro INAH Morelos* [Cave worship in Chimalacatepec. An interpretation, Report from the Third Internal Congress of the Morelos INAH Center] (Mexico City: UNAM, 1996).

24. Fray Bernadino de Sahagún, *Códice Florentino: Historia General de las cosas de Nueva España* [Florentine codex: General history of the things of New Spain], Tomo I, Josefina Quintana y Alfredo López Austin, estudio introductorio, paleografía y glosario, Conaculta, Alianza Editorial Mexicana, Mexico, 1989), 239–241. Second Book, Chapter XXXIII.

25. Johanna Broda, "El culto mexica de los cerros de la cuenca de México: apuntes para la discusión sobre graniceros,"en *Graniceros, Cosmovisión y meteorología indígena de Mesoamerica* [Mexica hill worship in the Mexican basin: Notes for discussion about rainmakers, in Rainmakers, cosmovision, and indigenous meteorology in Mesoamerica] (Mexico City: UNAM, 1997).

26. Fray Bernadino de Sahagún, *Códice Florentino: Historia General de las cosas de Nueva España* [Florentine codex: General history of the things of New Spain], Tomo I, Josefina Quintana y Alfredo López Austin, estudio introductorio, paleografía y glosario, Conaculta (México: Alianza Editorial Mexicana, 1989), Second Book: 93.

27. Víctor Flores Ayala, *Tepoztlán nuestra historia*. Testimonios de los habitantes de Tepoztlán, Morelos [Tepoztlán our history. Testimonies from the residents of Tepoztlán, Morelos] (Mexico: INAH, 1998), 35 and following.

28. Johanna Broda and Druzo Maldonado, "El culto en la cueva de Chimalacatepec. Una interpretación," *Memoria del tercer Congreso Interno del Centro INAH Morelos* [Cave worship in Chimalacatepec. An interpretation, Report from the Third Internal Confernece of the Morelos INAH Center] (Mexico: INAH, 1996).

29. *Las pinturas rupestres de Tepoztlán* [The cave paintings of Tepoztlán], VHS, directed by Inocencio Rodríguez and Eduardo Barrón (Mexico City: Centro de Investigaciones y Servicios Educativos, Universidad Nacional Autónoma de México, 1997).

30. Hernando Ruíz de Alarcón, *Tratado de las Superticiones y costumbres gentilicias* [Treatise on ethnic superstitions and customs] (Mexico City: Imprenta del Museo Nacional, 1892.)

31. Gordon Brotherston, *El Códice de Tepoztlán. Imagen de un pueblo resistente* [The Tepoztlán Codex. Image of a resistent people] (San Francisco: Editorial Pacífica, 1999).

32. René Acuña, ed., *Relaciones Geograficas del siglo XVI: México* [Geographic relationships of the 16th century: Mexico] (Mexico, UNAM, 1986), 191–192.

33. Translator's note: In Spanish, the article *la* and the suffix *-a* are feminine, while *el* and *-o* are masculine. Thus, male specialists would be referred as el Tlamazcaqui, *el granicero, el tiempero,* or *el rayado.*

34. A dish made with ground pumpkin seeds, chilies, garlic, and onions; sautéed in lard and accompanied by *alberjones* [dried peas]. Served with white tamales to sop up the sauce.

35. Translator's note: La Mexicanidad ("Mexicanness") is a contemporary, mostly urban religious movement that lays claim to knowing the indigenous origins/traditions and bringing the ancestral past to the present.

36. Alicia María Juárez Becerril, "Peticiones de lluvia y culto a los aires en San Andrés de la Cal, Morelos" [Rain invocations and worship of the airs in San Andrés de la Cal, Morelos] (MA Thesis, UNAM, 2005).

37. Alfredo López Austin, "Religión, magia y cosmovisión" in *Historia Antigua de México* [Ancient history of Mexico], ed. Linda Manzanilla and Leonaro López Lujan (Mexico: Instituto de Investigaciones Antropológicas, 2001), 227–272.

38. Cornelius Castoriadis, *Un mundo fragmentado* [A fragmented world] (Buenos Aires: Altamira, 1997).

39. Renato Ortíz, A moderna tradiçao brasileira. Cultura brasileira e Indústria cultural (Sao Paolo: Editorial brasiliense, 2001).

40. Julio Glockner, Los volcanes Sagrados. Mitos y rituales en el Popocatepetl y la Iztaccihuatl [Sacred volcanoes. Myths and rituals in the Popocatepetl and the Iztaccihuatl] (Mexico: Grijalbo, 1996).

41. Pedro Carrasco, "La transformación de la cultura indígena durante la colonia," en Los Pueblos de Indios y las comunidades (El Colegio de México, México, 1991).

42. Robert Haskett, "Activist or Adulteress? The Life and Struggle of Doña Josefa María of Tepoztlan," in Indian Women of Early Mexico, ed. Susan Schroeder, Stepanie Wood, and Robert Haskett (Norman: University of Oklahoma Press, 1997).

PART III

Body, Mind, and Spirit

Dressing up the Spirits: Costumes, Cross-Dressing, and Incarnation in Korea and Vietnam

Laurel Kendall and Hien Thi Nguyen

K*ut,* performed by costumed shamans in Korea, and *len dong,* performed by costumed spirit mediums in Vietnam, have both commonly been interpreted as practices of ritual compensation whereby women with forceful personalities perform masculine authority in drag and "effeminate" men temporarily become pretty female spirits. The development of more sophisticated gender theory, allowing for complex, inconsistent, and multiple combinations of "masculinities" and "femininities" allows us to look at these rituals with fresh eyes, both with respect to the spirit mediums and shamans who perform them and most critically, with respect to the range of gender styles enacted within the ritual itself. In this chapter we briefly examine the social and religious identities of female Korean shamans and Vietnamese spirit mediums before and after their initiations, then consider how the medium or shaman crosses and recrosses gender boundaries in alternating categories of deities, dressing and undressing the particular colorations of status, age, and ethnicity. As a further complication, shamans and spirit mediums manifest the spirits, recognizable by type, in distinctive individual styles. We will use the array of costumes deployed in both traditions as a means of understanding how a range of stock masculinities and femininities are realized, what is happening in terms of the ritual "work" of costumes in spirit manifestations, and how these costumes combine with other performance elements to convey a spirit presence. We will argue that rituals involving multiple sequential manifestations of costumed spirits, like the Vietnamese *len dong* and the Korean *kut,* suggest funhouse mirrors on multiple and sometimes contradictory ways of doing, being, and performing "masculine" and "feminine" in both societies.

Kut, performed by Korean shamans (*mudang, mansin,* male: *paksu mu-dang*), and *len dong,* performed by Vietnamese spirit mediums (male: *ong dong*; female: *ba dong*) are spectacular ritual events involving music, colorful costumes, and theatrical accoutrements.[1] The spirits' sequential costuming in antique fancy dress, the most striking similarity between these two ritual forms, makes an obvious contrast between them and the shamanisms of Northeast Asia where a single magical robe enables flight and protects the shaman from attack by malevolent forces.[2] In Vietnamese *len dong* and Korean *kut* spirits are called into the here and now, called into the space where the ritual takes place, when the *mansin* or *ba dong* manifests them in her own body. This incarnation is the most visible and dramatic sign of her relationship with the divine that makes her who she is.

Within the ritual frame of Korean *kut* and Vietnamese *len dong,* female shamans and mediums have occasion to stride in the costumes of warriors, wielding antique weaponry, and male shamans and mediums have occasion to preen coquettishly in feminine attire, rendering "masculinity" and "femininity" theatrical as they assume multiple forms of women and men. There is some indigenous wisdom in both places for the notion that opposites attract, some cultural expectation that practitioners exhibit personality attributes for cross-gendered spirits, but this is not the whole story; indeed, it simplifies and consequently obscures the array of gendering at play in the rituals that we will be describing. We will argue that this variety is itself an important part of how these rituals deal with gender. Although some female Korean *mansin* and some Vietnamese *ba dong* are forceful personalities and although the opportunity to perform as beautiful goddesses certainly enhances the creative potential of gay male subculture in both places, a reductionist interpretation—women and men become shamans and mediums because they want the prerogatives of their gender opposite—does not suffice to explain these traditions. The assumption that male spirit mediums and shamans want to be women and female spirit mediums and shamans want to be men obscures at least three critical dimensions of women's participation as shamans and spirit mediums in Korea and Vietnam: the depth of the religious commitment that Korean shamans and Vietnamese spirit mediums make when they accept this role, the complex possibilities of gendered mixing and matching that both of these traditions recognize in relationships between humans and spirits, and the range of different ways of performing "masculine" and "feminine" that shamans or spirit mediums enact during a single ritual. Gender studies have taught us that ways of doing "masculine" and "feminine" can be complex and multiple[3] and have saved us from the kinds of social-psychological reductions that were popular in anthropology some decades ago.[4] Judith Butler's interpretation of gendered behavior as "performance" allows us to look at the Korean *kut* and the Vietnamese *len dong* with fresh eyes, both with respect to the spirit mediums and shamans who perform them and the range of gender styles they enact within a single ritual.[5]

In South Korea, most shamans (*mansin, mudang*) are women and male shamans (*paksu mudang*) have traditionally put on women's clothing, down to the full slip and pantaloons, before donning the spirits' robes and performing *kut*.[6] In Vietnam, women (*ba dong*) and men (*ong dong*) seem equally likely to become spirit mediums in the Religion of the Four Palaces (*Tu Phu*), also called the Mother Goddess Religion (*Dao Mau*). No strong cultural expectation favors one gender over the other. Some South Korean shamans suggest, impressionistically, that the number of male shamans is on the rise, changes they attribute to the improved status of Korean shamanship, now widely recognized as "Korean culture" and celebrated in the media. Some shamans have been appointed by the government as official performers of national heritage. Some Vietnamese scholars, familiar with the world of *len dong*, suggest that since the opening of the market in 1986 and the gradual easing of other social constraints, more male mediums are being initiated than ever before and that they tend subsequently to form loosely organized groups defined by their dual identities as spirit mediums and gay men. The relationship of male shamanship and mediumship to emergent gay cultures in South Korea, Vietnam, and Burma as well is a fascinating topic but beyond the scope of this volume.[7] In this chapter, we will examine the (gendered) social and religious identities of female Korean *mansin* and Vietnamese *ba dong* before and after their initiations and how these identities link them to gods of masculine and feminine genders, then consider how the individual medium or shaman crosses and recrosses gender boundaries to incarnate different categories of deities, dressing and undressing the particular colorations of status, age, power and authority, and (in Vietnam) ethnicity. Because our primary subjects are women, we will use the feminine pronoun.

BECOMING A SHAMAN, BECOMING A MEDIUM

Adherents of popular religion in both Korea and Vietnam hold that when the spirits choose a woman, she cannot escape her destiny, although many initiates resist for years on end before capitulating to the inevitable. Korean *mansin* attribute their calling to an unlucky birth horoscope that brings them all manner of misfortune and causes them to lead miserable lives until they accept the will of the spirits. Vietnamese also hold that mediums experience a great deal of suffering in their lives. In both traditions, and in classic shamanic fashion, the spirits choose a prospective *mansin* or *ba dong* by afflicting her with mysterious illness, madness, poverty, broken family ties, and other misfortunes. In Vietnam, many destined *ba dong* also experience an unusual knotting and matting of their hair which they can only comb out with the spirits' permission, and if they neglect their obligations to the spirits, their hair becomes matted once again. In Korea, some destined shamans exhibit an uncanny knack of spontaneous prophecy, taken as a sign of powerful divine inspiration and for some the true mark of an authentic shaman, a shaman who has inspired speech suddenly burst out of her. In both Korea and Vietnam, the prospective initiate may experience disturbing dreams and spend periods of semicrazed, distracted wandering and other bizarre behavior, sometimes mistaken for insanity, and she may fall into spontaneous trances during other peoples' rituals.[8]

In Korea, would-be shamans and their families resist the calling, in part because this was traditionally an "outcast" (*ch'ônmin*) profession requiring women to sing and dance in other people's houses like courtesans and dancing girls, embarrassing their kin and compromising their children's and grandchildren's future marriage prospects. For much of the 20th century, different regimes mounted antisuperstition campaigns against the *mansin*, regarding them as practitioners of backward rural superstition and their rituals as the irrational squandering of material resources toward nonmaterial ends. The most vehement opposition came during the early 1970s New Community Movement of the Park Chung-hee regime when local authorities interrupted rituals and threatened shamans with arrest, local zealots burned down shrines, and urban development schemes caused other shrines to either relocate or disappear completely. The newly elevated status of Korean shamans as exemplars of "national culture" rather than "backward superstition" and the gradual liberalization of attitudes toward women's public behavior—including dance and performance as part of the liberal arts curriculum in the best women's universities—has somewhat alleviated the old onus against shamans in Korea, although hostility from within Korea's sizeable Christian community sometimes erupts in incidents of harassment. Owing to the relatively positive contemporary image of shamanship, *mansin* now complain that there are more initiates than ever before but that many of them are insufficiently inspired and inadequately trained.[9]

In Vietnam, the number of mediums has increased exponentially since the late 1980s with the gradual liberalization of many social policies, including those regarding popular religion and "superstitious practices," although mediums are still subject to periodic harassment by local authorities.[10] With the opening of the market economy since 1986, market traders, who were enthusiasts for spirit medium rituals in the 1950s have returned to popular religion, seeking the favor of the Mother Goddess and her pantheon as a hedge on their necessarily risky enterprises.[11] The Vietnamese media, however, has continued to portray spirit mediums as "liars and swindlers" and to describe them as "uneducated, ignorant people."[12] Even in a more liberal social climate, the government continued to discourage all rituals and practices that involved mustering supernatural forces in "dealing with human agonies and anxieties."[13] A tremendous change occurred on November 15, 2004, when a new ordinance on folk beliefs and religion legitimated the veneration of spirits in popular religion as an extension of the—generally favorably regarded—veneration of national heroes.[14] The ordinance recognized activities associated with folk belief including ancestor worship, the commemoration of historical figures, and the veneration of spirits.[15]

The physical, emotional, and economic demands of shamanship and mediumship are another reason for resistance. Accepting a divine calling requires a total life commitment, and shamans or mediums who break their relationship with their spirits risk illness and serious misfortune, afflicting both themselves and their families. In both traditions, shamans and mediums maintain shrines to their spirits, which they keep clean and replenished with fresh offerings; purify their bodies before performing *kut* or *len dong*; sponsor expensive periodic rituals for the benefit of their own spirits; and make pilgrimages to sacred sites (mountains in Korea, famous temples in Vietnam) to secure the spirits' favor and thereby enhance their own powers. Even minor infractions, such as a delay in performing a ritual or an inappropriate arrangement of ritual paraphernalia will bring divine displeasure.

DOING THE SPIRITS' WORK

In Korea, initiation as a *mansin* brings a new identity—social, religious, and professional. Experienced shamans will repeatedly tell the initiate, "You must change completely" in order to receive the spirits. Marriage is usually a casualty of the *mansin* profession, either because a destined shaman experiences early widowhood, divorce, or flight from an abusive marriage as part of her ill-fated destiny, or because husbands subsequently abandon shaman wives out of shame or jealousy. By cultural stereotype, the shaman's husband is a man who lives off of money earned by his wife, in effect a kept man, and a *mansin*'s work requires both days and nights away from home, provoking suspicion.[16] In *mansin* terms, male spirits are themselves jealous and make normal married life with a mortal man untenable so that even *mansin* who continue to live with husbands seldom share a common bed.[17] Typically, the destined *mansin* accepts her calling only when she has been forced into marginal and desperate circumstances and holds her initiation *kut* (*naerim kut*) out of desperation, usually by going into debt to cover the cost of the ritual and the requisite costumes and paraphernalia she must assemble in order to perform it. At the critical moment of a successful initiation, her "gates of speech" (*malmun*) open and she pours out divinations in "the true words of the spirits." With this ability, she not only receives clients for individual consultations but can begin to perform simple tasks at a *kut,* eventually gaining the ability to manifest all of the spirits and ancestors who appear, manifesting their persona and mannerisms in her own body and, most importantly, speaking in their voice. Speaking the spirits' words convincingly and shaping chaotic, random, or absent visions into a coherent divination is the most difficult task of an initiate, but without it, she is no *mansin*.[18] With the power to divine, a new *mansin* can begin to make a living, supporting herself and if necessary, her children and other family members, and paying back her debts.[19] Full competence in music, song, chants, performance business, and ritual lore requires years of apprenticeship under the tutelage of an experienced "great shaman" (*k'ŭn mansin*), ideally the "spirit mother" (*sin ŏmŏni*) who conducted her initiation *kut*. Many *mansin* complain that unseasoned shamans are greedy to conduct initiations for naïve clients, perpetuating a cycle of insufficiently inspired, badly initiated, and poorly trained shamans who do not really know how to serve the spirits and who, as a consequence, cause much mischief and unnecessary misfortune to themselves and their clients. Since the 1990s, some disappointed initiates have been turning to new shaman schools, trying to learn in a classroom setting the performing and ritual arts that their spirit mothers should have taught them.[20]

Vietnamese *ba dong* eschew any notion of paid professionalism, and in addition to their new identity as spirit mediums, they continue to think of themselves as the farmers, traders, or civil servants they were before their initiations. In effect, and in contrast to Korean *mansin*, they keep their day jobs. Many mediums, particularly Hanoi women market traders who consider their relationship with the spirits good for their own business, health, and general well-being, only perform periodic *len dong* for the sake of their own businesses and families; they do not receive clients. Even so, they feel an obligation to perform a *len dong* ritual at least twice a year. Their participation is somewhat analogous to the activities of the *mansin's* regular clients who make offerings in her shrine two or three times a year and dance in the shamans' clothing during interludes at a *kut* to achieve a mild euphoria or, more rarely, a full-on trance, engaging and entertaining their own body-governing spirits (*momju*) for similar personal and familial benefits.

Master mediums (*dong thay*) are mediums that have powerful connections to their spirits and are experienced and knowledgeable ritual performers somewhat analogous to *mansin*.[21] Depending on the spirits who work with them, master mediums can divine, exorcise, heal illness, and initiate other mediums, but most master mediums will insist that they receive only token compensation for these services. Sister Nga says that out of sympathy for poor and desperate patients, she assumes the cost of mounting their *len dong* ritual herself, including furnishing all of the offerings and votive paper sculptures. She assumes that these grateful people will pay her back later on. *Ba dong* complain that some master mediums have become greedy and charge too much when other mediums use their shrines for their own rituals, but even famous master mediums will point out that they give back to the spirits whatever they earn by performing their own *len dong* and by honoring their spirits with ever-more elaborate temple fittings and statues and more beautiful costumes. Master mediums frequently perform *len dong* for their own spirits, saying that they will feel ill for no otherwise explicable reason if they do not regularly "sit" for the incarnating spirits by performing *len dong*. *Mansin* also feel obliged to celebrate their own spirits, hosting a *kut* attended by their regular clients at least once a year if they can afford the expense, and also claim that neglecting this obligation will adversely affect their health, income, or family well-being. But with the exception of these special *kut*, the other *kut* that a *mansin* performs are her primary source of livelihood.

RITUALS, RITUAL OFFERINGS, AND CASH

As a central dynamic of *kut*, the spirits demand cash which the client supplies, usually with comic bantering. In and around Seoul, the client pays the cost of her *kut* up front with a significant sum given back to her to use as stage money in her dealings with gods and ancestors. The gods will also extract some previously uncommitted cash from her and encourage other spectators to spend small sums on divinations and on cups of "lucky" (*pok*) wine and sweets. In other words, the gods and ancestors draw wealth in and give back auspiciousness for a large or small fee. Although *len dong* also involves honoring the spirits with a tribute of cash and food, the dynamic is very different. The medium who performs *len dong* gives out all of the offerings and cash that have been piled on the altar and all of the offerings and cash that guests have offered on heaping trays. Mediums make some redistribution during every spirit incarnation, and in the end, everything gets shared out again to the assistants, the musicians, and all of the other participants as a bestowal of the spirits' auspicious favor (*loc*). Even a casual visitor returns home with a small sum of cash and a bag containing beer or soda, cookies, fruit, paper flowers, and some small plastic items like combs and pocket mirrors. A Korean *mansin* who had occasion to visit Vietnam and witnessed a *len dong* was profoundly impressed by what she saw as the mediums' extreme generosity which she contrasted with the dynamics of a *kut* where *mansin* and spirits make demands, but give little back.[22] These distinctions further underscore the *mansin's* identity as a professional practitioner who depends upon income from the rituals she performs, and the *ba dong's* denial of profit. These similar-seeming religious experiences have been shaped by different cultural expectations of what and how *mansin* as shamans and *ba dong* as spirit mediums are expected to perform.

The range of performance skills required of a *mansin,* and in particular, the necessity of exhibiting inspired speech, distinguish her from the *ba dong*. As a shaman, the *mansin* orchestrates her dealings with the gods and ances- tors, summoning them into the ritual space that she and her colleagues have purified, winning their good will on behalf of her clients, and sending the gods, ancestors, and any lingering noxious influences away in proper sequence. *Mansin* spell each other at drumming and making the percussive music that accompanies spirit manifestations. *Mansin* occasionally hire additional pro- fessional musicians who play the fiddle, flute, and Chinese military horn to please the spirits when the occasion and the client's pocketbook merit this ad- ditional expense, but these musicians are not essential to the critical work of invoking spirits and enabling the *mansin* to manifest them. A *mansin* is more nearly a shamanic "master of the spirits" than is the *ba dong,* who requires a ritual master to make appropriate petitions to summon the spirits for *len dong* and performers of *chau van* music and songs to call down particular spirits and later send them on their way at the end of an incarnation.[23] Although it is the medium who cues the musicians once she senses the presence of a particular spirit, Hien Nguyen's observations suggest that even when musicians miss their cue, the spirits wait for the singer to invite them to descend, and depart only when the singer bids them farewell.[24]

Both Korean and Vietnamese traditions encourage communities of adherents. In Vietnam, disciples of a particular master medium become a close circle, serving in their master's temple and assisting at or simply attending each other's *len dong* as happy, celebratory events. Mature me- diums who become masters themselves become the nuclei of new groups. In Korea, *mansin* make up teams to perform *kut* in shifting combinations of congenial colleagues ("sisters") and their respective apprentices, making networks and shifting alliances of people who work well together. With respect to clients, the country *kut* of a few decades past were boisterous parties that drew enthusiastic female kin and neighbors to the sponsors' house. Although *kut* are now performed in near privacy in commercial sha- man shrines, celebrations of Buddha's Birthday and the Seven Stars of the dipper on the seventh day of the seventh lunar month, and seeking divina- tions in the first two weeks of the new year bring celebratory crowds of long- time clients to a shaman's house as does her annual celebration of her own spirits. Like many other communities of coreligionists, the world of *mansin* or the world of *ba dong* creates occasions of social conviviality and pleasure and broadens the adherent's social networks.

SPIRITS AND SPIRITS' GENDER

Although she honors a full pantheon of deities in her shrine, a Korean *mansin* claims the special protection of a Body-governing God (*momju taesin*). The spirits in her shrine and in particular, her Body-governing God, demand fierce loyalty, sometimes expressed as "marriage" and while a few shamans describe this relationship in sexual terms, the idiom evokes more broadly the Confucian notion of life-long wifely fidelity. As Roberte Hamayon notes, many different shamanic traditions describe the relationship between a shaman and his or her spirits as marriage, but the expectations of a marital contract vary considerably across cultures.[25] A Confucian marriage bond may be the proper metaphor for the kind of loyalty a Body-governing Fairy Maid, a feminine spirit, exacts of a female shaman in a decidedly asexual relationship. A positive relationship with powerful spirits enables the *mansin* to practice as a *mansin,* a relationship closely bound up with her identity as a professional shaman who is paid for what she does; the spirits bring her clients and empower her to give accurate divinations and perform efficacious *kut. Mansin* read a sudden falling off of business as a symptom of divine displeasure, and more catastrophically, angry spirits can cause a *mansin* to lose her inspiration altogether. A *mansin* with an elaborate shrine, gold jewelry, and heavy rings on her fingers is a *mansin* whose spirits have brought her many satisfied clients. By stereotype, *mansin* are greedy, just as powerful and efficacious spirits are demanding spirits, and even loyal adherents assume that a *mansin* will encourage them to perform expensive rituals that might not be merited, even as an ambitious doctor might be suspected of advising unnecessary and costly medical procedures. The assumption of greed and potential charlatanry contributes to the negative image that *mansin* bear.

The relationship with a Body-governing God is complex because the spirit is both a "type"—a certain General, a Spirit Warrior, a Great Spirit Grandmother—and usually also a known ancestor who has more-or-less been appointed to this slot. Yongsu's Mother honors a Spirit Warrior (Sinjang) who is her own deceased husband and their prickly relationship continues. Because most *mansin* are women, and most spirits are men, female *mansin* usually have masculine spirits, sometimes characterized as jealous and possessive of their chosen *mansin*. By cultural expectation, female deities are attracted to male *paksu mudang*. But these lines are far from absolute. Man can have men and women can have women as their Body-governing Spirits. Deceased shaman kinswomen, or kinswomen who ought to have been initiated as shamans, often assume this role and possess a female descendant;

in the initiation *kut* filmed by Diana Lee and Laurel Kendall the shamans identify the initiate's dead sister in the role of Princess Hogu (Hogu Taesin) as her Body-governing God, retrospectively describing the dead girl as a destined shaman whose calling was not recognized.[26] Many female shamans have a special relationship with the Fairy Maid (Okwang Sŏngnyŏ), as the formidable Chatterbox Mansin once did. In addition to enjoying a particular spirit's favor, a *mansin* is said to "play well" when she manifests spirits of a similar type to her Body-governing God in *kut*. Many female *mansin* do masculine spirits particularly well, and many male shamans have a special penchant for prettily manifesting female spirits—performances that by the aptness of their characterization, testify to the alterity of spirits, their absolute difference or otherness, and to their uncanny presence in the here and now.

In Vietnam, the "root" of medium destiny (*can*) can also be gendered masculine or gendered feminine, and men or women may have the root of a spirit of either gender. Those men and women who have a male spirit root are said to have glowing faces and red, restless eyes, hot tempers and impulsive natures; those who have a female spirit are said to be "feminine" or in the case of men, "effeminate." When a woman initiate displays a hot-temper, the mediums call her "manly" (*dan ong*) and say that her root comes from a male spirit, a Mandarin (*can Quan*) or a Prince (*can Ong Hoang*), while the root of an effeminate male medium is attributed to a female deity. Mediums' identification with the personality traits of particular spirits (in the manner of a Korean Body-governing God) extend into the mediums' quotidian personalities. A *ba dong* with the Seventh Prince's root has a masculine look and is strong in mind and character. A male medium that is identified with the Ninth Damsel usually has a frail carriage and walks coquettishly; he is addressed as "Miss." In both Vietnam and Korea today, many young practitioners claim a special relationship with a Child Spirit (Tongja in Korean, Cau Be in Vietnamese) who is playful, mischievous, and likes to be indulged. In Vietnam, the Child Spirit is always a boy and in Korea, usually so, but these spirits are more nearly marked by age than gender and in Korea both boy and girl Child Spirits speak with the same falsetto voice.

SHAMAN ROBES AND SUITCASES FULL OF COSTUMES

This mixing and matching of spirits, shamans, and mediums of the same and of contrasting genders is hardly an ethnographic aberration particular to East and Southeast Asian state societies. In other places, Marjorie Mandelstam Balzer, Barbara Tedlock and Ana Mariella Bacigalupo[27] have drawn on their own fieldwork and on the shreds and patches of older ethnographies[28] to describe bigendered shamans, gender categories in permanent flux, and

shamans whose multiple or ambigendered identities are contingent on gene-
alogies of ritual transmission and upon the particular identities of spirits who
show up during a given performance. They have also shown how, in different
shamanic traditions separated by time and space, the empowering robes and
other accoutrements that shamans wear combine attributes of masculine
and feminine identity to enhance the powers of the shaman.

The robes or cloaks that have such a strong association with northern
Eurasian shamanisms are replaced in Korea and Vietnam by suitcases bursting with brightly colored costumes for rituals where Korean *mansin* and Vietnamese *ba dong* change their dress and accoutrements to receive a sequence
of spirits, both male and female, who give these rituals the air of costumed
historical dramas. In both Korea and Vietnam, the spirits come garbed in the
imagery of antique courts and armies, populating ritual imaginaries with an
imagery very different from that of North Asian shamanisms where power
emerges from a harsh natural landscape and spirits may have animal form.[29]
In both Korea and Vietnam, premodern states adapted Chinese statecraft
and some of its imagery to convey temporal power. Where spirit power appears in the idiom of state power, as it does in both *kut* and *len dong,* popular
religious imagery in Korea and Vietnam draws on similar historical models
for weapons, battle flags, and a five-element scheme of bold primary color,
although the cut of the clothing, the music, dance, historical allusions, and
even the aesthetics and flavors of offering food are unmistakably Vietnamese
or Korean. Vietnamese who see Korean *kut* and Koreans who see Vietnamese *len dong* are immediately struck by their many visual similarities and the
words "*kut*" and "*len dong*" have been deployed as reciprocal translations for
these rituals. In the remainder of our discussion, we will consider how the
bursting suitcases of costumes that accompany Vietnamese *len dong* and
Korean *kut* contain in their range of dress multiple masculinities and femininities that the *mansin* and *ba dong* perform into being.

We use the word "costume" because particular robes are identified with
specific spirits, but we want to also emphasize that in both traditions, these
are more than secular theatrical properties. The costume is also an offering, an item of religious transaction which, once it is dedicated, is closely
identified with the spirit who wears it and must be treated with respect as an
extension of the spirit's presence. It must be stored carefully and kept apart
from ordinary clothing. In Korea, shamans offer new robes to their spirits
on the strength of a dream or a divination from another shaman, but many
of their costumes are gifts from clients, marked with the client's name as a
durable sign of an active relationship between the shaman, the spirits in her
shrine, and the client and her own family's spirits. The costume is a sign and
extension of the spirit's presence; *mansin* dust clients with auspiciousness by
shaking the hems of their costumes into the client's clothing and when the

mansin removes her costume after manifesting a particular spirit, she casts it into the client's outstretched skirt as a sign that the spirit bestows blessings on the client. Each time the *mansin* wears the robe dedicated by a particular client to feast and play at *kut*, even *kut* for the benefit of a client other than the client who dedicated the robe she wears, the first client's spirit is satisfied by the dancing and play and consequently favorably disposed toward the client's household. An experienced Korean *mansin* with a large number of clients will have multiple robes for each of several spirits. When she performs her annual *kut* for her own spirits and her community of clients, she will bundle on multiple versions of the same robe to bestow simultaneous blessings on several clients. By so doing, she also evidences that her spirits are powerful spirits who have brought her much business over several years of practice, a thickening of client relations made literal through several layers of costume.

During an interval in the *kut,* clients are encouraged to dance to entertain their own personal spirits, either wearing the costumes that they have dedicated or in robes identified with spirits who are also powerful in the client's own household pantheon. Such dancing carries the risk that women who are destined to become shamans will be claimed by the spirits while they are dancing, and minor temporary possessions can also occur through the medium of dance, music, and clothing. During the initiation ritual that Lee and Kendall recorded on film, the experienced shamans urge the initiate to grab whatever robe strikes her fancy on the assumption that it would lead in an urgent spirit who will enable her to speak and act like a shaman.[30] Eventually, the presiding *mansin* covered the initiate in the robe of the Heavenly King whose powerful aura would overcome the troublesome spirits that were blocking her flow of inspiration.

In Vietnam, each spirit has a specific costume in which the medium's assistants (*tu tru,* meaning "four pillars") dress the medium once she has identified the spirit and while the singer invites the spirit to descend. At a *len dong* performed by master medium Tinh, one of the damsels expressed urgent rage when the attendants failed to produce the appropriate costume and would not dance until an inappropriate pink robe was replaced with the desired one; this happens often. Before her initiation into the service of the spirits (*ra dong* or *mo phu*), the medium must purchase suitable costumes, especially those of his or her patron spirits, those whose root she carries. Some Mother Goddess temples maintain extra costumes that poor mediums can use. A medium of the Mother Goddess Religion is supposed to possess all of the costumes for all of the spirits that she will potentially incarnate when she performs *len dong*. In addition to her obligation to perform appropriate rituals during the year, she must wear beautiful costumes to "dress up" the spirits in order to receive more favor and compassion, but some mediums will purchase costumes for only the most frequently incarnated spirits until they can afford to purchase the others. One medium told us, however, that if a spirit arrives and does not find the appropriate costume, the attendant must petition the spirit on the medium's behalf, asking the spirit to bless the medium with good fortune so that she will be able to purchase the costume in the future. (A similar transaction takes place in *kut* when an initiate or client cannot meet a god's unanticipated demand for clothing or accessories). A *ba dong* told us that she felt badly when she could not incarnate a spirit in the appropriate costume. When a *ba dong's* circumstances improve, she acknowledges the spirits' favor by buying them more spectacular and expensive costumes, carefully preserving the old ones and maybe allowing the mediums she has initiated to use them.

Devotees of the Mother Goddess religion will sometimes offer to provide costumes to a medium. Some mediums refuse this on the grounds that purchasing costumes is their own personal act of devotion to the Mother Goddess. One *ba dong* told us that she made an exception for a devotee who was also a close friend and this produced an interesting story about the relationship between spirits and clothing. The woman sold meat in the market. Being short on cash, she delayed in picking up the costume from the tailor on the specified day. As midday approached she had not sold most of her stock, which would spoil, forcing her to take a loss. She prayed to the Mother Goddess and asked for help selling her stock, promising to pick up the costume in the evening. That afternoon, her luck changed and she was able to sell out her stock and collect the costume. A young overseas *ba dong* described how the young damsel (*Co be*), her patron spirit, was not happy when the medium incarnated her in a borrowed costume rather than purchasing a robe for the damsel.

Now let us examine the range of spirit manifestations these different Korean and Vietnamese costumes enable.

The Performance of Gender

Both *kut* and *len dong* are theatrical, highly artistic popular religious forms, full of music, dance, and performative business, and both have links to more secular artistic genres.[31] At their most basic level, these rituals are intended to pleasure the spirits who bestow favor upon the human sponsors. Both rituals last for many hours and are said to make the participants feel better both during and after the performance. The spirits who appear are stock characters, types readily identified by their clothing and behavior.

Korean *mansin* say that the *kut* has twelve sequences or *kôri*, and can usually list them, but they will also admit that in contemporary practice, segments are combined and simplified and some of the spirits are conflated.

In the more recent *kut* Kendall observed in the tradition of Seoul (Hanyang *kut*, Hansông *kut*), each of three shamans might perform one major segment that lasts from 90 minutes to two hours, with preliminaries and denouement. Such *kut* are usually divided into a segment for the Mountain God and spirits associated with pure high places, prayers for fertility, and for the benefit of children; a segment for the family's ancestors who are led to the *kut* by an ancestral shaman; and a segment for warriors and officials, which involves feats such as balancing the offering meat on a battle trident and more spectacularly, may involve the shaman herself balancing on knife-blades. The *kut* begins with a long drum song expelling pollutions and inviting the spirits and ancestors into the house. It ends with manifestations of the House Tutelary, the Mountebank, and some minor gods and a final send-off of ghosts and other unclean entities. The dynamic for encounters between a spirit and a client typically begins with the spirit deriding the client for having ignored rituals and offerings in the past. The *mansin's* words combine stock phrases with pointed references to the client's current troubles. The language becomes more direct and less larded with archaic vocabulary as the encounter continues, with the client and the other *mansin* repeatedly asking for forgiveness and understanding, bestowing more cash on the spirit whose prognostications become increasingly benevolent as the spirit promises to shower blessings on the client.

When a shaman prepares to perform a segment, she dresses in layers of robes; some manifestations of spirits will be accomplished by removing layers of clothing, others by switching outer robes. The spirit with the highest status in the segment appears first, followed by spirits in descending order of status until the segment is complete, the costumes are all removed, and another shaman begins to costume herself for the next segment. As high spirits, Mountain Gods and Generals are the first to appear in their respective sequences. They stride regally to a processional clash of cymbals and assume an arrogant posture. They extend their fans in an elegant gesture to receive cash from the client. They would not deign to dun the client for cash. Officials, by contrast, are highly demanding, the greedy and corrupt underlings who appear with the other military spirits but may also show up as underlings in other sequences. Their performance is characterized by appetite: they demand wine, meat, cash, and dancing partners, and they exhibit their lust with phallic play, taking a dried fish or a drum stick and bouncing it up and down under their costume while leering at the giggling client. In other words, all of these spirits are "masculine" but they are masculine in different ways. Generals and Mountain Spirits have the demeanor of high officials (positions traditionally enjoyed by men, but a minority of men); their dignity is a measure of their status. Officials and Spirit Warriors have less couth personas, sometimes conflated with narrative portrayals of demanding husbands, a comically unflattering, bothersome, demanding masculinity.[32] Child Spirits are capricious—the source of potential trouble—and they can be mollified with sweets. A boy child's masculinity, where marked, is that of a spoiled child. The two authors witnessed a surprise appearance by Child Spirits who, in the manner of bothersome toddlers, announced to one of the shamans "I don't like you," chased another shaman around the offering table because she had failed to make a promised pilgrimage to Mount Paektu, and delayed the ritual by refusing to depart on schedule. While manifesting the boy Child God, the *mansin* kept twisting the cloth of her skirt into an approximation of a tiny phallus, the only distinction between her manifestation of the little girl and the little boy. When the segment was over, she was overheard to remark that she "couldn't help herself" from making the crude gesture with her clothing. Knowing that the Child Spirits always delay the ritual, she had not brought out their costumes, but they had come anyway and she had found herself involuntarily extracting their little sets of clothing from a zippered storage bag.

Most of the spirits who appear in *kut* are male, but Princes Hogu is a young woman, a virgin who died of smallpox and asks for "make-up" money to cover the scars on her face so that she can get married. She appears with a red skirt cast over her head, which is "opened"—a parallel to "opening" the client's luck, when the client gives her sufficient cash. This spirit is flighty and flirtatious; unattended she stirs up trouble between husband and wife. The Buddhist Sage, Seven Stars, and Birth Grandmother appear in the white robes and hoods of Buddhist liturgical dancing, and like Buddhas, they are vegetarian spirits, but also identified with ancestral family grandmothers who fasted, bathed with cold water, and prayed on mountains to conceive and raise healthy male children. Usually, they are addressed and referred to as "Grandmother" and appear in dreams and visions as "white-haired grandmothers." Their complaints over neglect are not unlike those of aging mothers-in-law. The Great Spirit Grandmother is a dead shaman, often a shaman known to the shaman participants, whose strong personality marks her continuing relationship with her former apprentice. In other words, the particular "femininity" of Korean spirits is colored by type as determined by age and social circumstance.

The spirits of *len dong* are historic or quasi-historic figures, described in legends and the stories that the *chau van* singers recount in the songs they sing to entertain each particular spirit who appears during the ritual. Over the course of several hours, a single spirit medium will incarnate multiple deities, evoking their presence with appropriate mannerisms, dance gestures, and sometimes verbal statements. Any of 36 spirits might possess a spirit medium during a *len dong* but only a few of them will appear in a single ritual and some make more regular appearances than others. The spirits come from the four palaces governed by the Mother Goddesses and their robes are in the color of each domain: red for the palace of heaven, yellow for earth, white for water, and blue or green for the mountains and forests. The spirits' offerings are also color-coded to match the palaces they inhabit. Spirit types are also ranked and mediums incarnate them in descending order and alternating gender: Mandarins, Dames, Princes, Damsels, and Boys.

The medium sits under a red cloth, awaiting the deity's presence, then signals with her hands to cue the musicians and *chau van* singers. The right hand signals for female spirits and the left hand for male spirits. For example, one finger of the left hand would signal the presence of the First Mandarin, two fingers of the right hand would signal the Second Dame. Switching hands, say from left to right, signals the appearance of deities from the next lowest rank. For example, if the medium were performing Mandarins, a switch to the right hand would signal the arrival of Dames; if performing Princes, then Damsels. Once a *ba dong* has cued the musicians, the four assistants scramble to assemble the appropriate costume and spend several minutes dressing the medium and decorating her turban with appropriate accessories. Now the medium is ready to dance and mime the spirit she has incarnated, but without the extended verbal encounters of a Korean *kut*.

Since each spirit has a distinctive quasi-historical biography, we find even more variation in type than in the Korean *kut*. The Second Mandarin, who bestows wishes for talent and a good career, is a General and appears as a strong, austere military figure. The Fifth Mandarin is a secret inspector, a powerful and righteous investigator. The dames, closely identified with the Mother Goddesses they serve as ladies in waiting, are elegant and, as mature women, more serious than the younger Damsels. The Second Dame has healing powers; she is identified with mountain-dwelling minority people who have herbal lore. Her lively dance with fire sticks suggests the lowlander's view of exotic mountain people. The Princes, who are all legendary figures, lack the military austerity of the mandarins. The Seventh Prince, a playboy who craves beautiful girls, drinks and smokes a great deal when he incarnates the medium. The Tenth Prince has more artistic tastes. A literary connoisseur, he enjoys the music of the *chau van* singers whose song describes him composing poetry with his friends. The Prince smiles and expresses his pleasure by tapping the pillowed arm rest that is part of the ritual paraphernalia, and shouting for joy. Then, he rewards the singers by showering them with money. The Tenth Prince is always open-handed in distributing favors in the form of money, cakes, sweets, and jewelry, particularly to women. Everybody receives his favors with deep respect, and some participants give him offerings, asking for his protection. He returns some of these offerings to the contributors, accompanied by good advice and good wishes.

Following the incarnations of the Princes, some of the 12 Damsels appear. The Damsels are young and unmarried, so their incarnations are always cheerful, with colorful costumes and fluttering dances. Like the Dames, the Damsels are usually portrayed as ethnic minorities. Their costumes use fabrics and accessories associated with ethnic minorities, albeit without ethnographic precision. The Second Damsel performs a coy dance, carrying flower baskets on a pole, flaunting her girlish femininity. The Third Damsel has a different style; wearing a long pink dress and a long scarf, her movements exhibit grace and beauty. This is a sweet and gentle spirit.

Among the 10 Boy attendants, only the Third Boy-attendant (Cau Bo) and the youngest Boy-attendant (Cau Be) often descend and are incarnated. The Boy's costumes, gestures, and words are childlike, reflecting his playful nature. In addition to the requisite rituals, today the little Boy attendant also performs unicorn and lion dances, shaking his belled *heo* stick to the amusement of the spectators.

Conclusion

We have described how Korean *mansin* become shamans and Vietnamese *ba dong* become spirit mediums through an idiom of unavoidable fate that enjoins a powerful obligation to their guardian spirits and affects other domains of their lives. They observe various ritual duties and thorough their relationships with the spirits, establish new social relationships with co-religionists. The Korean *mansin's* identification with her new role is total and requires mastery of a range of new and difficult skills, which she uses both to serve the spirits and make a living. In both traditions, the alterity of spirits and their powerful presence in the quotidian world is sometimes manifest in cross-gendered identification with male or female guardian gods, but as in many other shamanic and shaman-like traditions, the possibilities for gender identification are fluid and variable. Moreover, in the performance of *kut* and *len dong* as costumed and theatrical rituals, the spirits exhibit a variety of masculinities and femininities, dressing and undressing the particular colorations of status, age, and (in Vietnam) ethnicity, permitting a theatrical mimesis—the compelling evocation of what one is not—in a fun-house mirror of stock types, a sometimes humorous, sometimes seductive, sometimes overbearing commentary on gender itself.[33]

Notes

Our work together on this project was supported by the Jane Belo Tannenbaum Fund of the American Museum of Natural History and a Ford Foundation grant which provided Hien Nguyen with a postdoctoral fellowship at AMNH. We are grateful to the many shamans and mediums who allowed us to observe their rituals and discuss their work and to Seong-nae Kim, Sung Ja Kim, Pham Quynh Phuong, and Ngo Duc Thinh, who joined our conversation about the comparisons and contrasts between Korea and Vietnam. We, alone, are responsible for the shortcomings of this effort.

1. In both Korea and Vietnam, there is significant regional variation in these rituals. In general, we are describing *kut* in and around Seoul and *len dong* in and around Hanoi.

2. In English-language translations, the entities that Korean shamans manifest are conventionally "gods" (*sin, sinyŏng*) and "ancestors" (*chosang*). Vietnamese popular religion distinguishes between "gods" (*than*) and "saints" (*thanh*) who once had mortal lives. In this chapter, we use the less precise term "spirits," which is used in writing about shamans and mediums in many parts of the world, to override these differences of language in a manner that does no violence to the content of our descriptions.

3. Ortner, 1996.

4. Lewis, 1966, 1969; Spiro, 1967.

5. Butler, 1993.

6. We have met one exception to this general expectation, a male shaman who wore traditionalist-modern male clothing under his costume and performed masculine deities. There are undoubtedly others but men who favor feminine deities are far more numerous.

7. Kumada, 2003.

8. For accounts of shamanic destiny in Korea see Harvey, 1979, 1980; Kendall, 1985, 1988, 1996; and Kim, 1995. For Vietnam, see Fjelstad, 1995; Nguyen, 2002; and Pham, 2006.

9. Kendall, 2009.

10. Truong, 1998; Norton, 2000; Malarney, 2002.

11. Durand, 1959.

12. Norton, 2000.

13. Endress, 2006.

14. The policy document was actually passed by the Standing Committee of the National Assembly on June 18, 2004, but did not take effect until November 15, 2004.

15. Ordinance on Folk Beliefs, 2004.

16. Harvey, 1979.

17. Kendall, 2000.

18. See, for example, the struggles of Chini, the initiate described in Kendall, 1996, and in the accompanying film, *An Initiation* kut *for a Korean Shaman* (Lee and Kendall, 1991), who is repeatedly told that the gods will not move her tongue for her, that she has to make the manifestation happen, whether the spirits are present or not.

19. Until recently, Korean family law granted legal custody to fathers in the event of divorce. A woman abandoning an abusive spouse or fleeing an otherwise

untenable domestic situation was usually forced by circumstance to relinquish her children as well, a common circumstance for destined shamans.

20. However much *mansin* romanticize the relationship between a spirit mother and a spirit daughter "in the old days," these relationships were often brittle; then as now, many spirit daughters found other shamans to mentor them. The schools evidence both an individualization of shamanship and a commoditization of the shaman's training. See Guillemoz, 1998; Hogarth, 2003.

21. Larsson and Endres, 2006.

22. Ch'ŏn, 2001. In fact, clients at a Korean *kut* also take home fruit and rice cake and offer it to the spirits in their own households. At the end of a *kut,* shamans commonly offer fruit and rice cake to any other participants, but this is not part of the dynamic of the ritual itself which emphasizes the sprits' demands as a measure of their power. When *kut* were held in clients' houses, as was common in the 1970s, the rice cake and offerings would be the clients' to redistribute—with the expectation of generous portions to the shamans, but all of the cash, grain, and significant portions of meat would be the shamans' share.

23. Cf. Shirokogoroff, 1935 cited in Jakobsen, 1999.

24. There are also differences in what is supposed to happen to a *ba dong* when she incarnates a spirit and what happens when a *mansin* manifests a spirit, but we will reserve that discussion for another place. Many *chau van* musicians and ritual masters have a dual identity as initiated mediums.

25. Hamayon, 1998.

26. Lee and Kendall, 1991; Kendall, 1996.

27. Balzer, 1997; Tedlock, 2005; and Bacigalupo, 2004, 2007.

28. eg., Bogoras, 1904–1909.

29. Vitebsky, 1995a and b.

30. Lee and Kendall, 1991.

31. For Vietnam: Ngo, 1999; Nguyen, 2002; Norton, 2002; To et al., 1999. For Korea: Yim, 1970; Lee, 1969, 1982, 1996.

32. Kendall, 2000.

33. cf. Morris, 1995.

References

Bacigalupo, Ana Mariella. "The Mapuche Man Who Became a Woman Shaman: Selfhood, Gender Transgression, and Competing Cultural Norms." *American Ethnologist* 31, no. 3 (2004): 440–457.

Bacigalupo, Ana Mariella. *Shamans of the Foye Tree: Gender, Power and Healing Among Chilean Mapuche.* Austin: University of Texas Press, 2007.

Balzer, Marjorie Mandelstam. "Sacred Genders in Siberia: Shamans, Bear Festivals, and Androgyny." In *Gender Reversals and Gender Cultures,* edited by Petra Ramet, 164–182. London: Routledge, 1997.

Bogoras, Waldemar. The Chukchee. 3 vols. New York: American Museum of Natural History, 1904–1909.

Butler, Judith. *Bodies that Matter: On the Discursive Limits of "Sex."* New York: Routledge, 1993.

Ch'ŏn, Pokhua. *Mudang naeryŏk* (Mudang chronicles). Seoul: Minsogwŏn, 2001.

Durand, Maurice. *Technique et Panthéon des médiums viêtnamiens* (The Technique and Pantheon of Vietnamese Sprit Mediums). Vol. 45. Publications de l'École Française d'Extrême-Orient: Paris, 1959.

Endress, Kirsten. "Spirit Performance and the Ritual Construction of Personal Identity in Modern Vietnam." In *Possessed by the Spirits,* edited by K. Fjelstad and T. H. Nguyen, 77–94. Ithaca, NY: Southeast Asia Program Publications, Cornell University, 2006.

Fjelstad, Karen. "Tu Phu Cong Dong: Vietnamese Women and Mediumship in the San Francisco Bay Area." PhD diss., University of Hawaii, 1995.

Guillemoz, Alexandre. "What do the Naerim Mudang from Seoul Learn?" In *Korean Shamanism: Revivals, Survivals, and Change,* edited by K. Howard, 73–90. Seoul: Royal Asiatic Society, Korea Branch, 1998.

Hamayon, Roberte N. "Le Sens de l'alliance religieuse: 'Mari' d'espirt, 'femme' de Dieu (About Positions in Religious "Alliance" Relationship: 'Husband' of a spirit. 'Wife' of God.") *Anthropologie et Sociétés* 22, no. 2 (1998): 25–48.

Harvey, Youngsook Kim. "Possession Sickness and Women Shamans in Korea." In *Unspoken Worlds: Women's Religious Lives in Non-Western Cultures,* edited by N. A. Falk and R. M. Gross, 41–52. San Francisco: Harper and Row, 1980.

Harvey, Youngsook Kim. *Six Korean Women: The Socialization of Shamans.* St. Paul, MN: West Publishing, 1979.

Hogarth, Hyun-Key Kim. "Inspiration or Instruction? Shaman-training Institutes in Contemporary Korea." *Shaman* 11, nos. 1–2 (2003): 51–68.

Jakobsen, Merete Demant. *Shamanism: Traditional and Contemporary Approaches to the Mastery of Spirits and Healing.* New York and Oxford: Berghahn Books, 1999.

Kendall, Laurel. "But Isn't It Sexual? The Freudian Slip beneath the Ethnographic Gaze." In *Gender/Bodies/Religions,* edited by S. Marcos, 193–215. Cuernavaca, Mexico: Adler Publications, 2000.

Kendall, Laurel. "Initiating Performance: The Story of Chini, a Korean Shaman." In *The Performance of Healing,* edited by C. Laderman and M. Roseman, 17–58. New York: Routledge, 1996.

Kendall, Laurel. *The Life and Hard Times of a Korean Shaman: Of Tales and the Telling of Tales.* Honolulu: University of Hawaii Press, 1988.

Kendall, Laurel. *Shamans, Housewives, and Other Restless Spirits: Women in Korean Ritual Life.* Honolulu: University of Hawaii Press, 1985.

Kendall, Laurel. "Shamans, Nostalgias, and the IMF: South Korean Popular Religion in Motion." Honolulu: University of Hawaii Press, 2009.

Kim, Seong Nae. "The Iconic Power of Modernity: Reading a Cheju Shaman's Life History and Initiation Dream." In *South Korea's Minjung Movement:*

The Culture and Politics of Dissidence, edited by K. M. Wells, 155–165. Honolulu: University of Hawaii Press, 1995.

Kumada, Naoko. "Spirit Cult and Gender: Spirit Mediums in Post-socialist Burma." New and Old Religious Forms, annual meeting of The Society for the Anthropology of Religion and The American Ethnological Society, Providence, RI, April 24–26, 2003.

Larsson, Viveca and Kirsten W. Endres. "Children of the Spirits, Followers of a Master." In *Possessed by the Spirits: Mediumship in Contemporary Vietnamese Communities,* edited by K. Fjelstad and T. H. Nguyen, 143–160. Ithaca, NY: Southeast Asia Program Publications, Cornell University, 2006.

Lee, Diana S. and Laurel Kendall. *An Initiation Kut for a Korean Shaman.* Los Angeles: Produced at the Center for Visual Anthropology, University of California, and distributed by the University of Hawaii Press, 1991. Video.

Lee, Du-hyun (Yi Tuhyŏn). *Han'gugmusokkwa Kongyŏn* (Korean shaman practices and performance). Seoul: Seoul University Press, 1996.

Lee, Du-hyun (Yi Tuhyŏn). *Han'guk kamyŏn'guk* (Korean masked-dance drama). Seoul: Munhwa Kongbobu, Munhwaje Kwalliguk, 1969.

Lee, Du-hyun (Yi Tuhyôn). "Role Playing Through Trance Possession." Workshop on theater and ritual, Asia Society, New York City, 1982.

Lewis, I. M. Ecstatic Religion. Harmondsworth: Penguin, 1969.

Lewis, I. M. "Spirit Possession and Deprivation Cults." *Man* 1, no. 3 (1966): 307–329.

Malarney, Shaun Kinsgley. *Culture, Ritual, and Revolution in Vietnam.* New York: Routledge Curzon, 2002.

Morris, Rosalind C. "ALL MADE UP: Performance Theory and the New Anthropology of Sex and Gender." *Annual Review of Anthropology* 24 (1995): 567–592.

Ngo, Duc Thinh. "Hau Bong as Viewed from the Angle of the Performing Arts." *Vietnamese Studies* 12, no. 192 (1999): 56–60

Nguyen, Hien Thi. "The Religion of the Four Palaces: Mediumship and Therapy in Viet Culture." PhD diss., Indiana University, 2002.

Norton, Barley. "The Moon Remembers Uncle Ho: the Politics of Music and Mediumship in Northern Vietnam." *British Journal of Ethnomusicology* 11, no. 1 (2002): 69–98.

Norton, Barley. "Vietnamese Mediumship Rituals: The Musical Construction of the Spirits." *The World of Music* 42, no. 2 (2000): 75–97.

Ordinance on Folk Beliefs. "Ordinance on Folk Beliefs and Religion." In *21/2004/ PL-UBTVQH11,* edited by Standing Committee of the National Assembly, 2004.

Ortner, Sherry B. *Making Gender: The Politics and Erotics of Culture.* Boston: Beacon Press, 1996.

Pham, Quyen Phuong. "Tran Hung Dao and the Mother Goddess Religion." In *Possessed by the Spirits: Mediumship in Contemporary Vietnamese*

Communities, edited by K. Fjelstad and T. H. Nguyen, 31–54. Ithaca, NY: Southeast Asia Program Publications, Cornell University, 2006.

Spiro, Melford E. *Burmese Supernaturalism.* Englewood Cliffs, NJ: Prentice Hall, 1967.

Tedlock, Barbara. *The Woman in the Shaman's Body: Reclaiming the Feminine in Religion and Medicine.* New York: Bantam Books, 2005.

To, Dong Hai, et al. "Hymns of the cult of Holy Mothers." *Vietnamese Studies,* Special Issue: The Cult of Holy Mothers in Vietnam 12, no. 192 (1999): 61–72.

Truong, Thin. "Ton trong ttn nguong va bai tru me tin di doan" (Respect folk beliefs and abolish superstitions). In *Tin Nguong Me Tin* (Religious beliefs-superstition), edited by Ha, Van Tang and Truong Thin, 112–126. Hanoi: Nha Xuat ban Thanh nien, 1998.

Vitebsky, Piers. "From Cosmology to Environmentalism: Shamanism as Local Knowledge in a Global Setting." In *Counterworks: Managing the Diversity of Knowledge,* edited by R. Fardon, 182–203. London: Routledge, 1995a.

Vitebsky, Piers. *The Shaman: Voyages of the Soul, Trance, Ecstasy and Healing from Siberia to the Amazon.* London: Macmillan Reference Books, 1995b.

Yim, Seuk Jai (Im Sôk-chae). "Han'guk mosok yôn'gu sôsôl" (Introduction to Korean "mu-ism"). *Journal of Asian Women* 9 (1970):73–90.

CHAPTER 6

Women and Sacred Medicines among the Khasis in the Highlands of Northeast India

Darilyn Syiem

This chapter is based on information obtained from personal interviews, informal talks, the author's personal knowledge (she being part of the tradition), and available literature. At times you will find references to the past, which I have made with the intention of conveying the following message: *that the past cushions the present thus keeping alive these traditional practices in spite of criticism, resistance, and at times even prohibition.* Throughout I have focused largely on indigenous healing practices among the Khasi community

In a country as diverse as India, there are various systems of belief and worldviews, but the systems of medical religious practices can be divided primarily into a folk stream and a classical stream. Within this larger division there are myriad subdivisions, and each community brings to the tradition a distinctiveness and identity that are determined by the worldview of that community. With the advent of modernity and conversion to other religions, much about these traditions that is largely oral in nature is at risk of being lost. This is especially true of the northeastern region of the country, which is peopled by over 200 groups with distinct ethnic identities (Goswami et al., 2005, p. 3) that underwent rigorous proselytizing after the arrival of American Baptists in 1836, Welsh Calvinist Methodists in 1841, and Catholic priests in the latter part of the 19th century.

In the tiny state of Meghalaya in this northeast region, however, two major communities resisted total conversion to Christianity. These are the Khasis and the Jaintia (Pnar), tribes that follow a matrilineal system. As one scholar observed, "The Khasis are the only race or community of the Austro-Asiatic race who have been able to stand unchanged against the test of time and to resist against the forces of social and historical evolutionary processes" (Lyngdoh Nongbri, 2006). These few educated Khasi-Pnars, whom Christianity had not succeeded in drawing to its fold, started a revival movement in 1899, and established an organization called the *Seng Khasi* with the objective of keeping alive their ancestral customs, culture, and religion.[1]

Against this backdrop, this chapter will examine and analyze the customary beliefs that underlie the healing traditions of the Khasi tribe.

A BRIEF PROFILE OF NORTHEAST INDIA AND MEGHALAYA

Northeast India is bordered by Bangladesh in the south, Myanmar in the east, and China in the north. It is a landlocked region and connected to the rest of India by a thin strip of land commonly referred to as the chicken neck. The region comprises eight states: Arunachal Pradesh, Assam, Manipur, Meghalaya, Mizoram, Nagaland, Tripura, and Sikkim. It is different from the rest of the country in terms of culture, tradition, beliefs, lifestyle, landscapes, and people's appearance. The dialects spoken in each state and by each ethnic group differ from one to the other.

Meghalaya is squeezed between Bangladesh in the southwest, Burma in the east, and Bhutan in the north. This small hill state of the Indian nation is some 40,000 square kilometers, at an elevation between 4,000 and 6,000 feet. The seven districts of Meghalaya are inhabited by three tribes: the Khasis, the Jaintias and the Garos. Each speaks its own language and has its own culture. The Khasis are of Mongolian stock, and their speech has Mon-Khmer affinities and is connected with Cambodian. For centuries they lived intact, preserving their system of beliefs (Skolimowski, 1993). Anthropological, ethnological, sociological, and linguistic research shows that the Khasis belong to the Austro-Asiatic or the Austro race.

KHASIS LINEAGE

The Khasis are divided into a number of clans that are bound together by strict ties of religion, ancestor worship and funeral rites. The Khasis draw their lineage through the mother and trace their origin back to 'Ka' Iawbei ('Ka' is feminine). *Ka Iawbei* is the primeval ancestress of the clan (*kur*). She is to the Khasis what the "tribal mother" was to old Celtic and Teutonic genealogists, and we have an interesting parallel to the reverence of the Khasis for *Ka Iawbei* in the Celtic goddess Brigit, the tribal mother of the Brigantes (Gurdon, 1906, p. 112). Among the Khasis, *Ka Iawbei* is the ancestral mother who establishes a particular lineage or clan. She has the sacred trust of increasing and ensuring the preservation of her *kur* with the sanction and help of *ka Leilongkur ka Leilongjait* (goddess of clan preservation). Her daughters, known as *Ka Iawbei Khynraw,* are handed over this sacred trust for perpetuation and preservation of the clan. Oral traditions say that ancestral mothers of several clans have a supernatural origin and are a part of the tradition of ancestor-worship. *Hasting's Encyclopedia* notes: "Of the deceased ancestors the Khasis revere *Ka Iawbei* the most and a large number of the flat table-stones to be seen in front of the Khasi menhirs are erected in her honor" (Choudhury, 1993, p.110).

Again, the youngest daughter and the ancestral home—called *ka khadduh* and *ka iing seng iing khadduh,* respectively—are the focus of this spiritual heritage. Since religious activities related to the unity, preservation, and well-being of the clan center around the *khadduh* and her home, she can be seen as symbolically keeping alive the family ritual and worship She is, in this sense, the keeper of religion. On the other hand, the ancestral maternal uncle (*U Suidnia*) is the one who formally establishes and seals the sacred pact of God and man in his family worship and rituals. The ancestral father (*U Thawlang*) is the co-creator along with *Ka Iawbei.* He has the responsibility of providing and caring for the family (Lyngdoh Nongbri, 2006, p. 240).

Traditionally, the performance of sacrifices by a *Lyngdoh* (Khasi priest) requires the assistance of a female priestess known as *Ka Lyngdoh* (female priestess). This female collects all the articles and places them in the *Lyngdoh's* hands at the time of sacrifice. He merely acts as her deputy when sacrificing (Gurdon, 1906). Another venerated key figure is the mother or sister of the Chief (*Syiem*) in the Khasi native state. She is known as the *Syiem Sad.* As the nearest female relative of the Chief, the *Syiem Sad* is seen as a moral force behind the throne. Some scholars have even defined her as the High Priestess and Spiritual Head of the State (Nongbri, 2003).

THE BELIEF SYSTEM OF THE KHASIS

The Khasis are traditionally governed by a set of commandments that are orally and mentally pronounced from generation to generation. These are: (1) *Kamai ia ka hok,* connoting that people should live righteously; (2) *Tipbriew Tipblei,* connoting that people who know God are those who know their own fellow human beings; (3) *Tipkur Tipkha,* connoting that people should honor and respect their relations on the mother's side as well as the father's (Rymbai, 1993, p. 73). The Khasis believe that *U Blei*

(God) is the Creator, Protector, and the Provider. God to them is formless and is unidentifiable with any animate or inanimate object in nature. They believe in a single God whose gender changes contextually. God appears to be either female or male. So he is *U Leilongspah* (Male God of Prosperity) or *Ka Leilongkur ka Leilongjait* (Female Deity who increases and protects the clan, more specifically the matrilineal lineage). When a prayer is offered for the welfare of the house, the clan, or the community, God is addressed as *Ka Blei* (feminine gender). When a prayer is offered for the *hima* (state), God is addressed as *U Blei* (masculine gender). Other records also tell us that, to the Khasis, God has no gender. They explain their invocation of the various names of God as divine attributes. God dwells up and above the land; the land itself is referred to as *Ka Dwar u Blei,* or "where God stays." The temporal world is called *Ka Pyrthei Shong Basa* (a world of temporary sojourn) and it is believed that the soul of the dead can reach *Ka Dwar U Blei* only with the performance of rituals by the kinsmen of the deceased (Nongkynrih, 2002, p. 130).

The Khasis also believe in the unique gift of *Ka Rngiew.* They believe that every individual has in himself or herself an inner spirit in varying measures known as *Ka Rngiew*. An individual's well-being, good health, and longevity depend upon the strength of *Ka Rngiew* (Nongkynrih, 2002, p. 149). This is also the capacity to bring rational considerations to bear upon a person's understanding of his or her own situation. When a person has lost this inner spirit, which is like a spiritual amulet, he or she is virtually reduced to a lower species of creation, such as an insect or a bird. Even one's good fortune and material success in life desert a person on the loss of *Ka Rngiew.* In this case, it is said that *Ka Rngiew* has fled to the devils or to other evil powers, and the real cause of it is that the person has gone astray from God and so God must forsake him or her. The only power in this world that can restore a person's lost *Ka Rngiew* is his or her own sincere endeavor toward peace with God.

The intention of the focus on the religious aspect above is to highlight the interweaving of the social order with the religious order. The former cannot be promoted or maintained in abstraction from the latter. We can, in a certain sense, even go so far as to claim that the two are one and the same (Miri, 1981, p. 17).

THE CONCEPT OF HEALTH AMONG THE KHASIS

Human beings are compelled by necessity to find answers to questions of health and survival. Among the Khasis, there are no straightforward answers to good health and their approach to health is overarching and comprehensive. An understanding of the Khasi worldview and belief system is therefore necessary as it informs all practices of the Khasis and is the fundamental organizing principle of life of the entire community. The three command-ments mentioned earlier would, if followed rigorously, ensure health, wealth, and happiness, and would strengthen *Ka Rngiew*. The Khasis describe the experience of continually falling ill as *La Jem Ka Rngiew* (weakening of inner spirit). In this case it is the mind which must have the power to *Pynksan Ka Rngiew* (strengthen the inner spirit). It would appear then that the Khasi ap-proach to health is more from a mental and spiritual perspective. They believe that when the mind is calm and at peace, the body will also be healthy. Again, the focus on righteous conduct, it would seem, would also naturally ensure good health as well as entry into the Heavenly Abode (*Ka Dwar U Blei*).

Keeping the philosophy of complete well-being in mind, the Khasis also have a very sophisticated and practical understanding of the environment and the need for conservation. Traditionally, at the edge of every village, there would be an area of protected green cover called *law kyntang,* or the sacred grove. Even now these sacred groves still exist, and it is taboo to cut trees or even branches of living trees, although dead wood could be removed and greens from the ground could be gathered for home consumption only.[2] The traditional unwritten message is that anyone who cuts timber or any plant from these groves for a commercial purpose would be haunted by the evil spirit. No amount of education and awareness about deforestation and climate change could make the Khasis react as strongly as does this tradi-tional belief. These sacred forests thus guarantee the presence of water and greenery and fresh air for inhabitants of the village, as well as valuable herbs and plants that are widely used for medicinal purposes. The preservation of the sacred grove clearly has a positive impact on the health of the people.

Everyday life of the traditional Khasis also is governed by a whole list of *dos* and *don'ts* (*bit* and *ym bit*). The practices of washing their feet before entering the house, washing their hands outside, prohibiting the cutting of one's nails in the night or sleeping through the sunset have all been imposed with the sole intention of warding off disease. Nowadays, many of these *dos* and *don'ts* are no longer seriously adhered to, yet deep in the heart and mind of the Khasis, they still live and can be called to action anytime. I use this strategy to make young girls adopt civic sense: when I see them discarding used sanitary napkins carelessly I remind them that such actions expose their personal well-being and would bring ill fortune (*thad ia ka long rynieng bat jem daw*). As expected, it works!

ILLNESS, DISEASE, AND THE SACRED ROLE OF THE SYIEM SAD

When a person falls ill, relatives would usually give some kind of cure, be it within the traditional or the modern systems of medicine. The for-mer consists mostly of oral traditions, the carriers of which are millions of housewives, thousands of traditional birth attendants, bone setters, village practitioners, and herbal healers. In fact, before the Welsh missionaries came to these Khasi hills, this traditional system of medicine was the only health system among the Khasis. When the patient fails to respond to the long spell of medical treatment, the kinsmen begin to show anxiety and start suspecting that some evil is influencing the patient. In a manner similar to that of modern medicine—treating symptoms first, then performing tests and prescribing additional treatment—they continue the medical treatment while they contact the *nongduwai* (medicine man) for the diagnosis and cure of the problem. The *nongduwai* tries to find the cause (*ka daw*) of the suffering. He starts by looking for the cause within the household (*ka daw-üng*). He tries to find out whether any member of the household has ever committed *ka pap ka sang* (acts of sin and breaking of taboo, such as marrying within the same clan) for which no forgiveness has been asked from *U Blei* (God). If this is the case then the medicine man performs a prayer ritual whereby he implores God to exonerate the sinner and take away the disease.

If the suffering is diagnosed as caused by some keeper of *u thlen*, then no *nongduwai* has the power to affect a cure.[3] This power resides only with the *Syiem Sad,* and the patient has to be taken to her. The *Syiem Sad* heats up an iron rod in the fire of the hearth in the *üing sad* and touches the hairlock on the head of the patient with it while saying prayers to *U Blei*. She then dips the same rod in water, which is given to the patient to be used for drinking, massaging, and bathing. This ritual is believed to cure the patient by "burning away" the evil spell of *u thlen* (Nongkynrih, 2002, pp. 151–152). The *Syiem Sad* does not perform rituals and sacrifices; only males who are specifically sanctioned by their clan or by the indigenous religious community do these. As the caretaker of traditional religious ceremonies, however, she offers fervent prayers and chants to *U Blei*. From the beginning, the Khasi ancestors have relegated to her the power to dispose of any unclean aspect of life, evil existence, and so on, within her clan; hence, the *Syiem Sad* is expected to have the power to heal evil afflictions.

Other female members of the *Syiem* clan also practice rituals of burning, symbolic sanctifying using rice or water or even *ka kiad* (local liquor). For instance, a handful of rice that has been sanctified is given to the patient who then keeps it under the pillow until the illness disappears. Though these other women of the *Syiem* clan can effectively bring about a cure, the majority of the Khasis who believe in the efficacy of this kind of healing prefer to go to the *Syiem Sad*.

Another cause of illness or disaster is believed to be caused by the past wrongdoings of an ancestor or clan. Elderly people would often remark, "Beware of your ill doings for they may come back to you or your offspring in some form or the other." When such predictions come true, the clan to which the ailing person belongs appeals to the medicine man to offer prayers to a deity through rituals that include the practices of chanting, egg-breaking, and cock-sacrifice. Many times these rituals are performed in a nearby forest, grove, or river, as the Khasis closely associate their deities with nature. In "egg-breaking," known as *shat pylleng,* only the chicken's egg is used for it is considered improper to use any other egg (Wolflang, 2003, p. 120).

These kinds of beliefs and practices are slowly dying out with the increasing numbers of Khasis converting to Christianity. Ironically, however, people who are Christians by birth or by conversion often fall back on the indigenous beliefs and practices when everything else fails. Often, in case of sickness, "they [Christian villagers]still depend on the traditional medicinemen for diagnosing and curing the sickness by performing traditional rituals" (Nongkynrih, 2002, p.145). Rymbai (1993) also said: "Christianity follows now some of the aspects and rites of the old religion which its followers see as eternal truth of all religion." It is also interesting to note that in the Christian Bible, it is written that Jesus demystified the pagan belief that diseases occur due to the sins of parents but at the same time used symbolic items for healing. Jesus made a paste out of mud and spittle, applied it to the blind man's eyes, and then told him to wash his eyes—the blind man obeyed the instructions of Jesus and was able to see.[4] The use of elements such as water and mud is also traditional among the indigenous Khasi healers. These natural elements, however, are called upon by other local names. For instance a healer would call upon the name of the water followed by a chant, after which the person being treated is made to drink a liter of the water (Kharmawphlang, unpublished paper).

OTHER WOMEN HEALERS

Among the Khasis there are other women healers. These do not have the status of the *Syiem Sad* because they are not of the *Syiem* clan, but they are also gifted with the power to heal. These women, some of them Christians, often perform rites and call upon the deities in order to cure many illnesses and afflictions. Being viewed as ordinary women, some of them have received skeptical responses from their community when performing rituals considered to be the privilege of the *Syiem* clan. But many of these women have devised ways of practicing healing without raising objections from their community. For example, one woman, who as it happens was a Christian, healed the sick by praying, chanting, and even performing healing rituals She was questioned by her community, which considered her activities to be sorcery and branded her as one possessed by the devil. To enable herself to continue with the healing without criticisms and accusations, she announced that she saw the Holy Spirit in her dreams, who gave her sanctity to pray and chant to heal the sick. This declaration received the sanction of the community, and she was able to continue with her healing practices till her death.

This kind of healing usually begins with *ka jing phah peit* (diagnosis), where the female (or male) possessing god-given healing abilities would use rice, egg, or water to find out if the afflicted person has been possessed by any evil spirit. An image or vision (seen only by the healer) would appear if suspicions proved to be true. When this happens, the healer would offer fervent prayers to the respective deity, imploring the deity to remove the illness. Sometimes, the ailing person would be taken to a hillside or other secluded place and prayers and chanting would be performed. The indigenous faith healer would address the deity as *Blei Nongbuh, Nongthaw,* (deity who creates) and would implore the deity to take away the affliction. Other clinical problems like the *niang-sohpet* (pain in the umbilical area), common among infants, can be effectively cured by the woman healer other than the *Syiem Sad.* No fees are charged by her, but any token of gratitude and respect is graciously accepted.

Currently there are a number of Khasi women who use playing cards to read a person's problem and diagnose it, somewhat like the modern Tarot reader, but with the difference that they use normal playing cards and follow their own system of interpretation. They would even pray if the patient so wishes, and then refer the patient to other healers (who may be indigenous), herbal, or even allopathic doctors. Many of these women are Christians, but they engage in this kind of healing practice and their prayers address God (though not necessarily the Christian God). They claim that they were born with this gift and their mothers and grandmothers were involved in similar activities. One such woman (from North Shillong) said in an interview that she did not know that she had this healing power but stumbled upon it quite by chance when she jokingly tried to prophesize her friends' conditions and then discovered that her prophecies were true.[5] Her first husband barred her from this activity, but she did not stop and continued in secret. Many people claimed they were cured by her advice. Like most such healers, the woman is extremely diffident and reluctant to talk about her ability. It is difficult to say whether this reluctance is connected to fear of being branded a "witch" or fear of backlash from a woman who has "power."

THE GUARDED SACRED-SECRET KNOWLEDGE

Similarly, the women healers belonging to the *Syiem* clan were not willing to talk. They gave various reasons to avoid the interviews. Here, this reluctance could be interpreted as a feeling of fear of the divine or the wrath of the gods to whom they pray if the secret knowledge is shared with others or the prevailing Christian influence. It could also be connected to the belief that talking would take away the power and efficacy of the divine healing and cause it to become ineffective, thus depriving the many people who depend on them to take away illnesses and evil spirits. This analysis acknowledges the common belief among the Khasi indigenous healers that the power of healing should not be documented, nor should fees be charged for the services rendered. As tokens of gratitude, patients or their relatives usually offer gifts in kind or just place (*pynkham*) some amount of money in their hands without actually disclosing the amount.

From a conversation with a *Seng Khasi* man, who is actively involved in the preservation and conservation of Khasi culture, it is deduced that most indigenous faith healers avoid talking about their healing power mainly because the healers seem to be in a sort of trance when they pray, chant, and perform rituals to invoke the deity for a cure of the illness.[6] He said that, as such, they may be unaware of the process after its completion and thus cannot narrate it. There is also the probability that the indigenous healer may be unable to narrate such sacred performances because these come naturally, and only when the need arises. As Kharmawphlang of North Eastern Hill University, Department of Culture, said: "The healing ritual performed by the indigenous healers is such that it cannot be explained and can only be understood when observed."

GENDER ANALYSIS

Even though *Ka Iawbei,* the primeval ancestress of the clan, is not directly involved in social or religious rituals and practices, she is the perpetuator and the preserver of the clan, so she symbolically hands over the baton to her kinsmen and kinswomen. In this sense, the survival of *ka jaid bynriew khasi* (the khasi community) depends on *Ka Iawbei,* who spells out traditional norms and customs such as shunning from *ka pap ka sang* (acts of sin). Again, as the Khasi concept of health is embedded in the socioreligious fabric, committing *ka pap ka sang* would bring about affliction and disease. In this context, therefore, *Ka Iawbei* indirectly plays a critical role in the recovery from illness and disease. Further, we cannot belittle the role of *Ka Lyngdoh* which, on the surface, appears to be that of servitude to a male, a socially expected norm. However, as related earlier, she is the one whose presence is crucial for the smooth performance of rituals and sacrifices. But the striking observation is the power and influence of the *Syiem Sad* and the exalted office held by her. Since Khasi Chiefs are not only administrative and political heads, but also custodians of the religious cult of the state, the *Syiem Sad* is seen as the key figure in the rights and ceremonies that are performed (Nongbri, 2003).

Again, information from interviews with those who are not healers, but who follow the indigenous faith, shows that both women and men who possess the divine power of healing perform rituals and prayers in line with their faith. There is no bar for women though it is the *Syiem Sad* whom people prefer to go to as traditionally it is the *Syiems* who can cure afflictions by the evil spirits. Even among the males who belong to the *Syiem* clan, it is the ancestral maternal uncle who has the divine power to perform healing rituals and prayers; this further emphasizes the deep implications of the matrilineal lineage.

CONCLUSION

The Khasis are traditionally a people who respect and give due acknowledgement to their womenfolk. But the social and religious changes that have taken place are posing a serious threat to this unique culture and its practices. The adoption by a matrilineal community of a new religion that is essentially patriarchal in nature presents great challenges to fully understanding and retaining the centrality of the "feminine power and energy." The lack of sufficient literature does not help the cause, and a time will come when the beliefs and the practices will be history. For me writing this article was a dilemma, as I had to depend mostly on informal interviews with those who follow the indigenous Khasi faith, those who have been cured by the *Syiem Sad* or other women healers, and on personal observations and orally preserved traditional beliefs. Given a few exceptions, it was impossible to get interviews with indigenous faith healers. Portions of this article, therefore, have been based on conversations with academics from the North Eastern Hill University, Shillong, who have done studies on the Khasi society and on my own understanding of my own community. Until today, there is no literature on this form of healing which is characterized by the undaunted belief that it should only be preserved orally and handed down by word of mouth only to the next of kin.

My acknowledgement goes to all those who have shared their knowledge and thoughts with me. It has been very difficult to write this article, but I was inspired by those who spurred me on with the argument that there is always a beginning to everything and the beginning is the most intimidating. My sincere gratitude goes to Roshmi Goswami, who not only helped with the editing but, more importantly, presented challenging questions that I could not and did not want to pass by. Finally, I am indebted to my daughter Evanshainia Syiem, who helped me with the required referencing format, which I must admit, was unfamiliar to me.

NOTES

1. The *Seng Khasi* includes male and female members, who follow the Khasi indigenous faith.

2. For example the famous sacred groves of Mawphlang (a village in East Khasi Hills) and much referred to by environmentalists as good practices.

3. A *u thlen* is a devil in the form of a serpent that demands human blood from its keepers and in return showers them with wealth. One of the ways to get a human being into its grasp is by cutting off a little of his/her hair or a piece of garment and then offering this as a sacrifice by means of which the *rngiew* of the victim is captured to give as an offering to *u thlen*.

4. Gospel of John 9:1–8.

5. Shillong is the Capital of Meghalaya.

6. See note 1.

REFERENCES

Chowdhury, J. N. (1993). Indigenous Religion of the Khasis: An Anthropological Approach. In *Religion in North-East India* by S. Sen, 110. New Delhi: Uppal Publishing House.

Goswami, R., Sreekala, M. G., & Goswami, M. (eds.) (2005). *Women in Armed Conflict Situations (A Study by North East Network)*. Guwahati, Assam: North East Network.

Gurdon, P. R. (1906). *The Khasis*. Delhi: Low Price Publications.

Kharmawphlang, D. (unpublished article). *Healing Chants of the Khasis: A Study.*

Lyngdoh Nongbri, M. W. (2006). *Basic Foundation of Khasi Culture: Community and Change,* 240. Unpublished PhD thesis submitted to the North Eastern Hill University, Shillong, Meghalaya.

Miri, S. (1981). An Introduction to the Study of Tribal Religions. In *The Khasi Milieu* by H. O. Mawrie, 17. New Delhi: Concept Publishing Company.

Nongbri, T. (2003). Khasi Women and Matriliny: Transformation in Gender Relations. In *Gender Relations in Forest Societies in Asia: Patriarchy at Odds* by G. Kelkar, D. Nathan, & P. Walter. New Delhi: Sage Publications.

Nongkynrih, A. K. (2002). *Khasi Society of Meghalaya: A Sociological Understanding,* 130, 145, 149, 151–152. New Delhi: Indus Publishing Company.

Rymbai, R. T. (1993). Christian Missions and the Indigenous Religion of the Khasi-Pnar. In *Religion in North-East India* by S. Sen, 73. New Delhi: Uppal Publishing House.

Skolimowski, H. (1993). *Early Eco-Philosophers Among the Tribal People: Letter from India*. Trumpeter, Vol. 10, No. 4.

Wolflang, B. M. (2003). *Khasi Myths–An Interpretative Study,* 120. An unpublished PhD thesis submitted to the North Eastern Hill University, Shillong, Meghalaya.

CHAPTER 7

The Not-So-Subtle Body in Dais' Birth Imagery

Janet Chawla

D ais' imaging of the body, and their use of expressions such as *narak,*
nasae, and *nadi* (the latter terms shared by the more conventional
ideas of "subtle body"), have been considered in terms of imagery
serving them in their role as midwives, hands-on practitioners of indigenous birth knowledge and skills.[1] In this chapter Motherhood and Traditional Research, Information, Knowledge and Action (MATRIKA) data will
be examined—along with other scholarly material—from the perspective
of notions of the subtle body, using that term in its broadest sense.[2] The
woman-centered nature of this exploration is intended to challenge prevalent hierarchies that privilege the subtle body over the gross body and consequently the male "spiritual" body over the female material, reproductive,
and maternal body.

In Indian imagistic traditions, the female body and the earth (body) have
been abidingly conflated. This is not a symbolic relationship. The earth is
not a symbol of woman, nor is woman a symbol of the earth. Rather song,
image, myth, and medicine have all celebrated the fertility of both, in the
same breath, so to speak. The Sankhya philosophical system is foundational
to this imagery in which *Prakriti* represents the entire phenomenal world,
and *Purush,* consciousness. Strictly speaking the *Prakriti-Purush* dyad is conceptual, abstract, and ungendered. But in fact its exoteric, popular, and gendered manifestation has had disastrous consequences for what is commonly
termed "the status of women."

Woman is identified with the field/matter (*Prakriti*) and man, with "knowledge of the field" (*Purush*). Although, in pure Sankhya, this "knowledge of the field" is equivalent to consciousness," in social history it has played out as power, privilege, and patriarchy.

In a morning newspaper, the *Hindu,* on June 26, 2007, a religion column titled "Rise above the Gunas," exhorted the reader to detect the observer of the body-mind complex. This is the classical nonattachment teaching of Hindu text and practice. Krishna is invoked to describe the human dilemma utilizing the language of subtle and gross bodies and equating them with the "knower of the field" and the "field."

> Lord Krishna explains the difference between the observer and the observed in terms of Kshetrajna (the knower of the field) and Kshetra (field), where the two entities—the subtle soul and the gross body—are seen to be together and yet distinct. (p. 12)

From the perspective of a practitioner of yoga or meditation, one can experientially identify the terms "field-knower" and "field" as aspects of the inner *lila* of attention (*dhyan*) and objects toward which attention is directed. Society, however, is not composed exclusively of philosophers, yogis, and meditators.

Sociologist Leila Dube's *Seed and Earth: The Symbolism of Biological Reproduction and Sexual Relations of Production* (1986) exposes the sociopolitical consequences of this philosophic and folk homology. She quotes the *Narada Smriti*: "Women are created for offspring; a woman is the field and a man is the possessor of the field." Dube shows how this analogy has functioned to legitimize male rights over female sexuality (right to "plow" the field), rights to both agricultural land and children ("the crop should belong to him who has sown the seed").

Furthermore, the assumption is that the earth/woman can "bear" or support life—that women can suffer or bear pain in the support of life (i.e., children, family, domestic, and agricultural responsibilities). This image or conflation translates into the common perception that pain is somehow "natural" to woman in other domains as well as childbirth—and feminist writers have roundly critiqued that assumption. This naturalization of female pain is similar to the biblical curse on Eve for eating the apple in the Garden of Paradise: "To the woman he (Yahweh God) said I shall give you intense pain in childbearing, you will give birth to children in pain" (*New Jerusalem Bible,* 1985, p. 18). A review and reclamation of the woman-earth conflation need not valorize female suffering and victimization.

I have modified and elaborated on this essential equation of earth equals woman in "The Conflation of the Female Body and Earth in Indian Religious

Traditions: Gendered Representations of Seed, Earth and Grain" (2000), where I make a distinction between "earth" and "field." A scrutiny of the dais' traditional use of grain in a ritual performance facilitating birth displays a woman-centered conflation of earth body and female body, a conflation valorizing the fecundity of both earth and woman. The custom entailed *atta* being placed on a *tali* in one mound and the woman separating that mound of *atta* into two with her hand, invoking the goddess Bemata and the help of the dai. "With the power of Bemata, and the support of the dai, may the baby separate from me as easily as I separate this one mound into two." Interestingly the word "dai" derives from *dhatri,* also related to *dharti* (earth)—the key sense is "to support" or "to bear."

Foregrounding data from dais and birth traditions interrogate and challenge androcentric assumptions inherent in the "religion" propounded by the newspaper article quoted above, refining the feminist analyses of Dube's paper. Data from dais, privileging their voices and customs, lead us to other understandings of female physiological processes. Their perceptions of birth-giving and the conflation of earth and female bodies require us to make an epistemological shift—allowing us to empathetically access their knowledge skills and lives. We are also provided with an imagistic mapping of reproductive bodies earthy, whole, and sacred, which stands apart from the priestly, biomedical or "new age" views.

Geoffrey Samuel writes of the use of subtle body imagery and its power to situate the individual within culturally specific body praxis in both healing and birthing arenas (2005, pp. 121–135). He also writes:

> One of the more significant aspects of the subtle body language is the way in which it can open our picture of the individual out to include the relationship with others. It is particularly relevant to any consideration of subtle body practices in the context of healing, since healing is always at some level about relationships between people. Such an approach would involve looking at childbirth practices in South Asia simultaneously in terms of physiology, and in terms of what these practices communicate to the birthing mother and other participants in the childbirth about how to make sense of the process of childbirth. (Samuel, 2006, p. 123)

To paraphrase Samuel, "What a woman has between her ears (i.e., her mind-culture-beliefs) has more to do with the process of her labor than does the width of her pelvis And, of course, the labor is also affected by who is supporting and accompanying her, midwifing her. (And here I must acknowledge that in circumstances of poverty her all-too-real deprivation of basic bodily needs profoundly and negatively affects her at the time of parturition).

DIRTY OR FERTILE? BIRTH TRADITIONS AS A CONTESTED SITE

Today dais serve the poorest of the poor—and have always been associated with embodiment and not enlightenment—thus negotiating the energy flowing through the mother's body (not to mention the family!), getting the baby born, and ensuring the survival of mother and baby are their central concerns. Nevertheless, cosmos/body understandings have emerged from our analysis of their indigenous medical imagery and ritual enactments.

Sociopolitical and economic realities, however, do impinge on any consideration of birth attendants and practitioners. Dais and other birth workers in the informal sector still occupy the nether end of the caste hierarchy. Caste was a geographically varied social organization that was reinforced by Western imperial interventions. Privileged Indians in proximity to colonial powers and attitudes reflected and often exaggerated colonial disdain for lower caste birth work and women's health traditions. Katherine Mayo, in her now infamous, but then very influential, *Mother India* (1927)—a book Mahatma Ghandi referred to as "a gutter inspector's report"—devotes a chapter to motherhood. She quotes a Dr. N. N. Parikh: "Ignorance and the purdah system have brought the women of India to the level of animals. They are unable to look after themselves, nor have they any will of their own. They are slaves to their masculine owners" (1927, p. 119). Dais and birth customs were a terrain for bitter ideological writings about "backwardness" and "filth." Again to quote from Mayo:

> The first dhai that I saw in action tossed upon this coal-pot, as I entered the room, a handful of some special vile-smelling stuff to ward off the evil eye—my evil eye. The smoke of it rose thick—also a tongue of flame. By that light one saw her Witch-of-Endor face through its vermin-infested elf-locks, her handing rags, her dirty claws, as she peered with festered and almost sightless eyes out over the stink-cloud she had raised. (pp. 93–94)

I would argue that colonial ideologies segue into the contemporary scene. And that any kind of continuity or reclamation of "traditional" birth practices among middle and upper class women and their families are challenging because of attitudes and economics.

> The attack on dais was an aspect of the way in which the new middle class and upper caste elites were defining themselves and shaping their identity. Interwoven with this attack were questions of who were the high and the low of the society, and how spaces hitherto accessible to women and the lower castes were to be prized open and appropriated for middle class men and women.

Further, the newly worked out concept of cleanliness was important for the definition of the middle class as well as the lower caste. The colonial state, entering the competitive world inhabited by a number of medical and semi-medical practitioners, picked on the "dirt" and the "filth" of the lower caste dai and the customs related to birthing to assert its hygienic, scientific and moral superiority. The colonial state used the notion of aseptic cleanliness as a weapon to introduce Western medicine, while for the Punjabi upper castes, sanitized cleanliness became an ideology for asserting middle class identity as it worked in tandem with notions of caste purity and pollution. (Malhotra, 2006, p. 201)

Not only were dais and traditional birthing practices "dirty" aspect of low castes and classes, they were also harmful displays of female ignorance. Women and tradition needed to be revamped in the name of "ideal motherhood"; that is, nationalist reconstruction involved imported Western notions of ideal motherhood.

Lack of knowledge and education amongst women was seen as causing harm not only to the family but even to the nation. It was pointed out that women who were ignorant of the rules of the body would not only harm themselves, but by producing weak and deficient children, would also destroy the nation. Thus, with the emergence of the family as a site where nationalist restructuring was to be carried out, women were awarded a special augmented status in remodeling the private domain of the nation. In the twentieth-century reconstruction of ideal motherhood, and in the activities of women's organizations, we find a broadening of the class basis of future mothers of the nation and incorporation of the poorer classes as being in need of education in mothercraft. (Mukherjee, 2001, p. 209).

These ideological constructions were pervasive and still exist. A bulwark of "safe motherhood" trainings has been the "Five Cleans," a continuing attempt to clean up Mayo's filthy midwife—a project totally devoid of the cultural awareness put forward in this chapter. The enterprise of "development" extends these ideologies into domains of the modern and even the postmodern and globalization. It should not surprise us that today dais are considered dirty, ignorant, and superstitious by "educated" Indians and held primarily responsible for high maternal-infant mortality and morbidity by global health establishments. Women who handle birth occupy the nether regions (pun intended) of all hierarchies—class, caste, and even gender (thanks to the wholehearted acceptance by feminists of the biomedical, delivery-of-services approach to women's health).

MATRIKA research methodology and analyses invert these hierarchies, foregrounding the dais' worldview, philosophy and cosmology. Dais, demeaned with the term TBAs (traditional birth attendants) by the global and national health establishments, are the inheritors of India's birth knowledge, rituals, and hands-on skills. One woman Ayurvedic practitioner claimed, "Dais are the obstetricians of Ayurveda" (Dr. P. Girija in a seminar titled "Back to the Future: Indigenous Medicine in Contemporary India," Jawaharlal Nehru University, 2006.) Midwife literally means "with woman"—being *with* her and mediating her own cultural understanding of the birth process.

I once conducted a workshop for an NGO (nongovernmental organization) in Koraput District of south Orissa, helping them document a remote and primitive tribe's birth practices. I was told by the doctor and nurses who had worked in the area for 10 years that these women gave birth alone—no system of dais and certainly no biomedical practitioners or facilities existed in the area. The first day, in a role-play, an older tribal woman grabbed hold of a curtain (simulating a rope) with her legs straight out in front of her. Soon a neighbor came in and sat behind her, spooning her body with her own, then another and another—a train of laboring women. I felt in my own body the energy that would flow from one into the other, the laboring woman's back leaning against this literal support system—and I had been told that these women labored alone! These were "midwives" with laboring women. (I am not, however, making claims about these tribal women's body knowledge in this chapter.)

DIRTY MATTERS AND MATERNAL CONNECTIONS

When I first encountered the fact, confirmed in all our MATRIKA research locales, that traditional birth always involved severing the umbilical cord only after the placenta was delivered, I thought that such practice was so appropriate in this society that valued family bonds in general and the mother-child bond in particular. The dais reported their practical reasons for retaining this connection: they would stimulate the placenta with heat to revive a seemingly lifeless baby; the placenta was easier to deliver with the cord connected; and (illustrating the decentralized knowledge-culture system) the women attendants or family members would blame them if anything bad happened had they cut the cord!

On another level the umbilical cord is understood by dais to contain channels/*nadi* and it is through this thread that the *jee,* or life force, flows into the fetus. But the significance of this cord-connection is diverse. One dai in Rajasthan claimed to read the sex of women's subsequent births in the form and twists of the cord; one Punjabi dai said she would never cut the cord of women in her own family, because that would be like cutting off her own roots (those of her family). Another very elderly dai claimed that it was said by others that cutting the umbilical cord was a great *paap* or sin.

None of the dais would have, of their own volition, cut the cord before the placenta emerges. As one dai said, "The placenta and the baby have been together for nine months. What is the hurry to separate them?" It is unfortunate that most "dai training" teaches them to cut the cord immediately. The biomedical approach is a totally functional one. The purpose of the cord/bond has been served—now cut it. Delayed cord-cutting displays comfort with the "mess" of merger, birth, and the process of emerging slowly.

I have often speculated that the "sin," filth, disdain, and pollution associated with the cutting of the cord—and the extent of this "traditional belief" cannot be exaggerated in my experience—involve problematizing a form of violence. One can imagine a razor blade (or bamboo slice, sickle, or arrowhead) encountering the rubbery, fleshy cord-of-life connecting mother-placenta-newborn. One Rajasthani dai claimed:

> The new mother can also cut the cord. If she is not fully conscious then Dai cuts it. Dai Mai (Dai mother) is as loveable as a mother . . . but the dai is Mai, Vaid, Kasai (mother, Ayurvedic practitioner, butcher). Dai cuts the cord, nobody else because it's a dosh (blemish, transgression). There is life in the naala equivalent to the life of a baby—it has 72 naari and by cutting one commits *paap* (sin). (MATRIKA data)

As Sara Pinto writes of her respondents in Uttar Pradesh:

> Even if they do not refer to their tasks as sinful, their work and silences speak of the cutting of the umbilical cord as a momentary and permanent violence in which bringing-into-life entails a small act of death, the severing of a channel for jivan and the bond between the earthly baby and not-quite-earthly placenta . . . the placenta enters the realm of death and decay and the baby enters the world, becoming human, social, alive. (2006, p. 228)

The "stuff" of relationship, connection, is often not visible, acknowledged. The placenta in polite parlance (even in biomedical, public health, and safe motherhood discourses) is relegated to the domain of trash or the repulsive, the abject. It is the ultimate polluting substance in Brahmanical Hinduism.

A common practice is the dai's burial of the placenta in the house or the *angan*, or even in the fields. I once heard of a resident of one of the villages swallowed up by Delhi—his younger brother challenged his right to inherit the family home because his placenta was not buried on that land, the man having been born in Safdarjang Hospital. Often it is only the boy baby's placenta which will be buried—because he will stay (the land going to "he who has the seed"), but the girl's placenta, in Pinto's research, was tossed on the trash heap, because she will move on to another family, to "belong to" another place (Pinto, 2006, p. 206).

However we interpret it, the act of severing that "ma-babe" connection, and the handling of the placenta, is fraught with meaning in the subcontinent. Ayurveda provides us with a concept relevant to this exploration of the most primal of all relationships in nomenclature of the pregnant woman as *dauhrdaya*, or the "two-hearted one." Anuradha Singh writes of this seeming paradox:

> In this enigmatic state (of being both one and two persons) the usual distinction between self and other is obliterated. The embryo is not "other" nevertheless it is a different self. The umbilical cord that characterizes the one-who-is-two is said to have about 1600 nadi-s or channels. Interestingly both dais and texts make this claim. (2006, p. 155).

Advaita philosophy, found in its purest form in the Upanishads, is foundational to this epistemological and ontological system. What has been termed in some Western cultural analysts' parlance "cognitive dissonance" is actually a civilizational orientation toward both/and not either/or. Singh describes the Ayurvedic view of the maternal body during parturition as ". . . a microcosmic workplace, the site of creation and regeneration. Here macrocosmic forces were transacted in microcosmic bodily form." (2006, p. 137).

And yet the female bodily power to manifest new life had been usurped long before colonial ideologies: by Tantric male rites utilizing menstrual blood of virgins and semen retention in couplings; yoni worship with no consideration of women as persons; early coins with yoni image. All these are constructions that harness "barkat," or the energetics of the female power of manifestation, various forms of the "magic" of concretizing desire, to specific ends.

THE RELATIONAL BODY

Some feminist slogans make absolutely no sense to me. "My body is mine" is of limited value during parturition. Not only because of the baby but also because of the support a mother needs during that time. The following *sohar,* or birth song, sung at one of our MATRIKA workshops is blatantly proprietary of the *jachcha* (birth-giving woman). "My *jachcha*" is the first line. We don't know the relationship of the singer to the *jachcha*, allowing everyone to claim her.

> *My jachcha is the full moon of Sharad [as round/full/*
> *   bright/radiant/beautiful as]*
> *Beneath the mahal the dai waits*

With all that's needed for the jachcha.
Beneath the mahal saas (mother-in-law) waits
With all that's needed to make charua.
Beneath the mahal jethani (HBW) waits
With all that's needed to make laddoos.
Beneath the mahal nandi (HZ) waits
With all that's needed for sathiya.
Beneath the mahal devar (Hb) waits
Ready to play the flute.

Not only is the pregnant woman conflated with the most beautiful "full" moon of the year, but also the activities of all her attendants are listed: the mother-in-law makes the herbal concoction; the older sister-in-law makes the celebratory sweets; the husband's sister prepares to draw the auspicious symbols on the walls—and the husband's younger brother is ready to play the flute—and they are all *beneath* the *mahal*/woman/*jachcha* (Rao, 2006, p. 91).

This *sohar* exemplifies Samuel's notion of "modal states" or ways of being (and modes of action) that are both individual and cultural. Samuel sees these emotive states as "a repertoire of personal states . . . internalized during their lifetime" (Samuel, 2006, p. 123). Birth, especially if a son is born, is when the young wife reaps the benefits of her position in the family as mother.

The young wife has specific relations of deference, service, and compliance toward her husband, her mother-in-law, father-in-law, and other kinds of patterned relationships with her husband's elder brother and his wife, her husband's younger siblings and their spouses if any, and so on. Equally, she has expectations of specific forms of behavior in response from each of these persons (Samuel, 2006, p. 123).

The MATRIKA data are full of what we might term social or familial facilitations of birth. In one Bihar workshop, we were told that a laboring woman might be made to drink a glass of water in which her mother-in-law's big toe was dipped. We were rather aghast at that until we learned that in Ayurveda the *nadi* for *pran vayu* (understood to be the carrier of knowledge and experience) exited the body through the big toes. Touching the feet of the elders may transmit wisdom; drinking the toe-water grants permission for the birth to proceed. "The social hierarchy of mother-in-law/daughter-in-law is perhaps encoded in this rite, transmitting the respected female elder's permission for the birth to proceed—granting the status of maternity to the bahu, but at the same time asserting her authority and primacy" (Chawla, 2002a: 147–162).

Another fascinating ritual I encountered in the once polyandrous mountain area of Jaunpur in the state of Uttaranchal was *Matri masaan ka puja*.[3]

If a young woman had signs of a threatening miscarriage, she would walk back, with her male sasural kinsmen, dressed in a black blanket, to perform this *puja* at the water source, spring, river or tap, of her natal home—where she herself had drawn water as a child. The understanding was that she had been afflicted by the figure Matri Masaan, who resided there and needed to be worshipped and relinquished. *Matri* means mother, and *masaan* means the ashes-bone remnants of a cremated body in the cremation grounds. The woman performed *puja,* took off her *shringar ka saman: bindi,* bangles, earrings, *kumkum,* and so forth, which were offered, and she was not supposed to return to her *maike* throughout the pregnancy. I read the term *masaan* as referring to memories (now ashes) of life with mother in the natal home, before marriage—the girl's incomplete transfer emotionally to her sasural.

The emotionally and socially profound switch from her natal home to her married home is implicated here—"out-married daughters" leave their maternal home and enter that of strangers (often at a very young age). Obeisance is paid to this entity (*bhut, prêt,* deity), and also the marks of feminine beauty are left here—speaking the transition not only from daughter to wife, but also that of wife to mother. The ritual performance of *Matri Masaan ka puja* is a public display of the vulnerable state of the young woman. Wordlessly her anguish is showcased to family, neighbors, all in the vicinity, inviting their care and consideration.

Both mother-in-law's big toe ritual and *Matri Masaan* can be read together insofar as each bestows permission on the new mother for the labor to proceed, and to carry the pregnancy to term. There are two kinds of female lineages, that of the sasural and of the maike "mother's home"—which the new mother is betwixt and between. Reconciliation and relocation are ritually enacted; healing is effected.

COSMIC MOORINGS AND EARTHLY CONNECTION

Matri Masaan and another female deity/demon, Bemata, whom we will now consider, signify complex and multiple realities in what I have come to think of as geomysticism. According to some dais, Bemata lives deep within the earth (*narak*). She rules that domain and is responsible for the conception, growth, and birth of humans as well as all vegetation and animal life. Bemata, invoked at the onset of labor, must gradually leave the mother's body via the postpartum bleeding, lest she be responsible for problems for the mother. It seems that the Bemata figure functions as a tracking modality for women postpartum, in much the same way that the biomedical Apgar score is for the neonate.[4]

The meaning of *narak*, a residence of Bemata, is classically understood as one of the three worlds (*triloka*). The *triloka* are *swarg-bhu-narak,* or the celestial realms, the mundane earthly and visible, and the underground, unseen foundations of life—accepted categories of Puranic and classical Hinduism and folk culture as well. The dais' concept of *narak* allows for a mapping of the unseen, inner world of the body, privileging senses and capacities other than the visual, primarily touch and intuition. And indeed dais have practiced noninvasive techniques that negotiate and affect the inner body without violating the integrity of the skin/body/life force. Their holistic health modalities utilize touch (massage, pressure, manipulation) and natural resources (mud, baths and fomentation, herbs) and application of "hot and cold" (in food and drink, fomentation, etc.) and isolation and protection (from domestic, maternal, and sexual obligations).

In our MATRIKA data, the postbirth time, that of the "closing" body was inextricably entwined with conceptions of *narak*. What is normally closed (the vagina, cervix, psyche of the birthing woman), is now open, vulnerable and leaking bodily fluids along with new life. Women who attend birth are more comfortable with this openness and fluidity than the rest of us. *Narak ka samay*, voiced by dais, carries a totally different valence than that of the pundits—and this is what I investigate here in terms of body/matter (mother, matrix, material—all etymologically connected in Indo-European languages).

The concept of *narak* structures and gives meaning to the time, care, and social relations of the mother postpartum—and in keeping with the phenomenon of the "open" body, menstruation is included in this rubric. My intent in this chapter is to insert "fertility" into health and healing debates and discourses rather than simply jettison the "pollution" and uncleanness associated with menstruation and postpartum.

In our Bihar MATRIKA workshops we were told:

> Girls are considered holy before puberty. The marriage of a young girl (who has not had her periods) is performed with her sitting on her father's lap. After puberty the woman is considered unclean, and is unholy, because she bleeds, and this is *narak*.

The common term for the ritual that progresses the mother postpartum from the time of *narak* back into the social world is *chatti* or sixth—though this may have traditionally fallen on different days with different castes and in different areas. In the quote below we see the infant handed to the women who will co-mother him or her!

> On *Chhati* day (after birth) the *narak period* ends. The dai checks if the umbilical cord has fallen off. Then she bathes the baby and beats a *thaali* (plate) and gives the baby to *Chachi* (husband's younger brother's wife).

Chachi does *Namaskar* to God and gives the baby to *Jethani* (husband's elder brother's wife). Then the woman is bathed and she wears new clothes. The dai then cleans the room where the delivery took place and the mother was kept separately for six days.

And from Rajasthan, we heard that the place for dirt, blood, *narak* (and rest for the new mother) is located in her maternal home. Whereas the well worship is only done when she returns to her married home.

Rukma: It's the *jachcha's* mother's duty to have her daughter's birth in her *pihar*. Then her daughter gets rest. But jalwa puja is done only in sasural no matter how long the *jachcha* spends in her *pihar*.
   Manori: this is because after delivery *nau mahene ka narak nikalta hai* (nine months of *narak* comes out). This is also called *narak ka kund* (reservoir of *narak*).

The phrase *narak ka kund* speaks the language of what I have called geo-mysticism. A *kund* is a spring-fed pond, again an earth body analogy with the maternal reproductive body—ritually and socially "polluted" yet fertile.

A GENDERED POETICS OF REPRODUCTIVE BODIES

Martha Ann Selby's exploration of the Ayurvedic texts (2005) attends to the poetics of sexed bodies. The schema of maleness and femaleness she describes, especially the openness and susceptibility of the pregnant woman, is omnipresent in our MATRIKA data. Selby uses the word "poetics" in a broad cultural sense, which she claims is grounded both in texts as well as in practice; what she terms a "cultural semiotics."
   Women and the "feminine" are red; men and the "masculine" are white. The redness of women and the whiteness of men are based on the colors of their observable sexual effluents: menstrual fluid in the case of women, and semen in the case of men. White and red exist in a dominant/subordinate relationship, both in the medical texts themselves and within the larger and more articulated contexts of quasi-Hindu social hierarchy. In general, white always predominates, with red and other colors ranked below it. White is the color of coolness, celibacy, virility, purity and goodness, whereas red represents heat, sexuality, permeability, taint and energy (2005, p. 261).
   Selby's writing contributes to our consideration of the relational body.

The male body/self is more "individual" and the female body/self is more permeable: white is "male" and "closed"; red is "female" and "open." It is a woman's redness and openness that cause her susceptibility to all kinds of outside influences, both good and bad, and her porousness and fluidity allow for an exchange to occur in which elements in the environment— sights, sounds, and smells, as well as foods and medicines that are actually prescribed and ingested—all leave impressions in a woman's body that are incorporated into any embryo that she is actually carrying or might soon be carrying. (2005, p. 261)

The valuation of white over red hearkens back to the gendered polarity of the "field knower" and the field. Interestingly, in one of our Rajasthan workshops, discussions turned toward death. We learned that, in accordance with common funereal practice, a stillborn baby or dead neonate was ushered into the next life according to this poetics. "If a dead baby is born then we dig a place with hoe and bury it and plant a bush there. If the baby is a boy, then we cover him with a white cloth and if it is a baby girl, then a red cloth is used." And touchingly, it was mentioned that if the family was too poor, just a little square patch of red or white fabric was buried along with the tiny body.

THE COSMIC *NARAK*—NOT "HELL" BUT WOMB FOR THE UNBORN

I had always interpreted *narak* as referring to the innards of the female body and the earth body and made brief incursions into its Puranic meanings until I listened to teachings by Khentse Rimpoche at Deer Park in Himachal Pradesh.[5] There, the Tibetan text that he was teaching, used the term *narak* in its Sanskrit version, and I asked him the meaning of *narak* in this context. From his reply, I understood that *narak* was a kind of holding space for the *atma* of those awaiting rebirth.

If I consider *narak* in light of this more cosmic notion of the cycles of birth/death/rebirth, my understanding of dais meanings extends beyond the more "spiritual" concepts of the transcendent and escaping endless cycles of death and rebirth and the curse of the womb. From dais' mouths the phrase, in keeping with geomysticism, may denote the sacred cyclicity of cosmic processes (seasons, lunar and menstrual rhythms, reincarnations) of which human beings are a part. Geomystical, because the earth element, along with matter and mother is sacralized and not demonized. A seamless web of life and death, spirit (or rather *jee*, life force), and matter emerges from our data.

In the philosophical traditions of India, there has been an abiding merger between form and meaning, not only the fertility of woman and earth but also between the image and what is signified—there is wholeness, a oneness. The British colonizers perceived this as weakness and this cultural semiotics of representation has been deeply disturbed by modernity.

Dais, their sacrality and birth rituals, are dying, literally. Oxytocin injections are replacing rituals invoking Bemata—because the power to birth is increasingly understood not to reside in the mother's body, but rather "science"—the ritual use of scientific medicine.

NOTES

1. "Dai" as used in common parlance in India today means a woman (almost always poor) who cares for a woman (also poor) during labor and postpartum. Public health discourse uses the term "traditional birth attendant" to denote such women, assuming them to be unskilled. Latest data from the Indian National Family Health Survey uses the category "dai and 'other' women" and indicates that they attend more births than any other category of caregiver.

The dai today is not always a Dalit. What one could say with some amount of accuracy is that in most areas of India dais and other birth workers were traditionally low and outcaste (Dalit) women. Many scholars also suggest that health, healing, and body knowledge (including Ayurveda) probably originated with tribal and low and outcaste peoples—codified later by upper castes.

2. MATRIKA (Motherhood and Traditional Research, Information, Knowledge and Action) was a nongovernmental organization (NGO) research project devoted to documenting traditional midwives' skills, knowledge, and religio-cultural context. Workshops were conducted in four areas of North India—Bikaneer District, Rajasthan; Fategarh District, Punjab; Gomia District, Bihar; and the resettlement colonies of Delhi. See matrika-india.org.

3. For more about this ritual see Chawla and Pinto (2001).

4. See Chawla, Janet, "Understanding 'Narak' Rethinking Pollution: An Interpretation of Data from Dais in North India," 2007.

5. See Chawla, Janet, "Negotiating Narak and Writing Destiny: The Theology of Bemata in Dais' Handling of Birth," 2002.

REFERENCES

Chawla, J. 2000. "The Conflation of the Female Body and Earth in Indian Religious Traditions: Gendered Representations of Seed, Earth and Grain." *Gender / Bodies / Religions*. Ed. Sylvia Marcos. Mexico City: ALER Publications, 255–271.

Chawla, J. 2002a. "Hawa, Gola and Mother-in-law's Big Toe: On Understanding Dais' Imagery of the Female Body." *Daughters of Hariti: Childbirth and Female Healers in South and Southeast Asia*. Ed. Santi Rozario and Geoffrey Samuel. London: Routledge, 2002, 147–162.

Chawla, J. 2002b. "Negotiating Narak and Writing Destiny: The Theology of Bemata in Dais' Handling of Birth." *Invoking Goddesses, Gender Politics and Religion in India*. Ed. Nilima Chitgopetkar. New Delhi: Har-Anand Publications, 165–199.

Chawla, J. 2007. "Understanding "Narak" Rethinking Pollution: An Interpretation of Data from Dais in North India." *Exploring The Dirty Side of Women's Health*. Ed. Mavis Kirkham. London: Routledge, 165–176.

Chawla, J. and Sarah Pinto. 2001. "The Female Body as Battleground of Meaning." *Mental Health from a Gender Perspective*. Ed. Bhargavi V. Davar. New Delhi: Sage Publications, 155–180.

Dube, L. 1986. "Seed and Earth: The Symbolism of Biological Reproduction and Sexual Relations of Production." *Visibility and Power: Essays on Women in Society and Development*. Ed. Leila Dube, Eleanor Leacock, Shirley Ardener. Delhi: Oxford University Press, 67–128.

Malhotra, A. 2006. "Of Dais and Midwives: 'Middle Class' Interventions in the Management of Women's Reproductive Health in Colonial Punjab." *Reproductive Health in India: History, Politics, Controversies*. Ed. Sarah Hodges. Hyderabad: Orient Longman, 168–199.

Mayo, K. 1927. *Mother India*. 1977 edition. Delhi: Low Price Publications.

Mukherjee, S. 2001. "Disciplining the Body? Health Care for Women and Children in Early Twentieth-Century Bengal." *Disease & Medicine in India: A Historical Overview*. Ed. Deepak Kumar. New Delhi: Tulika Books, 198–214.

New Jerusalem Bible. "Genesis" 3:16. London: Darton, Longman and Todd, 1985.

Pinto, S. 2006. "Divisions of Labour: Rethinking the 'Midwife' in Rural Uttar Pradesh." *Birth and Birthgivers: The Power Behind the Shame*. Ed. Janet Chawla. New Delhi: Shakti Books, 203–238.

Rao, V. 2006. "Singing the Female Body." *Birth and Birthgivers: The Power Behind the Shame*. Ed. Janet Chawla. New Delhi: Shakti Books, 80–122

Samuel, G. 2005. "Subtle Bodies in Indian and Tibetan Yoga: Scientific and Spiritual Meanings." Conference Paper. 2nd International Conference on Religion and Cultures in the Indic Civilization, December 17–20, 2005, Delhi.

Samuel, G. 2006. "Healing and the Mind-Body Complex: Childbirth and Medical Pluralism in South Asia." *Multiple Medical Realities: Patients and Healers in Biomedical. Alternative and Traditional Medicine*. Ed. Helle Johannessen and Imre Lázár. New York and London: Berghahn Books, 121–135.

Selby, Martha Ann. 2005. "Narratives of Conception, Gestation and Labor in the Ayurvedic Texts." *Asian Medicine: Tradition and Modernity*, Volume 1, Number 2, 254–274.

Singh, A. 2006. "Her One Foot is in this World and One in the Other: Ayurveda, Dais and Maternity." *Birth and Birthgivers: The Power behind the Shame*. Ed. Janet Chawla. New Delhi: Shakti Books, 136–171.

PART IV

Sexuality, Power, and Vulnerability

CHAPTER 8

Ritual Gendered Relationships: Kinship, Marriage, Mastery, and Machi Modes of Personhood

Ana Mariella Bacigalupo

At this moment, I beg you to remain by my side, father of the sky, mother of the sky, old people from above, old grandmother, old grandfather. You who are the owner of all remedies that live in the blue sky, don't allow me to remain truncated. . . . I humble myself before you. Mount me on your horse and don't allow me to weaken. . . . You have remedies at the tip of your *rewe*. I ask you to give them to me for my work, to help people. I also ask you not to punish me as my only job is to use the remedies that you make me see. Isn't it you that made me be in this job to serve others? That is what I am saying, father God, mother God. (From *pelontun,* or divination, by machi José, December 21, 2001. Translated from Mapudungun to Spanish by Armando Marileo.)

From "Ritual Gendered Relationships: Kinship, Marriage, Mastery, and Machi Modes of Personhood." *Journal of Anthropological Research* (2004), 60(2): 203–229. Reprinted with permission from the *Journal of Anthropological Research*, University of New Mexico, NM, USA.

Mapuche shamans have different kinds of spiritual relationships that are shaped by the gendered power dynamics of colonial mastery and domination, marriage and seduction, possession and ecstasy, and hierarchical kinship systems. These spiritual relationships reflect a complex understanding of personal consciousness in which shamans are agents of their actions but at the same time share self with the spirits and are dominated by them.

Kinship, marriage, and mastery—the closest and most durable gendered social relationships among Mapuche in Southern Chile—are used by *machi* (Mapuche shamans) in ritual to create bonds with the spirit and animal world. Machi are individual women and men in their everyday lives, but in ritual contexts their sex and age becomes secondary as they engage in various relational personhoods that link machi, animals, and spirits. Elsewhere I have analyzed the role of gender in the ethnic identity, lives, and ritual practices of machi (Bacigalupo 2007). I have shown that machi are women or feminized, cross-dressed men, who assume multiple masculine, feminine and co-gender identities—people who embody and bring together the perspectives of both genders and combine the gendered occupations of both women and men—for the purpose of healing.[1] Machi "become" men, both young and old, to exorcize illness, bad thoughts, and suffering from their patients' bodies. They "become" women, again both young and old, to heal and reintegrate their patients back into their communities. They also embody the four aspects of the deity Ngünechen (male, female, young, and old) in order to transcend gender, and "become divine" to create new world orders and gain spiritual power (Bacigalupo 2005). Gender is one of the metaphors used by machi to mark polarizations, boundaries, and tensions between local and national identities as well as a way to express integration and create broader understandings of humanity, health, and healing.

In this chapter, spiritual kinships ties, spiritual marriages, and relationships of mastery between machi, animals, and spirits in initiation and healing rituals reflect historical ethnic/national relationships, social and gender dynamics, as well as complex understandings of personhood. Machi spiritual relationships reflect the gendered power dynamics of colonial mastery and domination, marriage and seduction, possession and ecstasy, and hierarchical kinship systems. These gendered spiritual relational personhoods and their associated altered states of consciousness are shaped by the legacy of colonization: political and religious authorities, the loss of autonomy of Mapuche communities, the incorporation of horses and sheep, the imposition of agriculture, and the reservation system and missionization. Machi are kin to their spirit animals and other machi who initiate them; they are spirit brides who seduce their machi husbands into possessing them; and they are masters of spirit animals and masculine mounted warriors who travel in ecstatic flight to other worlds. These spiritual relationships reflect a complex understanding of personal consciousness in which machi are agents of their actions but at the same time share self with the spirits and are dominated by them. Machi's gendered spiritual positionalities in ritual contexts are both embodied and ensouled. They gain varied forms of knowledge and power through the exchange of bodily substances as well as through spiritual means, and experience the world as different people offering a new perspective to current discussions on embodiment, ensoulment, and personhood.

Machi relational personhoods vary according to the region, machi school of practice, and the individual machi. Selected here are those machi initiation and healing rituals and narratives collected between 1991 and 2002 that best illustrate the gendered relationships machi hold with other spirit, human, and animal beings in communities near the towns of Temuco, Freire, Nueva Imperial, and Chol-Chol.

María Cecilia's Initiation: The Forging of Spiritual Kinship with Machi and Animals

Eighteen-year-old María Cecilia bowed her head as she sat beside her newly planted *rewe,* the step-notched trunk of a *pellin* tree which connects the human world with spiritual ones. María Cecilia wore a blue head scarf and an elegant black shawl with a pink stripe. Her necklaces of blood-red *kopiwe* flowers (Lapageria Rosa) and *llankalawen* leaves (Lycopodium Paniculatum) and her heavy silver breastplate (trapelakucha) swayed as she turned from side to side, beating her new drum, the *kultrun* with four red suns painted on its face. María Cecilia's machi spirit—her *machi püllu,* or *fileu* (literally the knowledgeable one)—lived simultaneously in the Wenu Mapu (the Mapuche sky), in María Cecilia's head, kultrun, and rewe, and in the spirit horse and sheep with whom she exchanged breath and blood. Possession, spiritual travel, dreams, and visions would give María Cecilia the knowledge to divine, heal, and grant blessings.

During her initiation ritual, María Cecilia has forged her spiritual kinship ties with animals and other machi by exchanging bodily substances with machi Javiera and machi Elena—her initiating machi—as well as with a cock, sheep, and horse who became her spirit animals.[2] Machi and animals share essences and qualities of being—as do family members. They gain various types of power from each other and protect each other from illness and sorcery. By virtue of her initiation, Maria Cecilia became part of the machi school headed by Javiera, where machi have similar symbols,

spiritual concepts and practices, and heal each other. In addition, Maria
Cecilia's initiation recognized her machi spiritual inheritance—which is or-
dinarily passed down through the mother's side of the family and stands in
opposition to social kinship, inheritance and succession, which is patrilineal.
María Cecilia had inherited her machi spirit from her great-grandmother.
She had experienced visions of drums and winter's bark trees (Drymis Win-
teri) and felt chronic pain in her bones and stomach. She finished secondary
school despite her illness and then went to live for a year with machi Javiera,
from whom she learned to control her altered states of consciousness, read
dreams, perform rituals, and prepare herbal remedies.[3]

I became close to María Cecilia and her family during the eight months
preceding her initiation ritual. I visited her natal home, where her father,
Edmundo, lived with his eldest wife, Marcela, his younger wife, Carolina,
and his and Carolina's two daughters and 10-year-old son. Eduardo and
María Cecilia asked me to photograph the initiation so that they would have
mementos of the event, despite Mapuche taboos on photographing rituals.
Mapuche often believe that photographs steal their soul and can be used for
sorcery or, as is often the case with tourists, to objectify them.[4] On April 16,
1992, the day of María Cecilia's *machiluwün* (machi initiation) machi Javiera and machi Elena visited María Cecilia in the community of Trarilonko.
For two days from dawn to dusk, they healed María Cecilia of the spiritual
illness (*machi kutran*) caused by a machi spirit to pressure the neophyte to
become a machi. Maria Cecilia legitimated her status as a machi by publicly
demonstrating her ability to drum, sing, and enter and exit altered states of
consciousness in order to speak to humans and spirits.

Edmundo, her father, tied the animals to stakes on the left-hand side of
her rewe. He circled their eyes, noses, and mouths with blue paint, the color
of the Wenu Mapu, or sky, so that their senses and skills would be put at the
service of María Cecilia's spiritual gifts. He then slit the ears of the sheep
and the cock's crest and collected the blood in a shallow wooden bowl. Some
of the blood he rubbed on the underside of the horse's stomach, and the rest,
María Cecilia drank. María Cecilia tried to strengthen the spiritual kinship
among her animals by making the horse drink sheep blood with her. The
horse resisted and bucked, so María Cecilia sprinkled blood over her rewe
instead to reinforce the connection between her spirit horse and her own
machi powers she inherited from her great-grandmother. A young man rode
María Cecilia's horse around the field, after which she inhaled the horse's
breath (*neyen*)—a source of *newen* (strength, power)—and forced her own
breath through its nostrils. The ritual exchange of blood (*molfuñ*) and breath
unites machi, animals, and spirits in kin relationships. Blood, breath, and saliva are spiritual foods that can be magically acted upon to give a machi or an
animal particular powers, but they are also profound indications of kinship

and life force shared among machi and between machi and spirit animals. Their symbolic dimension is inseparable from the ontological aspect of the machi, the spirit and animals that it signifies.[5]

Javiera and Elena moved slowly up the path toward María Cecilia's house, turning from side to side with each beat of the drum, each followed by an entourage of helpers: four *ñankan,* men to play flutes and dance with the machi while she was in *küymi,* or altered state of consciousness (ASC); a *dungumachife,* who spoke to the machi while she was in ASC and interpreted the metaphoric language spoken by spirits into a language understood by all; two *yegulfe,* or women helpers to heat and play the machi's drum and hand her herbal remedies; and four *afafanfe,* male helpers to crash *coligüe* (*koliu*) canes over the head of the patient, help the machi enter or exit ASC, and help her exorcise evil spirits.

María Cecilia mirrored the movements of her two machi professors. The three of them danced around the rewe in slow purposeful movements, playing sleigh bells and holding knives and foye branches to their ears in order to protect themselves from evil spirits. The three machi circled the rewe counterclockwise as they danced forward, side by side. Each machi faced a male partner who danced backward. Two young men led María Cecilia's sheep and cock around the rewe and made them "dance" to the kultrun rhythms played by the machi's helpers in order to endow these spirit animals with machi powers.

María Cecilia lay on the bed of herbal remedies while Javiera and Elena smoked and then rubbed her with the sacred leaves of the foye, triwe, and klon trees, spraying her periodically with mouthfuls of water. They sang and drummed over María Cecilia to heal her from her machi kutran. They begged her fileu to grant her power and healing knowledge and divined her future as a machi. Then, each machi prayed and played the kultrun. A cacophony of prayers, drumbeats, and flutes filled the air. The eight male helpers periodically clashed coligüe canes above María Cecilia's head to help her enter into ASC. Each dungumachife in turn conversed with his assigned machi, blocking out the words and sounds of the others. The dungumachife listened intently, memorizing the machi's words in order to repeat them later to the participants after the ritual. Any omission could cost him his health or that of the machi.

While possessed by fileu, each of the machi in turn climbed María Cecilia's rewe, her tree of life that would allow her to communicate effectively with other worlds; they swayed between the foye and triwe branches planted on either side. I danced counterclockwise around the rewe, too, holding hands with a group of Mapuche women. All of us wore blue head scarves and black shawls and carried *triwe iaf-iaf* (bunches of laurel leaves). A group of men danced clockwise around the circle of women. Javiera and Elena exhaled

over María Cecilia's head in order to grant her their powers and initiate her
into their machi school as spiritual kin. Two men slashed the neck of a sheep
and bled it into a bowl. The three machi drank the blood to consolidate their
personal and spiritual kinship ties and to feed their respective fileu.[6]

The participants celebrated the consolidation of María Cecilia's spiritual kinship ties over a dinner of roasted sheep meat and potatoes. The
dungumachife summarized and interpreted what each machi had said while
in ASC. They discussed similarities and differences in interpretation and
concluded that María Cecilia's ritual had been successful and that she now
belonged to Javiera's machi school of practice. The fileu was satisfied with
her performance and offerings but warned her that she must live a life of
sacrifice, or her fileu would leave her.

Kinship created by ritual sharing of breath and the blood of sacrifice
supersedes the blood ties of biological kinship. Just as Mapuche sons and
daughters are incorporated into the social patrilineage through blood ties with
the father, so María Cecilia was incorporated into the spiritual matrilineage
of machi by acknowledging the spirit of her machi great-grandmother and
by sharing breath and sacrificial animal blood with machi and spirit animals.
She often referred to machi Javiera as "mother" and to her cohorts within the
school as "sisters." María Cecilia's spiritual kinship ties express a larger notion
of an ordered social body comprised of various bodies and souls (human and
animal) and their social relationships. Once spiritual kinship is established
with spirit animals, machi bodies and those of their spirit animals become interchangeable. Machi animals can experience illnesses on the machi's behalf,
and machi become ill if their spirit animal or machi cohorts are hurt or killed.
As with the Kulina (Pollock 1996:320) bodies and souls are believed to share
the qualities of social relationships. Mapuche spiritual kinship is an expression of the relational dimensions of personhood that is acquired, shared, and
transformed rather than constrained in a single human body.

SEDUCING A SPIRIT, BECOMING A BRIDE

"Machi make necklaces out of kopiwe flowers and llankalawen, like jew-
els," said machi Rocío. "The fileu, the machi of the sky, looks down, he sees
these ancient jewel plants, and he likes it. He sees the silver shining in the
sun. 'Eeeeh, how pretty,' he says. It attracts him. He sees the machi's head,
all blue in the headscarf like an offering calling him, and down he comes into
the machi's head."

Machi passages from and between the spirit and human worlds are negotiated individually through intimate relationships with spirits involving seduction and marriage. Spirits and humans, like women and men, are people

with different qualities of being with various (culturally defined) interests and roles but are united as couples through marriage and seduction. The machi-bride is a human body dressed in women's clothes, open to the spirit world. Male and female machi become spiritual brides who seduce and call their fileu—at once husband and master—to possess their heads to grant them knowledge by wearing symbols of femininity and wifeliness: blue or purple head scarves, necklaces of red kopiwe flowers and llankalawen leaves, women's black shawls, and silver jewelry.[7] The fileu-husband is interested in the performance of wifeliness, not in the sex under the machi clothes. The ritual transvestism of male machi does not transcend the categories of woman and man but rather draws attention to the relational gender categories of spirit husband and machi wife as a couple (*kurewen*). María Cecilia, like most other machi, periodically renews her marriage ties with her spirit in a ritual called *ngeikurrewen*. The action of ngeikun refers to the machi swaying between the foye and triwe branches tied to the rewe and the term kurewen (couple) refers to the coupling of machi bride and spirit husband (Bacigalupo 1996a:83; Métraux 1942:201; Titiev 1951:120).

Perceptions of erotic relationships between machi and fileu and the symbolism of the head both mirror and transgress Mapuche gender relationships. Just as the community chief, or *lonko* (head), represents the community, so machi's heads are the loci of spiritual brideliness. Rural Mapuche women typically place great value on modesty so they hide their hair by braiding, tying, or covering it with head scarves, straw hats, or cloth baseball caps. They perceive young urban Mapuche women who cut their hair or wear it loose as seductive and promiscuous. Machi use traditional Mapuche women's head scarves, shawls, and silver jewelry in novel ways to attract and seduce the spirits. Contrary to Mapuche women's seduction of men, however, machi's seduction of fileu is positively valued as a skill available only to those who have power and enhances machi's reputations. Machi spiritual seduction offers a unique perspective on erotic spirituality that privileges gender identity and performance over anatomical sex or sexual penetration. Studies of gender identities in Latin America have focused on the ways in which specific sexual acts—that is, acts of penetrating or being penetrated by others—create gender.[8] They associate gender variance with sexual variance, whereas machi do not. Machi of either sex may, in their everyday lives, perform penetrating acts, receptive acts, or both with either men or women, or they may remain celibate, yet they still become spiritual brides in order to seduce the spirits. Male machi who do not construct themselves explicitly as brides of spirits or God in the same way that female machi do still view their commitment to machi practice as a marriage. Machi Sergio stated: "I cannot get married because I am a machi. All my time and dedication is to heal others. I am committed to my profession, and God does not allow me to have a family."

The power of spiritual seduction is so great that a machi can use it to delay initiation and alleviate spiritual punishment. On May 27, 1995, machi Pedro invited me to a healing ritual (*daahatun*) for a young girl who had a machi calling but who was being punished by her fileu because she had not yet been initiated. The girl's feet bled with open sores, and she went into an altered state of consciousness (ASC) frequently and uncontrollably for hours on end. Pedro drank a concoction made from the juice of foye leaves and metal particles scraped off a knife. He covered the girl's body and the four stakes of foye and triwe branches placed at each corner of her sheepskin bed on the dirt floor with silver jewelry and necklaces made from kopiwe flowers. This was in order to seduce the spirit and decrease the severity of the girl's spiritual illnesses. After the four introductory prayers (*llelipun*) in which Pedro narrated his calling to be a machi and described his powers, and the *metremtun* or calling of the spirits, Pedro rubbed the girls' body with triwe leaves. He then threw a knife toward the door four times to expel evil spirits that made the girl ill and to divine the outcome of the ritual. If the knife pointed toward the doorway, the spirit had accepted the offering but if it faced inward, the spirit was unhappy. The spirit's response was ambiguous. Twice the knife fell pointing toward the doorway and twice facing the inside. Pedro asked us all to donate some silver jewelry to the girl to wear in order for her to "look prettier for the spirit," and he repeated the ritual again at five AM the next morning. He asked the spirit to be patient, arguing that the girl would be initiated as a machi as soon as she learned to speak Mapudungun and her family saved enough money to pay for the initiation. This time the knife pointed toward the doorway three of the four times. Five years later the girl had learned to speak Mapudungun and became initiated as a machi.

There is a certain homology between machi spiritual marriages and human marriages. By marrying a machi püllu, a machi commits herself or himself to an exclusive lifelong relationship with a spirit which conflicts with machi sexual and romantic relationships with humans regardless of the sex of the machi and his or her sexual orientation. Jealous spirits punish machi who have romantic and sexual encounters with illness and must be appeased with offerings, gifts, and prayers (Bacigalupo 1995). Machi Pamela explained, "The machi püllu, God, does not like the smell of husband and wife together; he does not want it. One had to ask for forgiveness and give him prayers." The result is that machi are often widowed, single, or have exceptional partners who are willing to break away from the conventional gender roles and accept that machi must attend to their patients and ritual obligations over and above their families and partners. Scholars have often viewed the practices of female shamans as an extension of the reproductive processes of motherhood and fertility (Sered 1994; Glass-Coffin 1998). Mapuche shamans, on the contrary, believe that parenthood, fertility, sex, and family life conflict with a machi's spiritual roles and weaken their powers. As spiritual brides, machi participate in the cosmic process of fertility and reproduction which hold priority over and conflict with their own personal sexual and reproductive lives.

The relationship between a machi-bride and the fileu-husband who also possesses her reflects colonial hierarchical relationships where male colonial authorities—saints, apostles, mounted generals, Spanish kings (Bacigalupo 2004)—held power and authority over indigenous people and women. Machi brides express the limited participation of women in the patrilineal social and political realm. At the same time, machi brides demonstrate that through ritual practice, wives actively negotiate relationships between male lineages and between male-dominated structures of social and political power. Spirits do not spontaneously possess machi brides; machi seek to seduce them. Furthermore, machi control their altered state of consciousness and willfully embody the spirit and gendered hierarchies that order their worlds.

Machi's spiritual marriages are both similar and different from the sexualized hierarchical power relationships between Voodoo and Oyo-Yoruba Shango priests and the spirits that possess them. These priests are viewed as horses who are ridden by the spirits. The mounting action of the spirit rider suggests a form of control whereby horsemanship, spirit possession, and sexual penetration are homologous and the bride/horse is inferior to the master/husband and has no self-control (Bourguignon 1976; Matory 1994:7, 69). Machi brides are inferior to their spirit husbands, but their possession experiences are neither involuntary nor uncontrolled.[9] Machi are not horses penetrated and subsumed by the will of their riders but humans who control their interactions with their spirits husbands through seduction. A machi's seduction of spirits and deities who are superior to her is a way for her to gain control over the sociospiritual hierarchies that run her life. Furthermore, Mapuche spirit horses are not slaves or messengers for spirits but represent the power of the sky.

MASTER OF ANIMAL SOULS: THE MACHI MOUNTED WARRIOR

Father creator of the sky . . . take me over the earth, show me the earth above. "May he ride on his horses," you are saying, mother creator, father creator. May they protect me. The horse of the earth above has me with my head hanging. They lift my heart. They lift my head. I come from ancient grandparent machi. They gave me power. I want to ride on the horses from the upper worlds. Here I am, the child of the ancient people waiting for your horse to lift me . . . I am a being that rides on horses, that

knows herbal remedies. . . . My other self, my other power is riding on a
horse.

—Excerpt from machi José's divination prayers

Machi gain knowledge, power, and control over the spirit world through
horsemanship and mastery over spirit animals in the same way that Spanish horsemen and colonial institutions gained control over Mapuche people.
While machi brideliness reflects subtle forms of agency whereby machi gain
knowledge through feminine seduction, horsemanship is a spiritual relationship that involves explicit hierarchy and domination over spirits and is associated with masculinity and warfare. Horsemanship, mounting, and mastery
over animals are symbols of masculinity, fortitude, agility, and prestige for
machi, as they were for colonial Spanish and Mapuche warriors who battled
each other between the 16th and late-19th centuries. Mounted Spanish
conquistadores believed they were defeating infidels and evil while gaining
land and riches for Spain, and later Chilean mounted warriors defended
the independence of the new Chilean nation. Some machi mimic powerful
conquistadores on horseback to bring out their spiritual power. As masculine
mounted warriors and masters of animals, machi defeat evil spirits and for-
eignness and gallop to other worlds to gain knowledge of the universe. History is replayed and transformed in ritual. Machi gain sacred power from the
performance of the Spanish colonial and Chilean national armies and can
use it for healing or destruction.

In some contexts, Mapuche view horsemanship, dogs, horses, and bulls
as foreign and associate them with colonization and sorcery. Usually, however, machi view horses, sheep, and cattle as indigenous, associate them
with well-being and abundance, and value horsemanship and mastery over
animals. Mapuche warriors quickly incorporated Spanish horses, sheep, and
cattle into their livelihood. They created a cavalry to defend their land and
liberty. Cattle raising became a main source of sustenance for the Mapuche
until the imposition of reservations in 1883, when they turned to seden-
tary agriculture. Having many animals was a symbol of power, prestige, and
wealth (Alvarado 1991:84, 87, 89). Horses and, to a lesser extent, sheep and
cattle became important parts of Mapuche sociopolitical, ritual, mythical,
and military ideologies. In one version of the Mapuche deluge myth, only
humans who rode on horses were saved. Collective nguillatun rituals always
include the *awun*—an event in which Mapuche mounted warriors (*weichafe
pura kawellu*), carrying flags and lances and shouting war cries, gallop counterclockwise around the *nguillatuwe,* or altar. They do battle with the winds
in order to control the weather (Alvarado 1991:145) and celebrate the power
of horsemanship, the horse, and Mapuche identity.

Machi strengthen their bodily defenses and ability to heal by personifying male mounted warriors (*machi weichafe pura kawellu*), often referred to as "guardians," "nobles," and "kings," who shelter machi during ASC.[10] A machi must mount a spirit horse in order to become initiated: "I saw the saddled horse in my dream," said machi Rocío. "I knew that if I rode I would be a machi." After initiation, machi ride spirit horses during rituals in which they experience themselves as spirits that have knowledge and power (Juan Ñanculef, personal communication, September 26, 2002). Machi Ana argues that machi ride spiritual horses to other worlds in order to gain power and knowledge—to "know the situation of the universe."

Machi are also described as warriors who ride their rewe like a horse as they ascend the steps in their travel to other worlds in magical flight. Weapons and war imagery give the machi knowledge and strength. Machi view themselves as masculine mounted warriors who defeat evil, illness, and suffering. They use guns, knives, and war cries to kill illness or drive it from the bodies of their patients or from their lands, households, or communities. *Awinkamiento,* or becoming like a non-Mapuche, is often cited as the root of illness, evil, and alienation, three enemies that threaten the Mapuche individually and collectively. To help them defeat evil, machi often call on the power of *chueca* sticks—sticks used in playing the ritual game of chueca during nguillatun rituals and on other festive occasions. An all male game, chueca is semantically equivalent to warfare, and in the past it helped strengthen Mapuche warriors before battle. Machi perform spiritual warfare as a way of aggressively advocating the opposition between self, Mapuche tradition, and life, on one hand, and otherness, non-Mapuche culture, and death, on the other (Bacigalupo 1998). Traditional Mapuche norms dictate that ritual objects, deities, and ritual actions be referred to in sets of twos and fours, but the Catholic notion of the 12 apostles has also been incorporated into Mapuche sacred numerology. Machi Javiera prayed:

With all your teachings I will ride my horse for this ill son of mine. I will incense the horse with smoke; I will sweat knowledge. I will sweat petitions. . . . Come, become my tongue and come into my head. Come and live in my heart. . . . Take me, you twelve chueca sticks of war. My twelve arrows of war. My twelve knives of war that will allow me to travel through the universe and give me my knowledge. My twelve horse breaths. My twelve walking horses. My twelve spirit horses. . . . My superiors have given me my strength. They feed me with knowledge and advice. They take me to the sky. I shall go to the sky. I shall be doing war . . . knowledge of war, teachings of struggle. . . . This is the end of my greeting, my petitions, old woman of discourse, old man of discourse, warrior chiefs, wise people.[11]

Machi are also masters of other animals: they gain power, strength, and life force from special sheep, horses, chickens, and sometimes cows or bulls. Machi drink the saliva of their spirit animals and blood from the ears. They receive the animals' breath on their faces, heads, and backs, to strengthen them while the ritual participants eat horse and sheep meat. During initiation and nguillatun rituals, Mapuche tie a sheep, a horse, and sometimes a bull or cow to a stake near the nguillatuwe or rewe, and horsemen take their horses to the machi so that he or she can feel the horses' breath on the face, head, and back. Sometimes the horse's breath is the "breath of life" (Alvarado 1991:91) that restores the machi's strength after he or she enters into a ASC state, embodies a spirit, and travels to the Wenu Mapu. Machi also receive breath from their spirit animals daily. Machi José sang the life-giving qualities of his spirit horse's breath: "My heart has strength again. My head has strength again. Your breath has lifted my being."

Most machi choose a sheep, a horse, a chicken, a cow, or any combination thereof, and these spirit animals are initiated along with the machi, just as María Cecilia's were. Machi do not ride these spirit animals, make them work, or slaughter them. Instead, the animals are expected to protect and help the machi. The human machi's well-being receives higher priority than that of her spirit animal. If a machi is ill or is cursed, ideally the spirit animal will get sick or die on her behalf. If a spirit animal dies, the machi must replace it with another, or she will become weak and ill. The term *machi-fileu* or *püllu* refers to the machi spirit as such but also to the physical embodiment of the spirit, usually human, but sometimes animal.[12]

Not all machi can afford a spirit horse at home; they keep other animals with different power attributes to protect them. Machi Rocío, for example, kept a sheep and a cow. Instead of exchanging saliva with them or drinking their blood, she bathed them in herbal remedies. Machi Pamela had a machi-sheep with whom she exchanged breath. She prayed: "My heart is happy that my sheep has arrived again. By having my sheep I can scream louder. . . . Before, my tongue was stuck. My tongue was small. . . . Now this did not happen, I am revitalized. I have recovered my strength."

Bulls are strong and grant powers to machi, but horses are considered more powerful in the spiritual world because of their gracefulness and agility. Gloria, a Mapuche potter, said, "When bulls are castrated they lose their strength, but horses have much more power than any cattle. . . . The spirit asks the machi to have a horse. . . . Bulls are not as useful to machi." Other machi believe that the agility and spirituality of the horse can be combined with the strength of the bull. Machi María Cristina prayed, "I am looking for teachings. I implore for a horse-bull and for a ox-bull."[13]

Machi share spirit and life force with their spirit animals, and their lives are intertwined. If a machi's spirit animal is killed, part of the machi dies, too, and she suffers drastic physical and spiritual consequences. When 78-year-old machi Pamela's son died from heart failure in 1994, she ritually sacrificed her spirit horse to feed the mourners at the funeral and to ensure that her son would travel to the Wenu Mapu on the horse instead of lurking nearby and tormenting the living. Pamela became sad and weak after her son's death and felt pain in her chest, stomach, and head. She experienced fever, fainting, confusion, and amnesia, which she interpreted as soul loss. When Pamela fell into a cataleptic state, machi Ana came to heal her. After 40 minutes of massage, drumming, and prayers, Pamela regained consciousness. Ana said that Pamela's spirit horse was angry because she had killed it, and that in doing so had killed herself in the same way the horse had been slaughtered—stabbed with a knife in the heart and lung. Pamela had been hospitalized a few weeks before and diagnosed with cardiac weakness; blood and fluid were accumulating in her lungs. Pamela interpreted the diagnosis as a reflection of the spiritual suicide and soul loss she had experienced when her spirit horse was killed.

Ana obtained the power to heal Pamela from the deity Ngünechen in the guise of four mounted warriors. She asked them to revitalize machi Pamela: "Old Man mounted on your horse, Old Woman mounted on your horse, Young Man mounted on your horse, Young Woman mounted on your horse. . . . Come together with your four saddled horses to see this sister and strengthen her spirit of service, strengthen her heart. . . . This sick machi with a clean heart will mount her horse. . . . She must mount her horse with good faith to regain her vitality and the activities of her being." Machi Pamela agreed: "I need a horse to make me feel happier, stronger. I will not get sick, because Chau Dios will be watching over me. I will be invincible."

Machi share self with horses, master them, and become spiritual mounted warriors who appropriate the power of Spanish conquistadores and Chilean generals to literally or symbolically ascend the rewe, travel in ecstatic flight to other worlds, and kill evil spirits. At the same time, machi are neither horses nor riders but humans who propitiate the powers of the Wenu Mapu in the form of horses. They draw on the power of Ngünechen in the deity's guise of four mounted warriors. These multiple machi powers and positions, along with those of seduction and brideliness, are paired with different altered states of consciousness that grant machi a broad experience of the universe.

Machi's varied gendered relationships with spirit beings in ritual are both embodied and ensouled. The paradigm of embodiment alone—the lived experience of being in the body—is insufficient as a model for understanding machi ritual relationships. Rather, machi, like other non-Western people experience a continuum of states of being that include body, mind, personalities, consciousness, and self/soul (Halliburton 2002) where people possess not only bodies, but also multiple spirits (Laderman 1992; Pollock 1996).[14] Different states of individual and collective bodies (*trawa*), consciousness (*zuam*) and soul (*püllu*) are continuously interacting with each other in machi ritual relationships. Spiritual kinship and spiritual mastery are marked by exchange of bodily substances such as voice, breath, blood, and saliva while spiritual marriage involves shamanic illness and the symbolism of the mounting of the head. At the same time machi have many nontangible modes of experience separate from the body during altered states of consciousness in which their own soul, or püllu, remains distinct or merges with those of other spirit beings such as the fileu (the generic spirit of ancestral machi), machi püllu (the specific spirit that guides machi actions) and the Ngünechen (the Mapuche deity).

PERSONHOOD, POSSESSION, AND ECSTATIC TRAVEL

Machi's varied ritual gendered relationships with spirit beings offer new perspectives of shamanic altered states of consciousness. In this section, I analyze the problems with some of the previous approaches to gender and shamanism and explore how three different machi perceptions of self and their ritual gendered relationships with spirits contribute to current discussions on shamanic altered states of consciousness and personhood. First, I explore how machi view themselves as independent persons with symbiotic relationships with spirits in their everyday lives. Second, I examine how machi share personhood with spirits during ecstatic flight. And third, I analyze how machi have a persona separate from that of the spirit during possession, although it is the persona of the spirit that predominates temporarily.

Many ethnographers continue to accept older Euro-American assumptions about personhood, gender, and sexuality as natural, precultural universals and to project these concepts onto shamanic altered states of consciousness. Many ethnographers throughout the world still subscribe to the classic male-dominant paradigms proposed by Eliade (1964:328–329, 346–347, 411, 453, 507) and Lewis (1966:321–322; 1969:89), in which men are shamans because they travel to other worlds and experience ecstatic, transcendent spiritual knowledge, which they control and remember while women and passive homosexual men, who are like women in affect and dress (Matory 1994:228–229), are not defined as shamans, but as mediums because they are physically and spiritually mountable by the spirits who possess them.[15] These embodied possession experiences are characterized as unwilled, involving impersonation and a change of identity (Rouget 1985:3, 325), and therefore amnesic and uncontrolled (Bourguignon 1976:12).[16]

Some researchers of Mapuche shamanism replicate these older gendered notions of possession and ecstasy. They argue that spirits possess female and feminized male machi and that the machi's soul is displaced (Alonqueo 1979; Kuramochi 1990; Métraux 1973). San Martín (1976:192) argues that male machi do not experience possession but travel with their spirits in ecstatic flight to other worlds and gives no information on female machi. This perspective does not account for the fact that machi—male and female—experience both possession and ecstasy, engage with spirits of different genders, and incorporate both female and male symbols and roles in their practices. Anthropologists have viewed the distinction between ecstasy and possession as one of control or lack of control over ASC, but if the altered state is sought, however, "then the question of 'control' or 'possession' is a matter of ideology, techniques, theatrics, or audience perception" (Tedlock 2003:5). Machi entrance and exit from both possession and ecstasy is willed and controlled. When unwilled possession occurs among Mapuche, it is not considered shamanic. Those Mapuche who experience unwilled possession are either characterized as neophytes who have a spiritual calling but need training, or as people who are possessed by evil spirits.[17] Machi ecstasy is not superior to possession but involves greater risk and skill. The ecstatic machi may be captured by an evil spirit as it travels through different worlds and must be able to control her spirit horse. Machi do not cease to experience possession because they are shamans, but engage in possession and/or ecstasy according to the specific ritual situation.[18] Machi call their spirits and become possessed at the beginning of healing and initiation rituals and engage in ecstatic fight to gain more healing knowledge and to rescue lost souls in other worlds. These machi experiences are echoed by other scholars who argue that shamans engage in alternate states of consciousness (Frigerio 1988), and although the ability to undergo ecstatic magical flight may require greater skill than mastery of possession (Peters 1981:109), most shamans can experience ecstasy, possession, and visionary ASC (Hultkrantz 1973:29; Basilov 1976:149; Tedlock 2003:5).[19]

Many authors have linked the alleged predominance of female mediums and the lack of female shamanism with women's social or sexual deprivation. In societies where possession cults are "peripheral to the morality system," participants—namely women and effeminate men—are said to be drawn from the periphery (Lewis 1966: 321–322, 1969:89, Mircea Eliade (1964:507). According to Lewis (1969), women only become shamans in areas where state bureaucracies and doctrinal religions have discredited the practice of shamanism. Scholars have followed Lewis's lead to argue that the power female shamans gain in their families and communities from their spiritual callings to heal others compensates for women's peripheral social status (Basilov 1997; Lewis 1969; Harvey 1979; Wolf 1973). Female mediums too are often constructed as women who seek to heal themselves by compensating for sexual deprivation (Spiro 1967; Obeyesekere 1981), and resisting the power of men (Lambek 1981; Boddy 1989). Yet, if women are in fact universally deprived as Lewis argues, why is it that more women do not become shamans? (Kendall 1999: 893).

Contemporary authors have demonstrated that the deprivation hypothesis does not explain the predominance of female shamans around the globe (Balzer 1996; Basilov 1997; Humphrey and Onon 1996; Kendall 1985; Tedlock 2003) independently from the suppression and discrediting of shamanic practice by state authorities. Women are shown to become shamans because of specific historic conditions (Balzer 1996; Kendall 1999:894) and to create "new forms of speech and new local and global histories" (Tsing 1993:254) and work alongside male shamans (Tedlock 2003:2). This is particularly noticeable among the Mapuche where women and men shamans coexist with one or the other predominating according to specific economic, social, and political circumstances and the gendering of social and spiritual space (Bacigalupo 1996a, 2007).

Many scholars, however, continue to focus on the everyday gender identities of shamans as women or men neglecting the different gender identities assumed by shamans during altered states of consciousness. I argue that possession and ecstasy are expressions of different gendered relationships between spirits and hosts but that they are not direct comments on the everyday gender, sex, or sexuality of the machi practitioner. Rather, by rendering these everyday identities secondary, ritual personhoods use gender to express the hierarchical relationships between Mapuche authorities and Chilean authorities, masters and servants, parents and children, husbands and wives. I argue that machi's descriptions of their altered states as ecstatic flight as a masculine action or possession as a feminine action are contingent on machi's personal consciousness in relationship to that of spirits and deities.

In everyday life and in ordinary states of consciousness, machi are generally viewed as persons who possess zuam (consciousness) and are authors and agent of their own thoughts, actions and emotions. In order to be a person, a Mapuche must have a *piuke* (heart) the locus of *nünkün* (emotion) as well as *rakiduam*—thoughts, knowledge and wisdom. Seeing, knowing, and empathy are central to machi practice. Machi decide whether and whom to marry, make friends, vote, and are involved in politics. Machi autonomously decide which patients to see and what rituals to perform, how much to charge, and how to bolster their popularity and compete with other machi.

But although machi are held accountable for their actions in everyday life, they are never true agents of their destiny. After initiation, a machi's personhood is shaped by his or her relationship with spirits and their demands. Machi usually inherit a machi *püllu*, an individual spirit of an ancestral machi and also gain divinatory and healing knowledge from *fileu*, a generic powerful ancestral machi who guides them through their ecstatic travels to other worlds. Ngünechen, the Mapuche deity that fuses Mapuche ancestral spirits and colonial authorities with the Christian God, Jesus, and the Virgin, also provides advice and punishes machi who stray from traditional norms.

These spirit beings expect machi to live up to impossible ideals. They ask machi to dedicate their lives exclusively to the spirits, not to marry, to avoid modern technology, and to speak exclusively in the Mapuche language, Mapudungun, not in Spanish, the official language of Chile. Spirits place taboos on drinking, dancing, socializing, sex, and nontraditional clothing. Spirits are angered if machi have lovers or spouses, travel in cars, or use cellular phones, and punish them with illness and suffering.

Machi negotiate their needs and desires with those of their spirits, appeasing them continually with prayers and offerings. Machi Rocío described one of her struggles with her machi püllu in a dream narrative:

> In my dream there was a machi who didn't show her face. 'Extinguish the fire,' she said. 'No,' I said. And the spirit was mad. 'You are not your own owner,' the spirit said. 'I command you. Extinguish the fire. . . . Play your kultrun (drum) and pray for that poor ill man.' And that is what I did, because if one does not do what the spirit says in the dream, one becomes ill.

Some machi find the burden of spiritual marriage unbearable. Machi Fresia was unable to fulfill the demands of the spirit she inherited from her machi great-grandmother or to resolve the conflicts she had with her spirit. She finally decided to uproot her altar and abandon her machi practice (Bacigalupo 1995).

During ordinary states of consciousness, machi and their spirits are perceived as separate persons in symbiotic relationship. The fileu is the power, or *newen,* that makes the machi, and the machi is the human who makes the power tangible and effective through ritual practice. Thus, even human machi may be spoken of as fileu, just as fileu may be referred to as machi. Although machi are subject to the fileu's demands and desires, and the fileu influences the machi's personality, they remain separate persons. Ramiro, a Mapuche intellectual, elaborates on the relationship between machi personhood and that of spirits:

> RAMIRO: There are two elements to the machi person: the physical, which is individual, and the püllu, which is inherited. . . . Machi Jacinto is physically Jacinto. But his püllu is that of his great-grandmother. So when the püllu comes into him, which is the character who acts? The character of the machi—a great-grandmother.

MARIELLA: When machi Jacinto dies, which is the spirit that is inherited by another machi? That of machi Jacinto? That of the great-grand-mother machi? Or that of the great-grandmother machi transformed by machi Jacinto?

RAMIRO: That of the great-grandmother machi, because it is the machi identity that is inherited. But there is also the individual püllu of machi Jacinto, so the spirit says, I have also served this other fileu called So-and-So.

During ecstatic states, machi share self with the fileu. The fileu is the intermediary or messenger between humans and the deity Ngünechen, who speaks its demands, knowledge of remedies, and advice through the machi. Mapuche consider ecstatic flight (as a mounted Mapuche or Spanish warrior), a masculine action in which male and female machi travel to other worlds to obtain power objects, acquire knowledge about healing, and recover lost souls from the hands of evil spirits. Machi describe themselves as the fileu "flying to the sky," "riding the spirit horse," and "sitting beside Ngünechen to listen to his words." At the end of complex healing rituals or *daahatun,* machi experience an ecstatic state labeled *konpapüllu.* The term *konpapüllu* has multiple meanings: "the spirit who enters and does here" derived from the terms *konün* (to enter), *pa* (to do here), and *püllu* (living spirit); "the spirit who divines here" derived from the terms *koneu* (divination), *pa* (to do here), and *püllu* (living spirit); or simply "with the spirit." At this time the deity Ngünechen or the fileu merges with the machi to reveal the cause of the illness, and gives advice and knowledge about healing remedies. Machi remember their experiences as spirit beings in detail and recount them often.

The way in which machi share personhood with spirit beings during ecstatic flight is complex. Machi draw on the discourse of possession to describe ecstatic flight as multiple, multilayered possessions in which the machi and the fileu go into küymi (ASC), and the fileu "speaks the words of Ngünechen through the machi's mouth." Mapuche sometimes refer to machi in trance as fileu, or as Ngünechen. Ramiro, the Mapuche intellectual quoted earlier, argued that "the machi püllu, the fileu, and Ngünechen can be the same or different according to context." Machi Rocío explained this process:

MARIELLA: When you are possessed, what spirit comes?

ROCÍO: The spirit that one has, the machi püllu. A machi without power is no good. One has to have power.

MARIELLA: When your head becomes drunk and you go into küymi [ASC], who arrives?

Rocío: Fileu, Ngünechen, machi püllu. They are all the same.

Mariella: But if you inherit a machi spirit from your grandmother, that spirit is not Ngünechen.

Rocío: One has to inherit a spirit first to be a machi. That is the machi püllu. That is the spirit that comes to one. The words of Ngünechen, the fileu, come through the machi püllu. When the machi is in küymi, the machi püllu, fileu, and Ngünechen are the same. (Interview on December 28, 2001)

These multiple multilayered possessions between the machi person, the machi püllu, or fileu and Ngünechen are comparable to the two sets of mimesis observed by Taussig: one between the person and the copy represented by his or her soul; and the second, the mimetic conjunction between the soul and the spiritual cosmos (1993:120). Machi, like Panamenian Kuna chanters, have a decisively mimetic component built into their speech where the speaker is always retelling, reviewing, or reinterpreting something said before (Taussig 1993:109). Machi hear the message of Ngünechen through the words of the fileu and the machi püllu who interpret them. The machi repeats and interprets the words of the fileu and the machi püllu in her ecstatic discourse and gains power. The machi's words in turn are repeated and interpreted by the *dungumachife*, or master of words, on behalf of the community.

During possession states, the machi becomes a feminine bride and her or his head is mounted by a spirit, a process labeled *lonkoluupan*. The machi's personhood remains distinct from that of her spirit and the spirit speaks directly through the machi's mouth and body while he or she remains absent.[20] While possession thickens the interpersonal ties between spirits and their human spouses (Boddy 1994:421), it also keeps their personhood separate. Machi claim they do not remember the possession experience because they separate themselves from the spirit, who speaks. In practice, however, machi possession states are always under control, and machi are both aware and unaware in what Carol Laderman calls "a balance between remembering and forgetting" (1991:88). Machi distinguish between light and deep possession and consider the latter more prestigious, and powerful.

During light possession, the spirit inhabits the body of the machi but does not replace his or her soul, a phenomenon that Rolf Foerster refers to as "revelation"(1993:106). Machi are aware of the spirit's presence and understand its advice and demands, but it is the spirit, not the machi, who speaks. The possessed machi serves as a spokesperson for spirits. Machi forget their own persona but remember the ritual, the performance, and sometimes the actions and words of the possessing spirit. Machi Pamela describes her personal soul, or püllu, as "sitting beside" her body while she is being possessed by the fileu. Machi Marta described the experience this way: "The fileu is up in the sky but also in the rewe guarding the püllu. When the fileu comes to me I feel a heat rising in my body and I am gone. I stay at the rewe, I am Marta. The fileu takes over. While God talks to the fileu, the machi talks to the people. The word of God is repeated."

During deep possession, there is a complete separation between the machi's person and that of the spirit who takes over and replaces the machi's soul. Machi rarely remember anything about what transpired except for the drumming rhythms. Machi Fresia explained: "When the spirit is here I disappear. So there is a change. When the spirit is not with me then I am here. When the spirit arrives then I am not here where the spirit is talking. Machi are double persons because sometimes she is here and sometimes she is not the person with whom people are talking" (Interview on November 24, 1991). Like the Voodoo practitioners observed by Erika Bourguignon, machi view a continuity between the identity of the subject and the possessing spirit but a discontinuity between the latter and the human vehicle, who does not have memory or responsibility for the actions carried out by her or his body when it becomes the residence for a more powerful spirit. At the same time, some cases of possession show an obvious continuity with the conscious motivation of the possessed (Bourguignon 1965:47, 53, 57). In this case, the temporary substitution of the machi's self with that of a spirit does not challenge the integrity of the machi self but rather provides increased scope for fulfillment by providing the self with an alternate set of roles. Possession becomes an idiom of communication where spirits have a place not only during public ceremonies but in their everyday domestic life as well (Crapanzano and Garrison 1977:10–12; Lambek 1980:121–123).

During Mapuche rituals, machi or candidates to machihood (*machil*) are the only people who are possessed or who engage in ecstatic travel. Knowledgeable elder Mapuche, ngenpin, dungumachife, and some dancers and musicians understand the power and meaning of Mapuche ritual prayers, songs, and dances, but the machi alone is responsible for establishing the connection between the Wenu Mapu and the Earth. Machi criticize, for example, the collective possessions that typically take place in Cuban *santería*. When machi Abel participated in an international folk music festival in Germany, he was struck by the Afro-Cuban music and dance troop: "Not everyone can be a communicator, a spiritual messenger. How it is that one spirit possesses all those people at once? They must be possessed by the devil."

Machi stress the relational nature of humans, animals, and spirits, but in practice they operate in both relational and individual modes of personhood. They stress their relational selves in order to legitimate themselves as machi with strong spiritual powers who gain power from colonial authorities, ancestral spirits and spirit animals. But they emphasize their individual personhood when asserting their agency and volition in everyday life and in distancing themselves from possessing spirits who take over their bodies and speak through them.

Conclusion

Machi operate in both relational and individual modes of personhood, and their ritual experiences are embodied and ensouled. The complex workings of machi personhood offer a new way to think about the relationship between body, mind, and spirit and the ways in which shamanic altered states of consciousness are gendered. Mapuche consider out-of-body ecstatic flight a masculine action associated with the image of mounted conquistadores and Mapuche warriors, and embodied possession as a feminine action associated with brideliness to possessing spirits. Machi, however, experience both of these drum-induced ASC regardless of their sex, using one or another according to purpose and the specific ritual context. Contrary to classic theories of shamanism, Mapuche do not view ecstasy as superior, more controlled, or more transcendent than possession, nor does possession involve a loss of self. In fact, machi experiences of possession and ecstatic flight have much in common. Both altered states of consciousness are voluntarily induced and controlled. Possessed machi are double persons who have certain awareness of the ritual performance, while machi conceive of ecstatic flight as multiple, multilayered possessions where the shaman's self merges with that of their spirit while this spirit in turn is possessed by other deities and spirits.

Shamanism, however, is not just a question of varying altered states of consciousness nor about expressions of power and resistance (Comaroff 1995; Stoller 1995; Boddy 1989). Shamanism is not a "desiccated and insipid category" (Geertz 1966) but a widespread "historically situated and culturally mediated social practice" (Atkinson 1992) connected both to local circumstances and histories as well as to national and transnational contexts (Atkinson 1992; Balzer 1996; Joralemon 1990; Kendall 1998; Taussig 1987; Tsing 1993). The different relational personhoods and positionalities of shamans, animals, and spirits are expressions of cultural meaning, ethnic/national relationships in various social and political contexts. Machi ritual relationships through kinship, marriage, and mastery and their associated altered states of consciousness reflect the complex and contradictory relationships between Mapuche and Spaniards, women and men, humans, animals, and spirits. These relationships can be hierarchical or complementary and highlight the agency of the machi or merge her personhood with that of other spiritual beings. On the one hand, kinship merges human, animal, and spirit worlds. I have demonstrated that exchange of bodily substances among machi and between machi and spirit animals creates an ordered social body where machi and animal bodies and souls share the qualities of spiritual kinship. On the other hand, social kinship, inheritance, and succession remain independent from spiritual kinship. Machi inherit the spirits of machi on the mother's side of the family and share personhood with her independently from the social patrilineages.

Machi spiritual marriage represents the contradictions over feminine control and power in a patriarchal social system. When machi brides are possessed by husband spirits they illustrate the superiority of spirits and deities over humans, of Chilean authorities over Mapuche ones, as well as the limited participation of women in the patrilineal social and political realm. At the same time, spiritual betrothal illustrates how women are able to negotiate pragmatically with local male authorities in the same manner that Mapuche negotiate with Chilean ones. Machi's positive valuation of spiritual seduction as the tool for entering the spirit world and the prioritization of spiritual marriage over social marriages set machi apart from other women and offer a new reading of feminine sexuality in a spiritual context.

As masters of animals and mounted warriors who travel in ecstatic flight, machi gain control over the hierarchical institutions that regulate Mapuche people and use their power for their own purposes. Multiple, multilayered possessions provide the context for the merging of machi personhood with that of mounted masculine Mapuche and Spanish warriors as well as the Chilean religious and civil authorities that control their lives and futures. In this context shamans are not the children or brides of hierarchical spirits and deities, but deities and authorities themselves. It is from this position of power that shamans know about the universe and are able to change situations. By becoming male authorities in order to change the world, machi reverse the inferior position that Mapuche hold in relation to the Chilean state in an attempt to define their own destinies. At the same time, machi masters' powers, destinies, and lives are intertwined with the animals they dominate. Machi are part of a larger social body where Mapuche and non-Mapuche, masters and animals, share personhood and where foreign authorities and beings become part of and transform the Mapuche self.

NOTES

1. Barbara Tedlock introduced the term *co-gendered* to refer to a partly feminine and partly masculine personality (Tedlock 2003:6).
2. Alfred Métraux (1942) and Robles Rodríguez (1911, 1912) described machi initiation and renewal rituals.
3. Machi such as María Cecilia, who belong to a machi school of practice, invite their cohorts to heal them and grant them blessings. Machi who do not belong to a school of practice hire other machi to perform these functions in

their rituals. Machi initiation and renewal rituals are grouped together under the generic term *machi purrun* or *baile de machi* (dance of the machi).

4. Photographing María Cecilia's ritual could be particularly dangerous. Her relationship with her spirit was new and tenuous, and I was uncertain which soul would be captured on film when she was in an altered state of consciousness (ASC), and her personal soul might be traveling or displaced by a possessing spirit. I expressed my concerns to her, but she responded, "We know you. You are not a Mapuche and you have no power or bad intentions. . . . The photo captures the soul when the photo is taken close up and the eyes are open. Take photos when the machi's heads are covered with the headscarf, from behind, from far away, or when the eyes are closed. . . . If someone else tells you to stop taking photos, don't stop. If the machi tell you to stop, then stop." I followed her instructions and took photographs during the first day of the ritual.

5. Michael Taussig observes a similar process where semen and pubic hair are used to effect love magic through contagion, but they are also profound indices of sexual attachment, impregnation, and the making of children. "It becomes virtually impossible to separate their being sign from their being ontologically part of the sexually partnered" (Taussig 1993:55).

6. Some machi transfer power to their initiates by cutting crosses into the palms of their hands and rubbing them together in order to mix their blood. Javiera and Elena considered the ritual exchange of animal blood and breath to breath to be sufficient.

7. The kopiwe flowers and llankalawen vines that machi wear during initiation rituals have explicit spiritual, sexual, and reproductive connotations. Kopiwes are viewed as female symbols of traditional lore and machi practice, which resist urbanity and modernization. Crushed kopiwe flowers are used to help machi with the symptoms of initial calling and sudden encounters with evil spirits. Llankalawen, a wild plant that grows intertwined with the kopiwe vine, is the male counterpart of the kopiwe and is often associated with the fileu. It serves as the masculine complement to the machi, who is perceived as feminine when seducing the fileu.

8. Studies that have explored the way in which gender identities are negotiated in various Latin American contexts have centered on male transgendered prostitutes (Kulick 1998; Prieur 1998; Schifter 1998) or ordinary men (Lancaster 1992) but not on male and female shamans. The focus of these studies has been on the way specific sexual acts—penetrating or being penetrated by others— creates gender. They associate "gender variance" with "sexual variance."

9. The involuntary and uncontrolled possession common to Voodoo and Oyo-Yoruba priests only occurs among Mapuche neophytes who experience a calling or among Mapuche who are possessed by evil spirits.

10. Carol Laderman (1992:191) describes a similar phenomenon among Malay shamans, who mobilize their inner resources, personified as the Four Sultans, the Four Heroes, the Four Guardians, and the Four Nobles.

11. Prayer collected by Juan Ñanculef.

12. Pollock notes a similar process among the Kulina where the term *dzupi-nahe* refers to the physical embodiment of the spirit either by humans or animals (1996:330).

13. Prayer collected by Juan Ñanculef.

14. In the last two decades, anthropologists have focused on the phenomenology of the body and used the paradigm of embodiment in an effort to compensate for previous mentalistic perspectives and transcend the Cartesian mind-body dualism (Scheper-Hughes and Lock 1987; Stoller 1989; Roseman 1991; Csordas 1999; Lock 1993; Stewart and Strathern 2001). These perspectives often view non-Western people as grounding their experience in the body and not distinguishing between mind and body (Scheper-Hughes and Lock 1987; Scheper Hughes 1992; Low 1994; Pandolfi 1993; Strathern 1996) while nonmarginal European American groups are depicted as unaware of their bodies and failing to distinguish between mind and body. Many anthropologists interested in the relationship between personhood and spirits have drawn on the paradigm of embodiment to focus on the relationship between bodies and persons (Lambek and Strathern 1998), the personification of bodies (Lamb 2000; Lambek and Strathern 1998; Scheper-Hughes 1992) and the relationship between bodies and spirits (Boddy 1998; Rasmussen 1995:155; Corin 1998:89).

15. Mastery of control is viewed as the central element of shamanism and is described as "voluntary" by Oesterreich (1966), "solicited" by Lewis (1969), and "desired" by Bourguignon (1968).

16. Erika Bourguignon recently stated that uncontrolled possession is characteristic of first possession or occurs during "crisis situations" and is rare among Voodoo and Oyo Yoruba priests (Bourguignon e-mail message, January 26, 2004).

17. These two forms of possession are easily confused. Machi Marta, for example, began training a young woman whom she thought would become a machi but gradually realized she was possessed by an evil spirits because she danced like a *meulen* (a *wekufe* whirlwind).

18. Most machi argue that they experience diverse levels of consciousness, including ecstasy and possession, but machi Sergio believes machi can be grouped according to their different altered states of consciousness:

> Only select groups of machi are possessed by the fileu. The fileu is an ancient spirit, the biggest and wisest machi of the Wenu Mapu, the central head of all machi that takes machi to the magnetic field. The fileu looks for worthy machi heads in which to deposit its tradition. This takes many years. The fileu protects all machi who inherit this tradition. A machi who is possessed by the fileu remembers nothing afterward because the words come from God. It takes over the machi's mind and body completely. The fileu is a messenger for Ngünechen,

who tells it what it has to do. The fileu transmits the machi's prayers, and it also speaks the messages and prayers from Ngünechen. Those that are possessed by machi püllu are different. They are earthly, pagan machi. They learn from the knowledges of other machi. They learn from perimontun [visions], and they remember what they said or did while possessed because the spirit is also from this earth, like them. The spirit wanders around the mountains and the forests, but it does not go up to the Wenu Mapu. They have less power. (Excerpt from telephone interview, May 18, 2002)

Mapuche intellectual Juan Ñanculef, on the other hand, encountered machi who view the term *fileu* as something excessively mysterious and powerful to the point that it is sometimes associated with sorcery (Phone interview, September 26, 2002).

19. According to Larry Peters (1981), male Nepalese shamans are possessed in some instances and engage in spirit travel in others, but women never become shamans at all. He characterizes possession as an inferior form of involvement experienced by male neophytes while advanced men shamans gain control of their spirits and have encounters with them in ecstatic flight.

20. I disagree with several researchers who have argued that machi share personhood with the spirit that possesses them (Alonqueo 1979; Kuramochi 1990; Métraux 1973).

References

Alonqueo, Martín. 1979. *Instituciones Religiosas del Pueblo Mapuche*. Santiago: Ediciones Nueva Universidad.

Alvarado, Margarita, Ema de Ramón, and Cecilia Peñaloza. 1991. *Weichan, La Guerra de Arauco: Una Mirada Desde la Estética 1536–1656*. Unpublished Manuscript: Santiago.

Appadurai, Arjun. 1990. "Topographies of the Self: Praise and Emotion in Hindu India." In *Language and the Politics of Emotion,* ed. Catherine Lutz and Leila Abu-Lughod, pp. 92–112. Cambridge: Cambridge University Press.

Atkinson, Jane. 1992. "Shamanisms Today." *Annual Review of Anthropology* 21: 307–330.

Augusta, Félix José. 1934. (1910). *Lecturas Araucanas*. Padre De Las Casas, Chile: Editorial San Francisco.

Bacigalupo, Ana Mariella. 1994a. "Variación de Rol de *Machi* en la Cultura Mapuche. Tipología Geográfica, Adaptiva e Iniciática." *Revista de Antropología Universidad de Chile* 12: 19–43. Santiago, Chile.

Bacigalupo, Ana Mariella. 1994b. "The Power of the *Machi*: "The Rise of Female Shaman/Healers and Priestesses in Mapuche Society." Dissertation, University of California, Los Angeles.

Bacigalupo, Ana Mariella. 1995. "Renouncing Shamanistic Practice: The Conflict of Individual and Culture Experienced by a Mapuche *Machi*." *Anthropology of Consciousness* 6 (3): 1–16.

Bacigalupo, Ana Mariella. 1996a. "Identidad, Espacio y Dualidad en los *Perimontun* (Visiones) de *Machi* Mapuche." *Scripta Ethnologica* 18: 37–63. Buenos Aires, Argentina.

Bacigalupo, Ana Mariella. 1996b. "Mapuche Women's Empowerment as Shaman/Healers." *Annual Review of Women in World Religions* 4: 57–129.

Bacigalupo, Ana Mariella. 1998. "The Exorcising Sounds of Warfare: Shamanic Healing and The Struggle to Remain Mapuche." *Anthropology of Consciousness* 9 (5): 1–16.

Bacigalupo, Ana Mariella. 2001 *La Voz del Kultrun en la Modernidad: Tradición y Cambio en La Terapéutica de Siete Machi Mapuche*. Santiago, Chile: Editorial Universidad Católica de Chile.

Bacigalupo, Ana Mariella. 2002. "Mapuche Shamanic Bodies and the Chilean State: Polemic Gendered Representations and Indigenous Responses." In *Violence and the Body: Race, Gender and the State*. Bloomington: Indiana University Press.

Bacigalupo, Ana Mariella. 2004. "The Struggle for *Machi* Masculinities: Colonial Politics of Gender, Sexuality and Power in Chile." *Ethnohistory* 51 (3): 489–533.

Bacigalupo, Ana Mariella. 2005 "Gendered Rituals for Cosmic Order: Mapuche Shamanic Struggles for Healing and Fertility." *Journal of Ritual Studies* 19 (2): 53–69.

Bacigalupo, Ana Mariella. 2007. *Shamans of the Cinnamon Tree: Gender, Power, and Healing Among the Chilean Mapuche*. Austin: University of Texas Press.

Balzer, Marjorie. 1996. "Sacred Genders in Siberia: Shamans, Bear Festivals, and Androgyny." In *Gender Reversals and Gender Cultures,* ed. Sabrina Ramet, pp. 164–182. London: Routledge.

Basilov, Vladimir. 1976. "Shamanism in Central Asia." In *The Realm of the Extra-Human: Agents and Audiences,* edited by Agehananda Bharati, pp. 149–157. The Hague: Mouton.

Basilov, Vladimir. 1997. "Chosen by the Spirits." In *Shamanic Worlds: Rituals and Lore of Siberia and Central Asia,* ed. Marjorie Balzer, Armonk, NY: Sharpe.

Boddy, Janice. 1989. *Wombs and Alien Spirits: Women, Men, and the Zar Cult in Northern Sudan*. Madison: University of Wisconsin Press.

Boddy, Janice. 1994. "Spirit Possession Revisited: Beyond Instrumentality." *Annual Review of Anthropology* 23: 407–434.

Boddy, Janice. 1998. "Afterword: Embodying Ethnography." In *Bodies and Persons: Comparative Perspectives from Africa and Melanesia,* ed. Michael Lambek and Andrew Strathern, pp. 252–273. Cambridge: Cambridge University Press.

Bourguignon, Erika. 1965. "The Self, the Behavioural Environment, and the Theory of Spirit Possession." In *Context and Meaning in Cultural Anthropology,* ed. Melford Spiro, pp. 39–60. London: Macmillan.

Bourguignon, Erika. 1968. *Cross-Cultural Study on Dissociational States.* Columbus: Ohio State University Press.

Bourguignon, Erika. 1976. *Possession.* San Francisco: Chandler and Sharp Publishers.

Brown, Michael. 1997. *The Channeling Zone: American Spirituality in an Anxious Age.* Cambridge, MA: Harvard University Press.

Butler, Judith. 1990. *Gender Trouble: Feminism and the Subversion of Identity.* New York: Routledge.

Comaroff, Jean.1985. *Body of Power, Spirit of Resistance.* Chicago: University of Chicago Press.

Cooper, Johan. 1946. *Handbook of South American Indians.* Bureau of American Ethnology II. Washington, DC: Smithsonian Institution Press.

Corin, Ellen. 1998. "Refiguring the Person: the Dynamics of Affects and Symbols in an African Spirit Possession Cult." In *Bodies and Persons: Comparative Perspectives from Africa and Melanesia,* ed. Michael Lambek and Andrew Strathern. Cambridge: Cambridge University Press.

Crapanzano, Vincent, and V. Garrison, eds. 1977. *Case Studies in Spirit Possession.* New York: John Wiley & Sons.

Csordas, Thomas. 1994. *The Sacred Self: A Cultural Phenomenology of Charismatic Healing.* Berkeley: University of California Press.

Csordas, Thomas.1999. "Ritual Healing and the Politics of Identity in Contemporary Navajo Society." *American Ethnologist* 26 (1): 3–23.

Desjarlais, Robert. 2000. "The Makings of Personhood in a Shelter for People Considered Homeless and Mentally Ill." *Ethos* 27 (4): 466–489.

Dillehay Tom. 1985. "La Influencia Política de los Chamanes Mapuches." *CUHSO* 2 (2): 141–157.

Eliade, Mircea. 1964. (1974). *Shamanism: Archaic Techniques Of Ecstasy.* Princeton, NJ: Princeton University Press.

Ercilla y Zuñiga, Alonso De. 1569. (1933). *La Araucana.* Santiago, Chile: Editorial Nacimiento.

Ewing, Katherine. 1990. "The Illusion of Wholeness: Culture, Self, and the Experience of Inconsistency." *Ethos* 18: 251–278.

Faron, Louis. 1964. *Hawks of the Sun: Mapuche Morality And Its Ritual Attributes.* Pittsburgh: University of Pittsburgh Press.

Foerster, Rolf. 1993. *Introduccion a la Religiosidad Mapuche.* Santiago, Chile: Editorial Universitaria.

Foerster, Rolf. 1996. *Jesuitas y Mapuches, 1593–1767.* Santiago, Chile: Editorial Universitaria.

Frigerio, Alejandro. 1988. "Faking: Possession Trance Behavior and Afro-Brazilian Religions in Argentina." Paper presented at the meeting of the South-Western Anthropological Association, March. Monterey, California.

Geertz, Clifford. 1966. "Religion as a Cultural System." In *A Reader in the Anthropology of Religion,* ed. Michael Lambek, pp. 61–82. Oxford: Blackwell.

Geertz, Clifford. 1973. *The Interpretation of Cultures.* New York: Basic Books.

Geertz, Clifford. 1983. *Local Knowledge: Further Essays in Interpretive Anthropology.* New York: Basic Books.

Glass-Coffin, Bonnie. 1998. The Gift of Life: Female Spirituality and Healing in Northern Peru. Albuquerque: University of New Mexico Press.

Gómez de Vidaurre. 1789. (1889). *Historia Geográfica, Natural y Civil del Reino de Chile.* Volumes 14 and 15. Santiago, Chile: Imprenta Ercilla.

Guevara, Tomás. 1908. *Psicología del Pueblo Araucano.* Santiago, Chile: Imprenta Cervantes.

Gumucio, Juan Carlos. 1999. *Hierarchy, Utility and Metaphor in Mapuche Botany.* Uppsala Studies in Cultural Anthropology, 27. Uppsala: Acta Universitatis Upsaliensis.

Halliburton, Murphy. 2002. "Rethinking Anthropological Studies of the Body: Manas and Bôdham in Kerala." *American Anthropologist* 104 (4): 1123–1134.

Harvey, Youngsook Kim. 1979. *Six Korean Women: The Socialization of Shamans.* St. Paul, MN: West Publishing Company.

Harner, Michael. 1980. *The Way of the Shaman.* Harper & Row. New York.

Hilger, María Inez. 1957. *Araucanian Child Life and Its Cultural Background.* Washington: Smithsonian Miscellaneous Collection, Volume 133.

Hultkrantz, Ake. 1973. "A Definition of Shamanism." *Temeneos.* 9: 25–37.

Humphrey, Carol, and Urgunge Onon. 1996. *Shamans and Elders: Experience, Knowledge, and Power among the Daur Mongols.* Oxford: Oxford University Press.

Joralemon, Don. 1990. "The Selling of the Shaman and the Problem of Informant Legitimacy." *Journal of Anthropological Research* 46 (2): 105–117.

Kendall, Laurel. 1985. *Shamans, Housewives and Other Restless Spirits. Women in Korean Ritual Life.* Honolulu: University of Hawaii Press.

Kendall, Laurel. 1998. *Who Speaks For Korean Shamans When Shamans Speak Of The Nation? In Making Majorities: Constituting the Nation in Japan, Korea, China, Malaysia, Fiji, Turkey and the United States,* ed. Dru C. Gladney. Stanford, CA: Stanford University Press.

Kendall, Laurel. 1999. "Shamans." In *Encyclopedia of Women and World Religions,* ed. Serenity Young, pp. 892–895. New York: Macmillan.

Kulick, Don. 1998. *Travestí: Sex, Gender and Culture Among Brazilian Transgendered Prostitutes.* Chicago and London: University of Chicago Press.

Kuramochi, Yosuke. 1990. "Contribuciones Etnográficas al Estudio del *Machitun.*" Paper presented at the *Cuartas Jornadas de Lengua y Literatura Mapuche.*

Laderman, Carol.1991. *Taming the Wind of Desire: Psychology, Medicine, and Aesthetics in Malay Shamanistic Performance.* Berkeley: University of California Press.

Laderman, Carol. 1992. "Malay Medicine, Maly Person." In *Anthropological Approaches to the Study of Ethnomedicine*, ed. M. Nichter, pp. 191–206. Amsterdam: Gordon and Breach Science Publishers.

Lamb, Sarah. 2000. *White Saris and Sweet Mangoes: Aging, Gender and Body in North India*. Berkeley: University of California Press.

Lambek, Michael. 1980. "Spirits and Spouses: Possession as a System of Communication among Malagasy Speakers of Mayotte." *American Ethnologist* 7 (2): 318–331.

Lambek, Michael. 1981. *Human Spirits: A Cultural Account of Trance in Mayotte*. Cambridge: Cambridge University Press.

Lambek, Michael, and Andrew Strathern. 1998. *Bodies and Persons: Comparative Perspectives from African and Melanesia*. Cambridge: Cambridge University Press.

Lancaster, Roger. 1992. *Life is Hard: Machismo, Danger and the Intimacy of Power in Nicaragua*. Berkeley, Los Angeles, and London: University of California Press.

Langness, Lewis. 1987. *The Study of Culture*. Revised Edition. California: Chandler and Sharp.

Latcham, Ricardo. 1922. *La Organización Social y las Creencias Religiosas. de Los Antiguos Araucanos*. Santiago, Chile: Publicaciones del Museo de Etnología y Antropología de Chile.

Lewis, Ioan. 1966. "Spirit Possession and Deprivation Cults." *Man* 1 (3): 306–329.

Lewis, Ioan. 1969. "Spirit Possession in Northern Somaliland." In *Spirit Mediumship and Society in Africa*, ed. J. Beattie and J. Middleton, pp. 188–219. London: Routledge.

Lewis, Ioan. 1971. *Ecstatic Religion: An Anthropological Study of Spirit Possession and Shamanism*. Baltimore, MD: Penguin.

Low, Setha. 1994. "Embodied Metaphors: Nerves as Lived Experience." In *Embodiment and Experience: The Existential Ground of Culture and Self*, ed. Thomas Csordas, pp. 139–162. Cambridge: Cambridge University Press.

Marileo, Armando. 1995. "Mundo Mapuche." In *Medicinas y Culturas en la Araucanía*, ed. Luca Citarella. Editorial Sudamericana.

Mascia-Lees, Frances, and Patricia Sharpe. 1992. *Tattoo, Torture, Mutilation and Adornment: The Denaturalization of the Body in Culture and Text*. Albany: State University of New York Press.

Matory, Lorand. 1994. *Sex and the Empire That is No More: Gender and Politics of Metaphor in Oyo Yoruba Religion*. Minneapolis: University of Minnesota Press.

Métraux, Alfred. 1942. "El Chamanismo Araucano." *Revista del Instituto de Antropología de la Universidad Nacional de Tucumán* 2 (10): 309–362.

Métraux, Alfred. 1973. *Religión y Magias Indígenas de América del Sur*. Ediciones Aguilar: Madrid.

Moesbach, Wilhelm de. 1929–1931. (1936). *Vida y Costumbres de los Indígenas Araucanos en la Segunda Mitad del siglo XIX*. Santiago, Chile: Imprenta
Universitaria.

Murray, David. 1993. "What Is the Western Concept of the Self? On Forgetting
David Hume." *Ethos* 21 (1): 3–23.

Obeyesekere, Gannanath. 1981. *Medusa's Hair: A Essay on Personal Symbols and
Religious Experience*. Chicago: University of Chicago Press.

Oesterreich, T. K. 1966. *Possession*. Demoniacal and Other. Secaucus, NJ: Cita-
del Press.

Oña, Pedro de. 1596. (1975). Arauco Domado. Santiago: Editorial Universitaria.

Ovalle, Alonso de. 1888. (1646). *Histórica Relación del Reino de Chile y de las
Misiones que Ejercita en el la Compañia de Jesus*. Santiago, Chile: Imprenta
Ercilla.

Pandolfi, Mariella. 1993. "Le Self, le corps, la crise de la présence." *Anthropologie et Sociétes* 17 (1–2): 57–78.

Peters, Larry. 1981. *Ecstasy and Healing in Nepal: An Ethnopsychiatric Study of
Tamang Shamanism*. Malibu, CA: Undena Publications.

Pinto, Jorge. 1991. *Misticismo y Violencia en la Temprana Evangelización de
Chile*. Temuco: Ediciones Universidad de la Frontera.

Pollock, Don. 1996. Personhood and Illness among the Kulina. *Medical Anthropology Quarterly* 10 (3): 319–341.

Prieur, Annette. 1998. *Mema's House, Mexico City: On Transvestites, Queens, and
Machos*. Chicago: University of Chicago Press.

Rasmussen, Susan. 1995. Spirit Possession and Personhood Among the Kel
Ewey Tuareg. Cambridge: Cambridge University Press.

Robles, Eugenio. 1942. *Costumbre y Creencias Araucanas*. Santiago: Ediciones
Universidad de Chile.

Robles Rodriguez, Eulogio. 1911. "Costumbres y Creencias Araucanas. *Neigure-
huen* Baile de *Machi*s." *Revista de Folklore Chileno*. Entrega 3ra. Santiago de
Chile. Imprenta Cervantes.

Robles Rodriguez, Eulogio. 1912. "Costumbres y Creencias Araucanas. *Machi-
luhun* Iniciación de *Machi*." *Revista de Folklore Chileno*. Entrega 4ta. Santiago de Chile. Imprenta Cervantes.

Rosales, Diego de. 1989. (1674). *Historia General Del Reino De Chile*. Volume 1. Santiago: Editorial Andres Bello.

Roscoe, William. 1998. *Third and Fourth Genders in Native North America*. New
York: Saint Martin's Press.

Roseman, Marina. 1991. *Healings Sounds from the Malaysian Forest: Temiar
Music and Medicine*. Berkeley: University of California Press.

Rouget, G. 1980. (1985). *Music and Trance: A Theory of Relations between Music
and Possession*. Chicago: University of Chicago Press.

Sered, Susan. 1994. *Priestess Mother, Sacred Sister: Religions Dominated by
Women*. New York: Oxford University Press.

San Martín, René. 1976. "Machitun: Una ceremonia mapuche." In *Estudios antropológicos sobre los Mapuches de Chile sur-central,* ed. Tom Dillehay, pp. 83–97. Temuco, Chile: Universidad Católica.

Scheper Hughes, Nancy. 1992. *Death without Weeping: The Violence of Everyday Life in Brazil.* Berkeley: University of California Press.

Scheper Hughes, Nancy, and Margaret Lock. 1987. "The Mindful Body: A Prolegomenon to Future Work in Medical Anthropology." *Medical Anthropology Quarterly* 1: 6–41.

Schifter, Jacobo. 1998. *Lila's House: Male Prostitution in Latin America.* Translated by Irene Artavia Fernández and Sharon Mulheren. New York: Haworth.

Smith, Edmund Reul. 1855. *The Araucanians or Notes of a Tour among the Indian Tribes of Southern Chili.* New York: Harper & Row.

Spiro, Milford. 1967. *Burmese Supernaturalism: A Study in the Explanation and Reduction of Suffering.* Englewood Cliffs, NJ: Prentice-Hall.

Stoller, Paul. 1989. *The Taste of Ethnographic Things: The Senses in Anthropology.* Philadelphia: University of Pennsylvania Press.

Stoller, Paul. 1995. *Embodying Colonial Memories: Spirit Possession, Power, and the Hauka in West Africa.* New York: Routledge.

Strathern, Andrew. 1996. *Body Thoughts.* Ann Arbor: University of Michigan Press.

Strathern, Marilyn. 1988. *The Gender of the Gift.* Berkeley: University of California Press.

Taussig, Michael. 1987. *Shamanism, Colonialism, and the Wild Man: A Study in Terror and Healing.* Chicago: University of Chicago Press.

Taussig, Michael. 1993. *Mimesis and Alterity: A Particular History of the Senses.* New York: Routledge.

Tedlock, Barbara. 2003. *The Woman in the Shaman's Body: Reclaiming the Feminine in Religion and Medicine.* New York: Bantam (forthcoming).

Titiev, Mischa. 1951. *Araucanian Culture in Transition.* Ann Arbor: University of Michigan Press.

Tsing, Anna Lowenhaupt. 1993. *In the Realm of the Diamond Queen.* Princeton, NJ: Princeton University Press.

Vivar, Gerónimo de. 1558. (1966). *Crónica y Relación Copiosa y Verdadera.* Santiago, Chile: Fondo José Toribio Medina.

Wolf, Margery. 1973. "Chinese Women: Old Skills in a New Context." In *Women, Culture, and Society,* ed. Michelle Rosaldo and Louise Lamphere, pp. 157–172. Stanford, CA: Stanford University Press.

CHAPTER 9

Sexuality and Ritual: Indigenous Women Recreating Their Identities in Contemporary Mexico

Nuvia Balderrama Vara

In many forms of community organization, what stands out are the rituals, ceremonies, and different religious practices that are associated and closely linked with so-called *usos y costumbres* (custom and usage). Many community customs are mainly carried out or exercised by the male gender, who stake out their territory and at times limit the participation of the female gender.

This custom of creating unique spaces based on gender does not allow for a broad view of the community dynamic, or it is just that we only "see" it from one side.

Seeing my community from one side is what inspired me to want to see the other side. It made me seek, research, question, in a word, investigate, in many other words, attempt to know *why* there was such limited and under-valued participation of women in some of the Tepoztlán's community rituals.

My initial question was: "Why can't we as women direct the event Reto al Tepozteco (Tepozteco Challenge)?[1] That's how I began to see "this other side" of my community. I became interested in understanding the principle of women's nonparticipation, or, better said, their relegation to secondary roles and responsibilities. I also wanted to understand why the men refused to share this territory.

The denial of feminine spaces in the community of Tepoztlán has to do with the exercise of political power and the symbolic representation of authority. Not seeing women in the Reto al Tepozteco event is not seeing the importance of women's participation and community work in Tepoztlán and their contribution to Tepoztlán's identity.

As this ritual is so key for the indigenous identity of the collectivity (town), being active participants as women, and playing an important role in it, enhances the visibility of women's prestige, value, and contributions to the community.

In the town of Tepoztlán, whoever has power controls traditional spaces. How can we make these physical and symbolic community spaces also belong to women? In the Tepozteco legend, a 16th *cacique* (chieftain), sometimes called God-Man, was converted to Christianity. On one occasion he was eaten by the King-Monster of Xochicalco to satisfy his hunger. In the monster's stomach, the Tepozteco began to cut and scratch the monster's innards with obsidian stones in order to get out and not die. Only in this way, from inside, was he able to overpower the King-Monster of Xochicalco to then protect and guide the people of Tepoztlán.

In light of the metaphor *struggle from within,* I was able to focus on the dynamic that is repeated every year in preparation for this event. First, I became interested in the Náhuatl language and studied it to be able to understand the dialogue. Then I read part of my people's history. I began to establish social relationships with certain moral authorities of my community. I attended my neighborhood's meetings and assemblies, in which affairs and problems exclusively related to the neighborhood are discussed. I accompanied community and *ejido* (communal land) authorities on walks to identify the physical borders of Tepoztlán's municipal territory. I participated in improvement tasks. In other words, I became involved in my town.

Moved by my interest in learning about Tepoztlán in-depth, I wanted to know if its current population still had something in common with the Tepoztlán the grandmothers talk about, the one that is seen in old photographs, and beyond that, the one that is documented in the codices. I dared to take on positions and responsibilities traditionally reserved for men, which allowed me to better recognize, even in generational terms, how certain rituals, beliefs, customs, and traditions can change and become modified. I was bold enough to open up opportunities for many women, to encourage them to take leadership positions that were previously reserved for men. I studied the consequences of these changes.

By breaking into public spaces traditionally reserved for men, voicing our opinions in the assemblies, deciding and suggesting modifications regarding participation in some of Tepoztlán's rituals, I have been able to contribute to a certain reinvention of Tepoztlán's feminine identity. Thus new spaces for feminine public participation were made possible, and more importantly, people in the process of liberation, women and young people, were given a voice.

The Reto al Tepozteco is now an example of a situation in which men and women complement each other, in which girls, boys, the elderly, and disabled people express themselves. It's a space in which people can interact freely, in which the main role represents intelligence and the ability to transcend time. It's a space in which beliefs are made present and religions are fused into one. In the exercise and practice of my community's rituals, I have been able to see the essence of the dualities, of coming and going, of the recomposition of genders without modern conflicts.

COMMUNITY AWARENESS BUILDING

MY CHILDHOOD

The Hairdo: An Initiation to a Girl's Participation in Ritual

A gourd bowl full of water, tomato juice, and colorful ribbons are what my mother put in my hair. In front of me, a mirror reflected my small, bored, and angry face. Bored because of what my mother always did with me, and my not knowing what she was doing, or why she was doing it, or where she was going to take me. Angry because of the hair pulling and the rigid position I had to adopt for the hairdo to come out just like it had been requested of my mother.

Every once in a while, I listened to the talk of adult women, especially during preparations for the festivals. They would be in a circle, sitting around the fire where they were cooking the food and talking "women's talk." The laughter and tears gave flavor to the banquet that would later be eaten as an offering to God, but they always said nobody should get angry so the tamales wouldn't turn into *mocahuix*.[2]

Mixcoton Pipiltzín, The Boys and Girls Party

"Can I borrow your daughter?" is what a neighbor woman asked my mother, who had just finished with my hairdo. I was surprised: how could she loan me out? I was not a toy but a little five-year old *girl*, a little solitary, that liked to dance even then and it could be said that I was a little introverted. I listened attentively to the entire request and then realized that, more than a loan, it was an invitation to an exclusive party for girls and boys.

The hairdo ritual was repeated several times. The second time, I was once again in front of a mirror, but unlike the first time, my face had a smile but also signs of concern that the hairdo might not come out just right. Dressed in white and holding my mother's hand, we arrived at the party at the house of the neighbor who had wanted to "borrow" me. One room was decorated with colorful cut paper and full of smoke from the copal incense. The hostess asked us to sit down on *petates* (straw floor mats). They sat me down between a boy and another girl, and we made a circle with girls and boys combined in this way.

My mother and the other women were in a nearby room. I heard that the party was for a boy who ate raw meat, a lot of meat, and that this made him very grouchy and not able to concentrate on boy things.

They began by giving us some kind of sweet food. That's when the boy we were celebrating came in with his mother, who put him in the center of the circle. He was given the same food as everybody else. A woman prayed continuously at the boy's side. She threw bougainvillea and *cocoxochitl* flowers on him and continued praying. Then she threw candy on him and continued praying. Every time this happened, we were given the same thing as the boy.

At the end, they brought us green mole (a sauce) and white lard tamales without salt on small plates. They gave us toys in the shape of small animals, baskets, cars, and little flutes. The boy ate a chicken leg (and I imagined it was raw!) and the woman who was praying asked him to put it in the plate of mole. She came close to him and made him throw the mole all over his clothes, which he did repeatedly as if it were a game. At that moment, the woman invited all of us children to do the same and we all ended up covered in green mole, eating with our hands, decorated with flowers, and happy that the boy was cured. We played and a red *mixcoton* was placed on the boy, which he had to wear for several days until he was completely cured.[3]

The gesture of throwing food on one's clothes reminds me of part of the legend of the Tepozteco, the god-man and king Tepoztecatl-Ciztli who governed the town of Tepoztlán during the time of the conquest. It is said that when he was invited to eat together with the neighboring kings from Tlayacapan, Oaxtepec, and Yautepec in the kingdom of Cuahunahuac, he arrived wearing his best clothes, with a large entourage of guards accompanying him and the best *chimalli* to show his rank.[4] According to the legend, they were well into the feast when the king of Tepoztlán threw food on his clothes. Surprised, the other kings asked him why he was doing this and Tepoztecatl responded by saying that it seemed like they cared more about clothes than the person wearing them, because a few hours earlier he had gone to the Palace of Cuahunahuac dressed in common, simple clothes. When he said he was the King of Tepoztlán, they didn't believe him and wouldn't let him in.

Years later, when I brought up the subject of the girls and boys party with my mother and aunt, they wouldn't confirm it with me. To the contrary, they asked if I hadn't maybe dreamt it up. I responded that it wasn't a dream, that even my mother was at the party with me. After a few days my mother admitted to remembering the ceremony and my aunt shared that when she was little, they did a *chachahuate* for her because she had no appetite, was pale, wouldn't eat and was weak.[5] *Chachahuate* is a ceremonial meal they made especially for her. In order to prepare it, one must hunt a field mouse, cook it in a small clay pot with garlic, and add ground cilantro. Then, while the person without an appetite is eating it, everyone asks the mouse to cure the person and the *aigres* (wind) to make the person well again.

The Virgin-Girls

The colorful ribbons became part of my memories. But now it was flowers that my mother hurried to put in my hair. I was wearing a white dress, *huaraches* (sandals), and my first gold earrings. I asked my mother why she was dressing me like this and why I couldn't eat whatever I wanted. Hurriedly, my mother explained that we had to be present in the church to accompany the Virgin and that I would be guiding her with the *sahumerio* (incense) during the procession.

With the *sahumerio* in my hands and the copal smoke, I could barely breathe. The sun was in my eyes and, since I couldn't look up, I couldn't see beyond my feet. I felt like I wasn't fulfilling the task my mother had given me and for a moment I lost the hope of being recognized by the virgin.

Several girls who were no older than 15 or 16, dressed in black, with sandals and a hairdo similar to mine, carried the virgin on their shoulders with a look of suffering. I didn't want to suffer and during one of the most difficult moments for me, I gave the *sahumerio* to my mother and refused to continue with the procession. My mother calmed me down by saying that if I finished the procession, the virgin would take care of me and that when I became a young woman I could carry her. When I heard this promise, my lips trembled with fear and anger and I said loudly to my mother: "I don't want to be one of those girls who suffer. Don't bring me back to the church."

We spent all afternoon next to the virgin and the women in charge of the procession were with me, commenting about the privilege of being chosen to serve the virgin, about how the girls dressed in black had given themselves over to her since they were young and that, when they were adults, they would be in charge of taking care of her. I listened and watched the girls dressed in black who were quiet, with sore, swollen feet from walking so much, trying to keep their hairdos intact, and mainly serious, very serious.

I could not understand why they didn't play or laugh, nor could I understand why, since I was dressed in white, the same was demanded of me.

Ixpocatl, A Young Man and Woman

"They've come to get you for the virgin of Tlayacapan," my mother told me. Days later I was with a group of teenage girls trying to learn the *danza de las pastoras* (dance of the shepherd girls). When we were ready, we would walk to the church of the Virgin del Tránsito in the town of Tlayacapan. I had gone to the practices only a few times because I was more interested in the dance classes.

At about 5 AM in Tepoztlán I was in front of a mirror, making sure that the woven flowers in my hair didn't fall due to the white veil that my mother had just placed on my head. My first gold earrings matched my dress and white sweater. My cane, which my father had decorated, was beautiful and with it I would make the music to dance in front of the virgin. My family and I arrived by car at the church of the Virgin in Tlayacapan. The other "shepherds" hadn't arrived yet because they were walking. My mother and I entered the church.

The entire church was decorated with white agave flowers and was full of copal smoke that didn't stop flowing. My mother and I were alone in front of the Virgin. We got on our knees and began to pray. I repeated what my mother said. At a certain moment, she took me by the hands and began to say the following: "Young Virgin, my mother, virgin of the water . . . I bring my daughter to you so you will guide her way . . . So you will take care of her now that she is yours . . . don't leave her alone during the night or day you who understand us, make her a strong woman" . . . and she took off my veil.

Sometime later, the "shepherds" arrived and we began to dance, sing, and make figures with our canes. During the first break, I left the church. My mother didn't say anything and my father hugged me, put his sweater on me, and they let me sleep. When I opened my eyes, the sun was with me. I no longer was wearing my veil, or anything I owed to my mother or to the virgin. I was a girl dressed in white who had fulfilled her responsibility to give herself over to the virgin without protest. We ate red mole and milk candy, then I changed clothes and played all afternoon around the trees until I was exhausted and fell again into my father's arms, who took the last of the flowers out of my hair.

Ichpocame, Telpocame Xinelotl, Girls and Boys Moving Their Hips

After seeing the colors of my blouse reflected in the mirror, I left my house. I had a childhood friend and he was waiting for me at the corner in our neighborhood. We were about to leave when my mother's voice offering her final indications stopped me: "Be careful and don't do good things that seem bad." Those were her words before seeing us leave alone for the first time to go to a *carnaval* celebration. I was 15 years old; the church was behind me, and the introverted, solitary girl no longer existed. I was now a young woman from Tepoztlán, willing to discover what happens at *carnaval*, how you do the *chinelo* jump and why it made everyone happy.[6] What made people jump and jump the *chinelo* without getting tired?

My body began to move to the rhythm of the music; my shoulders went up on one side and the other; I felt my strong abdomen and my hips rocking in harmony with my legs; my feet found the exact moment to lift and my breathing got lost; it was lost between my breasts that jumped, expressing my happiness. I felt like something was running down my back. I touched it with my hands and it was the sweat that wet my body. I was doing the *chinelo* jump!

I got lost and then found myself in the midst of hundreds of people. There was laughter, breathing, sounds, colors, shouts, music, rhythms, colored fabric and feathers; it was like a windmill of emotions and I couldn't leave, nor did I want to. Some arms picked me up and put me on top of some shoulders—my brother invited me to be on top of a human pyramid. Without realizing it, I was in the center of one of the dance groups called "Central America of the Ants." One of the "ants" from my neighborhood and I were among the few women "ants" who dared to be in the middle of that windmill of masculine emotions. Feeling excitement and suspense, I got up to the highest part of the human pyramid. I got on my knees and in an instant the group flag was waving in my hands. I heard more shouts, applause, and that's how I became a *zicatl*, an ant together with other ants. I was a subversive right in the middle of *carnaval*. No woman before me had done what I had just done.

For a moment I felt confused. I didn't know if what I was doing was correct, but the excitement invaded me. It was the first time I entered a space that was just for men, where physical strength was what distinguished someone. I continued because I didn't feel it was a competition. I didn't feel excluded. In some way, I felt like this was my complement, like it became part of me. After this, I wondered why women didn't participate or have a role in these festivals, why there were no women musicians, women *chinelas, mayordomas* (church leaders); after all, we were women and men at the festival.

With this reflection in mind, I thought about other areas. I asked myself similar questions about school, dance, neighborhood festivals, soccer. Here I must recognize that in order to enter into mainly masculine spaces, I had to simulate their attitudes, because by imitating masculine attitudes and poses it was easier for me to access these spaces.

"It's better to dance the *xochipizahuatl,* which is just for women," I was told. And I danced it, but it seemed slow, like a decoration. Nothing changed when it was danced, and then I realized that activities in which women participated in Tepoztlán were like that; nothing transcended. It was just repeating something and nothing really exciting was offered to the women.

I started wondering why there was no presence of women in different rituals and ceremonies, or why the few women who did participate had inferior activities, why women participated by transferring domestic activities to public spaces. Why their opinions were hardly ever considered or were only vaguely taken into account. Why they didn't make decisions about community organization and why women were not represented in municipal politics.

That's how, with these types of questions and reflections in mind, I began to physically install myself in spaces that were not for women. Later, some friends helped me to be able to participate, mainly in sports. I began my entry into male spaces through sports. I was one of the first women to become a member of the only gym in Tepoztlán. I was the woman who played soccer with the men, who talked with friends in the streets at night and had some beers with them, who ran up the mountain to the Tepozteco (archaeological site) alone.

Maybe now these activities are common in my town, but while I was running in the mountains in the mornings, I thought a lot about the activities and things women could not do. In my case, I was already seen as strange because I ran so much, because I dressed in the colors of light and because I didn't accept what people said about the way things should be. Sitting on top of the mountain and viewing the diversity that surrounded me, my series of doubts and suspicions began to emerge regarding rituals, festivals, and ceremonies of Tepoztlán. Had they always been the way they are today? How had women participated in the past? Did men participate in the same way they do today? If there are priests now, were there priestesses then? Why do the young maidens who now participate in the Reto al Tepozteco ceremony look fragile, without presence, just there to fill in a gap. At another time, were the maidens the priestesses who walked and created the Tepozteco together, the place where I live?

With these doubts and suspicions, I began to participate in political and social spaces. I saw how people took a position.

New Spaces

Among a group of friends, we decided to attend the organizational meetings for the Reto al Tepozteco ceremony. At first we just listened to the people who had participated for years. We observed the group dynamic and understood that the first thing we had to do was to respect the opinions of the elderly, that they couldn't be questioned, contradicted, or challenged. It was a small group of no more than 15 people, all adult men from Tepoztlán, some with professions such as teachers, accountants; others had significant community representation, such as *mayordomos* or neighborhood representatives. Due to this situation, our patience and our desire to participate and make proposals kept us from intervening in any way.

After some time (between a month and a half or two), they finally realized we were there. First they asked us: "What family are you from? Who is your father/mother?" And then, "What do you think about this?" This opened the door for us to begin to offer our own opinions and later suggestions.

I felt uneasy and had doubts about how to intervene, how to ask for the floor, because as a young woman I couldn't do it directly. Only an older adult could grant me permission to speak. I knew I had the right to state my opinions and make suggestions as a woman, but the dynamic of the group didn't allow it. So I began to speak with each older person before and after each meeting. We spoke about their youth, their achievements, their characterizations in the Reto al Tepozteco, the ceremony, the offering, and how they would like to carry out this ritual now. We spoke of how the community should participate, the authorities, and what they thought about the town's politics. With these words in the air, I made my presence noticed at the meetings.

FESTIVALS AND RITUALS: WOMEN REINVENTING OUR IDENTITIES

How Everything Began: The Origin, Cause . . . Why?

On the main street in the center of Tepoztlán, more people than usual can be observed. It's six o'clock in the afternoon and night is upon us. It's September and the rains, together with a soft wind, are constant company. We can hear the far-away sound of the *teponaztli* echoing in the mountains.[7] It's been almost a week since many people sleep and awaken to this rhythm, almost a week that the hearts of many people who live in Tepoztlán beat to the sound of the *teponaztli*. Today is September 7, the day of benedictions for the Tepozteco God, and I wonder:

- Who gives this offering?
- How did this ritual come about?
- How is the Tepozteco God represented?
- What is needed in order to be chosen?
- Why is it only the men who are in charge of this ritual and festival on September 7 and 8?
- Why do the women who represent the maidens look so weak?

- What does it mean to be a maiden in this representation?
- Why don't they allow women to touch the shells?
- Who prepares the offering that is deposited at the house of the Tepozteco?
- Who was the mother of the Tepozteco?

Asking myself one question after another, I walked up the mountain, questioning the form and act of this ancestral ritual. I arrived at the pyramid on top of the mountain, called "the Tepozteco" in honor of this pre-Hispanic god. Some authors mention that Tepoztlán . . .

"was a religious center of importance . . . in 1532 Fray Domingo de la Anunciación arrived in Tepoztlán and . . . destroyed a famous idol, which was celebrated all over this kingdom and visited by outsiders through pilgrimages made in its service. They brought it offerings from the kingdoms of Chiapas and Guatemala. This idol was called Ometochtli, which means two rabbits." (Davila Padilla, 1955, Book.2:617–618)

Juan Dubernard Chauveau commented that

[t]he Tepoztécatl statue was destroyed by the missionary Fray Domingo de la Anunciación before September of 1532, because by the 8th of September, the last cacique of Tepoztlán, named *Cihtli* (hare), received the baptismal water from the hands of this evangelizer at the site called *Axihtla* (where the water comes from), in a place called *Tlacualoyan* (place where one eats) . . . According to tradition preserved in the town, this place continued to be used for awhile to celebrate baptisms and weddings until the first chapel was built. (1983: 47)

After doing some reading, I realized nighttime had arrived and I went up the mountain to the Tepozteco. There I saw many people. We lit each other up with torches and flashlights. The smell of copal inundated the space and the sounds of the *teponaztli,* the *chirimilla,* and the drums gave the signal to start dancing. People from the town and neighboring areas came together to follow the rhythm. At one side of the pyramid, another group of people was listening to stories and legends of the Tepozteco. At the pyramid's main altar, the "offering" could be seen, which had been placed there hours earlier by those in charge of the ritual. Two men were guarding this area so no one could enter.

I looked in and asked for permission to get closer, which was granted. Then I could see that the offering had bougainvillea flowers all around it. At the center was a gourd full of water, a sling, and an agave fiber (*ixtle* or *lazo*) rucksack, a bottle of mescal, tobacco, gourds full of pulque (a drink made from fermented agave sap), small candles . . . that was all I could see because the men wouldn't let me stay.

A little bothered by their attitude, I walked toward the steps to leave. It began to rain again and I walked quicker. I went by a lit *tlecuil*.[8] Some women offered me *atole* (a hot corn drink) and tamales. They offered this in outstretched hands, with a smile that made it impossible to say no. I remained while the rain came down. Suddenly everything began to move: some people were running, others were covering themselves from the rain with plastic, and the two men who were guarding the offering came to shelter themselves from the rain under the same cloth roof where the women and I were. The women gave the men food and we all ate together. I asked the men why they hadn't let me stay longer to look at the offering, and one of them said, without taking his eyes off his tamales, "Women can't get close to the offering or touch it because it's a man's thing," quickly adding, "The Tepozteco can get mad and then this water that's falling turns into a storm; bad water can fall."

It was only because my mouth was full of tamales that I didn't say anything else, but my eyes opened wide. Then my eyes met with those of one of the women and, in a language of gestures and signs, she made me understand that not all of this was true. We finished eating, the rain had stopped and many people had left. I got up from the floor, the women finished picking up their utensils and with a firm voice said to the men present:

"Let's go because tomorrow you need to be rested and so do we. We have to sleep this is all for today." The men took the baskets and without saying anything, we began to walk down the mountain. I had been eating in the company of the person who would represent the Tepozteco God the next day, September 8. I had begun to question part of my town's history. Something in me began to question the role of women in the community's custom and usage, rituals and practices.

To take a look at the social and gender roles played by women in Tepoztlán is to open one's way of seeing things and be sensitive enough to appreciate their role. Tepoztlán is a territory that has transformed itself within a context of political construction, of temporality (where history is always present). It's a region with political forces and a place where a social network is beginning to be built that sustains economic, political, social, and cultural structures. We are told that the territory is part of what allows us to have an identity, and the reason why we can answer questions like, "Where am I from?" or "Where do I come from?" "Who am I?" To speak of territory is to speak of more than a piece of land.

Being rhetorical about my culture allowed me to realize that the myths, sociocultural premises, religions, and sociostructural determinants involve the woman and convert her into a reproductive agent of the dominant

ideologies; thus, the woman is the main reproducer of much of the patriarchal system. By questioning this role with the women in Tepoztlán, I was
able not only to go beyond researching the structure of women's personalities based on men's perceptions, what others impose on them, but also to
discover who they are based on what they say, propose, resolve, do, and feel
themselves. This is why I speak of looking at the woman of Tepoztlán with
sensitivity. These are women with a high level of psychological resistance
and a high level of dignity. The women of Tepoztlán identify themselves as
struggling and not only do they have this characteristic, they have also been
able to change their personalities in accordance with the intensity of the
social movements they have participated in and the way in which they have
been involved.

El Reto al Tepozteco

The main players of the Reto al Tepozteco are men; those who play the
teponaztli, musical instrument of prehispanic origin used in practices and
rituals, as well as the *chirimilla* and the drums, are men. Those who organize
and manage the budget for this event are men. Those who do the casting for
the roles of maidens and the Tepozteco are men. Those who correct, propose
or limit . . . are men. What was happening with the women? When did they
come onto the scene?

By mandate, the women were given secondary or classic tasks supposed
to correspond to their gender: making the tamales, preparing the offering,
sewing the dresses, among other tasks in which they didn't have to make
decisions or give opinions about what happens in the Reto al Tepozteco.

This moved many things inside of me. I couldn't accept that women's
opinions were not taken into account. Women were always present but didn't
give their opinions. I decided to offer my opinion about this ritual for the first
time. I began by speaking about the stage, the infrastructure of the Tepozteco
pyramid's replica raised in Tepoztlán's plaza. I did this on purpose, since the
members of the Tepozteco Association were interested in knowing how the
replica looked and if it could be improved. Then I voiced my opinion about
the clothes worn by the characters representing the kings and how they
should be worn, the dances, the maidens' dress, the veil dance. Little by little,
without interfering in their original plans, I gave my opinions and expressed
my concerns. All of this took time, involving meetings, lobbying, practices,
visits, festivals, interviews, talks. I also spent a lot of time researching the
rituals, ceremonies, clothing, gods and goddesses, and ways of life during
pre-Hispanic times in central Mexico, mainly among *nahua* and *xochimilca*
cultures. My goal was to be able to defend my proposals since two teachers,
who were the main leaders, didn't allow any changes in this ritual and their
argument was: *"this is the way it's always been and it can't be changed."*

I asked older people who had participated in the Reto al Tepozteco many years ago to remember what it was like. I had long conversations with older men, with grandmothers and grandfathers. I asked them many things and they were glad to listen and respond. I think this step was decisive for me to be allowed into this event. I was interested in knowing about these people's experiences, what they had felt, what they thought, and what they would do now for things to be better.

The grandparents were excited when they spoke to me about how they saw the Reto al Tepozteco 30 or 40 years ago and how they saw it now, what had been taken out, what had been added. I included their comments and proposals in my talks with the authorities, especially with the Tepozteco Association. Each time I dared to express an opinion or make a proposal, I emphasized the fact that I had consulted previously with a grandfather, or that such and such a codex indicated this. One example was the issue of adding color to the clothing. Usually the clothing was not dyed but had the natural colors of the cloth, which was usually white cotton. Through my research, I discovered that the clothing of the *mexica* royalty, and thus that of the *tepozteca*, was multicolored and consisted, in a beautiful way, of embroidery, feathers, calico cloth, *huipiles,* and *maxtlas* that were painted in a style similar to tie-dye. Decorations and body painting, jewelry with gold, jade, silver, and seeds complemented the women's and men's clothing.

Altepehuitl, the Town's Festival

By organizing, we were able to participate in the Reto al Tepozteco. Young men and women participated in moderate numbers, but in a way that hadn't occurred in a long time. Preparations for a festival implies a community organization strategy. It also offers an opportune place for the exchange of roles. Now, with the thought on my lips and as a representative of this ceremony, I didn't forget that listening and having patience were the main ingredients for the success of my participation and my proposals.

I felt the community consciousness. when I was at the meetings of the representatives from the neighborhoods, towns and colonies that make up the municipality of Tepoztlán. I felt it when I asked my companions point blank if they liked what we were doing. When we played around during breaks and were able to chat, when all of the participants sat around to listen to a legend while eating roasted corn on the cob, when something was requested and always provided. The general lesson I learned can be summarized in these words: "always what is just and necessary."

Success came with the growing presence of women in this ritual. By transcending their traditional roles, they revealed themselves as women with confident bodies, with long looks and with pride for being their own women and not just the Tepozteco's maidens. Women with clothes that spoke for themselves, girls and boys who were happy to be girls and boys, men who were happy to be able to share their roles, men and women accompanying each other in a ritual.

These achievements have affected the lives of each person who has participated in the Reto al Tepozteco that I call *El reto nuevo del Tepozteco* (the new Tepozteco challenge). They have grown to include participation of women in public and political spaces, in the nomination and election of *mayordomas* and municipal assistants, in the constant search for men and women to be equal but not the same.

Those of us who participated in *El reto nuevo del Tepozteco* first took ourselves back to historic, pre-Hispanic times. We collectively situated ourselves without losing our individuality. We each made a commitment to be ourselves in order to become integrated as a group. We asked ourselves how we wanted to live, how we wanted to transcend, where we wanted to go after we die.

This ceremony is one of the many open windows for observing and understanding the indigenous cosmo-vision, in this case, a way of seeing life in the community of Tepoztlán, a way of reinhabiting the earth.

NOTES

1. The Reto al Tepozteco (Tepozteco Challenge), which is celebrated every September 8 in the town of Tepoztlán, is the theatrical interpretation, in the indigenous Náhuatl language, of a mythical-historical event. The *cacique* who was converted to Christianity was also, according to legend, a manifestation of the Tepoztecatl god, born from a virgin maiden, and associated with the moon and with *pulque*, a drink made from fermented agave (cactus) sap. After his conversion, at the beginning of the Conquest, Tepoztecatl ("the Tepozteco") was challenged by the *caciques* of neighboring villages to go back to following ancestral beliefs, especially by the cannibal king of Xochicalco, the main sacred place of the region's ancient religion. After he escaped from the monster's stomach, the Tepozteco brought the people of Tepoztlán to the Catholic faith and, with his good manners, converted the neighboring villages by showing them that Christian conversion is compatible with respect for their own customs and the Nahuatl culture's own values.

2. *Mocahuix* is a Nahuatl word that means "to remain raw, to not be cooked."

3. *Mixcoton* is a Nahuatl word that refers to a piece of clothing similar to an overcoat or poncho.

4. *Chimalli* is a Nahuatl word that means "shield."

5. *Chachahuate* is a Nahuatl word that refers to a ceremonial dish made with a field mouse (*teporingo*).

6. The *brinco del chinelo* is a dance that integrates indigenous, cultural elements (dancing, rhythm and, in part, the hat that is used), African elements

(rhythm, musical instruments) and Spanish elements (dress and masks). *Xinelotl* is a Nahuatl word that means *movements of the hip*. The word became *chinelo* in Spanish and is the name of the dance we just described, in which the indigenous people make a parody of the hip movements of the Spaniards.

7. Pre-Hispanic instrument with strong sounds, similar to a drum, used in ceremonies and rituals.

8. Pre-Hispanic kitchen made of stones, mud, and wood. It is still used today in some homes or in an improvised manner in the field.

REFERENCES

Davila, Padilla, *Agustín Historia de la fundación y discurso de la provincia de Santiago de México de la orden de predicadores*, título 2, pp.617–618. Edit. Academia Literaria, Mexico, 1955.

Dubernard, Juan. *Apuntes. ara la historia de Tepoztlán (Morelos)*, p. 47. Edición del autor, Cuernavaca Morelos, México, 1983.

Maldonado Druzo, *Cuauhnáhuac y Huaxtepec (Tlahuicas)* México: UNAM. Centro Regional de Investigaciones Multidiciplinarias, 1990. 296 pp.

INTERVIEWS

Sr. Camerino "n" Barrio de la Santisima Tepoztlan, Morelos, México, 2001.

Dra. Bertha Baheza Gallardo Barrio de San Miguel Tepoztlán, Morelos, México, 2002.

Sr. Ramiro Rodriguez Barrio de Santo Domingo Tepoztlán, Morelos, Mexico, 2001.

PART V

Women, World View, and Religious Practice

Drawing the Connections: Mayan Women's Quest for a Gendered Spirituality

Morna Macleod

Over the last decade (1996–2006), there has been a growing tendency among indigenous women in Guatemala to deepen their sense of dignity and self-worth, and promote gender equity through Mayan cosmovision or worldview. Cosmovision comprises cultural values and beliefs, concepts of time, space and order, spirituality and practices in which human beings, every element of nature, the universe and the cosmos are all interconnected and therefore affect one another, thus opposing the prevailing western assumption of the centrality of human beings and their belief in dominating nature. This does not mean that all indigenous people today still share this worldview: the extent of Guatemalan Mayans being "culturally shaped" by cosmovision depends on a complex mix of factors, including their varying contact with modernity, the handing down and practice of ancestral knowledge, and customs in their families,[1] and their desire or not to reclaim culture.[2] Resignifying the values or principles of complementarity, duality, and equilibrium has been a way chosen by indigenous women of enhancing their empowerment, and for struggling for equitable relations between men and women. It consists in a strategy rooted in—rather than contesting—Mayan culture, philosophy, and cosmovision.

Whereas feminism has tended to regard culture as the main cause of women's subordination,[3] through which practices against women's well-being and rights are legitimized and naturalized, many Mayan women see culture and cosmovision as sites of resistance and liberation,[4] or, as members of the Mayan movement put it, a horizon to *"Build a future for our Past."*[5] However, Latin American indigenous movement appeals to cosmovision and the philosophical concepts of duality, complementarity, and equilibrium can discursively conceal unequal power relations between men and women; and indeed these movement claims are often pitted against feminism and gender analysis. The few feminists who have addressed the term "complementarity" conclude that the concept does not redress the issue of gender inequity, that is, while men occupy public spaces and leadership roles, women hold "complementary" roles in the private sphere of the household.[6] However, a growing number of Mayan women—with different levels of appropriation of international human rights and women's rights discourse and acceptance of gender analysis—are resignifying these cosmogonic precepts. In so doing, they not only urge Mayan men to "walk the talk" and put these principles into practice, but they also decenter feminist discourses and demands, by insisting on the recognition of difference and diversity amongst women, and questioning their narrow and regulatory definitions of culture.[7] While cosmogonic discourse has great resonance and an increasing appeal to many Mayan women, some are more wary, cautioning that though it sounds wonderful in theory, it has little to do with everyday lived experience.

Thus, the meanings of complementarity and duality are contested and negotiated in the Mayan movement in Guatemala, often through regulatory and emancipatory discourses,[8] with a range of intermediate positions, giving rise to what Carrasco—in the introduction to the present volume calls *"the creative possibilities of incomplete, open-ended contact zones and narratives."* In recent years, Mayan women in particular are gaining strength and recognition in their emancipatory reading and positioning of this discourse, and are beginning to permeate international women's movements, as the following declaration of the International Indigenous Women's Forum at the Association of Women in Development's (AWID) meeting in Bangkok (October 2005) suggests:

> *We cannot work for changes in gender inequality in our communities if we do not incorporate the dual vision of indigenous cosmovision, where men and women are complementary. . . . As indigenous women are recognized in our communities as the basis for preserving the cultural and social patrimony of our peoples, it is important that our demands to improve our situation take on the cultural aspects which give meaning to our collective identity.*
>
> *The redefining of feminism by indigenous women seeks to break with the racist and discriminatory legacy of traditional feminism, which does not take into consideration the specific needs of indigenous women (as well as other*

*traditionally excluded ethnic groups). Traditional feminism has set out a sys-
tem of centre and periphery, and indigenous, black, poor women have always
been on the margins; we have had to accept the ideas and ways of conceiving feminist struggle with their homogenizing and discriminating bias; their
analysis establishes hidden power relations and hierarchies within the feminist movement which exclude indigenous women.* (International Indigenous
Women's Forum, Bangkok, October 2005: 4–5, my translation)

This does not mean that feminists from different parts of the world accept and agree with the views expressed by indigenous women during the international conference in Thailand, but it does mean that indigenous women
are gradually having more voice in global women's movements, and are increasingly able to publicly articulate their grievances as well as their specific
demands and claims.

In this chapter, after first exploring the concepts of complementarity,
duality, and equilibrium in philosophical and spiritual terms, I set out—
through interviews with and articles written by organized Mayan women—to
understand how different Mayan women understand these concepts, how
they relate them to their own lives, and to their visions of gender equity and
social transformation.[9] Self-representation and the political-cultural production of meaning, ideas and demands by Mayan women are central to this
aim, although I recognize the role I play and the risks of (mis)translation.[10]
By creating "dialogue and debate" between different Mayan women, I seek to
draw out some of the more contentious issues, as well as highlight the similarities and differences these concepts hold, particularly in view to emancipatory strategies toward social justice and gender equity. The essay draws
on my experience of collaboration with the Mayan movement in Guatemala
as a nonindigenous foreign woman, first as an international aid agency field
representative, trying to work—in consultation with its indigenous counter-
parts—from an indigenous perspective; from an ongoing process over many
years of sharing with and learning from Mayan friends and mentors; and
more recently, in the research work for my doctoral thesis, "*Cultural-Political
Struggles and Mayan Self-Representation in Guatemala.*"

THE COSMOGONIC PRINCIPLES OF DUALITY, COMPLEMENTARITY, AND EQUILIBRIUM

There seems to be a common need as well as a real problem in translat-
ing Mayan hermeneutics into western thought and interpreting meaning, as
the following rather pat attempt illustrates: "*These concepts can rather sim-
plistically be defined accordingly: complementarity signifies that all people, including men and women, are an important part of the cosmos; duality implies*

that everything in the cosmos has two sides, or presents positive or negative energies; equilibrium refers to the harmony between all elements and their energy." The following description of complementarity is even more problematic: "*that men and women are different, have complementary roles and that it is indeed this difference and complementarity that brings balance and harmony into society.*"[11] The need for precise and clearly defined explanations—and the corollary criticism leveled at Mayans as to their inability to successfully convey meaning, and to individually analyze or describe "complementarity, duality, and equilibrium" as separate, discrete concepts—would appear at odds with a less verbal apprehension of spirituality, and such efforts tend to render flat, rigid, and nonmalleable readings of concepts that defy translation.[12]

Another rather surprising initiative comes from a group of European anthropologists who set out to "*define and perhaps resolve, some of the problems which arise in the use of the notion of complementarity*" (Perrin and Perruchon, editors, 1997: 7), basing themselves on what has been written on the subject by social anthropologists, without asking indigenous intellectuals how they perceive and understand the concept.[13] On the other hand, attempts by Mayans to translate these complex notions into Spanish (here retranslated into English) can prove quite obscure to a western audience. These difficulties are not simply due to language differences, but to trying to span different epistemologies and worldviews.

Doña Virginia Ajxup and her husband Juan Zapil, Maya K'iche' spiritual guides living in Guatemala City, attempt to bring Mayan cosmovision to life both through their practice of Mayan spirituality—ceremonies, divination with the *Tz'ite,*'[14] and living according to Mayan values and principles—as well as by nurturing their own learning processes by accompanying and learning from spiritual guides in communities, whose longstanding practice and millenary knowledge has been handed down from generation to generation.[15] They also study the written literature on the subject and promote the teaching of Mayan cosmovision. Doña Virginia writes:

Each person is an essential being with his or her own dynamism. Each person is dependent on time and space, and exists in relation to others, sharing together common experiences. These experiences permit us to grow and develop our true Countenance and Heart, the primary basis of our individual identity. A person is also duality and complement. Our hearts preserve and refine knowledge . . . Our grandmothers and grandfathers, mothers and fathers created concepts which enhance the quality of life and of society, capturing the essence of life's energies, the environment's elements. Father sun summons the dawn and takes part in the intricacies of biological dynamics with his clarity (daylight). Mother moon looks after the darkness, the tranquility and complexity of the night. The understanding of new concepts regarding the profile of humanity in all its specificities emanates from her. Thus harmony provides a basis for new ideas in the social fabric woven by the daughters and sons of time. They live together amid their differences, understanding the complementary and dual nature of being. Through this process, desirable norms are derived from the experience of great events. These are handed down with the quality of representation and transcendence to the new generations. (Ajxup, 2003: 68, 69–70)

Through her description, Doña Virginia draws out the interconnections between nature, human beings and the cosmos, and a particular sense of time—which at once contains permanence and change—through the handing down of experience and wisdom from generation to generation. In her writing, she continually makes reference to the practice of her Mayan ancestors in observing nature and the stars, as the main source on which Mayan wisdom is based and recorded in glyphs and codices.[16] She also refers to the duality of "countenance" and "heart";[17] Sylvia Marcos notes that for indigenous peoples, the heart *"is the seat of the highest intellectual activities. Memory and reason reside in it. The heart is not a reference to feelings and love; it is the origin of life"* (Marcos, 2005: 91).

Don Juan, presently doing a degree in linguistics, gives an insight into the interconnected nature of the cosmovision, through his analysis of language. He takes the example of *kotz'i'j*, the Maya K'iche' word for flower, to illustrate the interconnections between nature, cosmos and human beings:

- ***Kotz'i'j*** = *flower*
- ***Kotz'i'jaal*** = *the nature of flowering*
- ***Kotz'i'jab'al*** = *the place where Mayan ceremonies are held*
- ***Kotz'i'janeem o Kotz'i'janik*** = *the flowering of plants, previous to their reproduction; human sexual relations*
- ***Kotz'ijab'alil q'ij*** = *the day to philosophize*
- ***Kotz'i'jal riij, Kotz'i'jal uwach*** = *the terms used to refer to mothers and fathers who live in the same house as their married children*
- ***Kotz'i'jam raqan uq'ab'*** = *the term used to refer to persons chosen to carry out an important authority role in the community*
- ***Kotz'i'janinaq upam ub'e upam ujook*** = *said of persons who have achieved a life of plenitude and harmony in their family, society and community*
- ***Kotz'i'jaxik*** = *the act of decorating a place for a special activity* (Zapil, 2006)

This gives a clear insight into the crossovers and linkages between nature and human beings, nature, culture and intellect, and the way authority and respect are envisaged and conveyed in metaphors drawing upon nature.

Complementarity, duality, and equilibrium, each in their way, all refer to this interconnection; "*complementarity*," writes Maya Poqomam María Estela Jocón, "*refers to the interrelation between environment and being (physical, cosmogonic and spiritual); men and women; it cannot be reduced to the idea of sexual complement, but rather refers to a wider scope of exchange and interrelation between animals, human beings, the cosmos, nature and energy*" (Jocón, 2005: 36). The idea of interconnection or intersubjectivity as Lenkersdorf calls it (1999),[18] is expressed in the principles of *kulaj* and *tzaqat*, explained by Maya Kaqchikel Juana Batzibal: "*I am you and you are me. This also means: I am your mirror and you are my mirror. It is a fundamental principle to maintain respect for our personal identities in view to the collective identity. As I respect the identity of my brother, so too, he will respect my identity. Furthermore, the exercise of my freedom is equally conditioned to others' freedom*" (Batzibal, 2003: 28). Doña Virginia Ajxup explains that *kulaj tz'aqat*—meaning duality and complement—is the principle of life, that is, all life is based on the principle of dual and differing energies (e-mail correspondence June 2007). Duality is the integration and relational articulation between opposites as a life-giving and life-conserving principle: "*Feminine and masculine energies are both necessary to be able to live, to generate life, this is understood as 'kulaj' and 'tz'aqat' in K'iche.' The two energies are necessary, it is the 'other I' that seeks the other. When one says 'kulaj', one is asking 'have you found your other countenance? Or your other 'I' necessary in order to prosper; both male and female are necessary for nature and for persons*"[19] (Interview, July 2003). Finally, equilibrium "*implies equality, equity and harmony or well-being of the cosmos. The lived experience of equilibrium permits equal opportunities to live, love, feel, create, debate, contribute, work*" (Jocón, op. cit.: 37).

When I mentioned to María Estela Jocón that some feminists criticize the idea of complementarity as they consider it regulatory not only socially but in terms of sexuality (permitting only heterosexual married couples), and thus excluding and actively invisibilizing single mothers, single men and women, gay and lesbian couples, María Estela explained that duality and complementarity do not just refer to, but rather go beyond relationships between men and women:

Duality refers to the way elements interrelate and cannot exist without the other. If we are speaking of nature, we talk about the sun and the moon, the sky and the earth, water and fire; everything in terms of two, men and women. But I cannot say that single mothers don't partake of duality; they are incomplete as no one is complete, that would imply that we are all perfect, and we're not. Because if you were complete, you wouldn't need this interview, nor your other interviews. Why? Because if I were self-sufficient, I would be able to write the document on my own; but I need help, that's the

*complement, that's the relation. But the relation is two-way, because you are
contributing with your questions, and I am contributing with my answers.
That is complementarity.* (Interview, July 2003)

In this sense, the concept of complementarity is less regulatory than
feminists often believe, although this is not to deny that single mothers,
homosexuality, and promiscuity are often censured, and indeed complementarity can be mobilized with a regulatory bias. It is also difficult to disen-
tangle Mayan values from moral values arising from the church, the state,
and community life, as these are not pure and discrete sets of principles,
reproduced in a vacuum. However, indigenous people are understandably
incensed when critics go to the opposite extreme denying difference (that is,
indigenous epistemologies and hermeneutics), or considering that everyone
is hybrid or *mestizo* (see numerous newspaper columns by Mario Roberto
Morales, Siglo Veintiuno, especially 1996–1997, Guatemala).[20] Indigenous
movement reaction to this homogenizing inclusion into modernity stimulates
strategic essentialism and resistance positioning (Macleod, 2006).

COMPLEMENTARITY, DUALITY, AND EQUILIBRIUM IN MAYAN WOMEN'S LIVES

During the interviews I held with Mayan women one of the things
that struck me time and again was that rather than eliciting theoretical explanations when I asked about complementarity, duality, and equilibrium,
the women always answered by relating them to specific experiences in
their own lives, often referring to their grandparents and particularly to their
grandmothers. As Marta Juana López says: "*Spirituality is knowledge gained
from experience, it is practice, it is human, it refers to values. It is more about
action: 'more verb and less noun.' It implies being congruent between discourse
and practice*" (Interview, December 2004). The importance placed on the
spoken word, on doing what you preach and gaining moral authority through
setting the example, suggests that the gap between "discourse" and "practice" is particularly deplorable for Mayan women and men.

Complementarity can refer specifically to what women and men do, but
it cannot be reduced to gender roles. Marta Juana López, thinking back to
her own childhood, considers that the different roles assigned to boys and
girls did not imply a lack of equality, whereas in other cases, it very much
does. The following two texts show these differences:

*When I analyze my childhood experience, my parents would always say to us:
"girls have to do this, but boys also have to do the other" both in domestic and
social roles. A girl needs to be more modest, more careful, but boys need to*

respect girls highly. We had very specific chores, but we also had joint tasks. I had to wash the dishes, but my brother had to sweep the patio. My brother had to feed the horses, I had to feed the pigs and chickens, because this was less dangerous than feeding the horses as they could kick, boys are better trained for this and can run faster. Often, when my brother finished first, he would help me, we negotiated. I didn't feel uncomfortable, they were domestic chores, perhaps mine involved more time, but in any case, we'd help each other out. And we were treated as equals in everything to do with education and health. In other families we knew it was the same. Families were more interested in constructing the identity of "being a woman" or "being a man," but I don't think this is happening any more, which is worrying. This was the family context . . . but there was also school, and school is patriarchal and racist. And then, the role of the church is also important: school/church is a secondary space of social relation, and they are very strong, very determining. (Interview with Marta Juana López, op. cit.)

Marta Juana recognizes the difference between women's and men's roles, but in her own experience considers that the inequality in gender arises from socializing outside the home; other professional Mayan women I interviewed felt the same way.[21] However, Lucía Willis's experience was quite different:

From adolescence on, I was taught my role as a woman. This included having household responsibilities, looking after our livestock and crops, gathering firewood, fetching water, making tortillas [corn pancakes], washing, cooking, and seeking the strength to do all this with enthusiasm. I was also taught the proper way to act and speak to people and the right way of doing things. If a woman does not adhere to these codes, she gives herself a bad image. What I found hard to accept was that my brother was free to go out, to work and play, and he never had to do household chores. Sometimes we would go out together to sell home grown fruit and vegetables.

My mother did not take a very broad view of the usefulness of me receiving a formal education. For her it sufficed that I learn my signature and to read and write. This way people would not take advantage of me, which is often the case when one is illiterate. She did not think that a school education would be useful to me, but only to my brother, as being a man he would seek work outside the home. In practice, we as women are more prepared, as we learn to do women and men's work. From that time on, I was aware of the different access men and women had to education. (Willis Paau, 2002: 85–86)

Whereas Marta Juana and Lucía refer to gender roles when talking about complementarity, Ixtz'ulu' Elsa Son relates it to the bicultural formation and education she received from her parents. Asking what complementarity means to her, she answered:

*I don't know if my lived experience helps. My father only attended the first year of primary school; he practically taught himself to read and write. I have no idea whether my grandfather went to school, but he did write and speak Spanish; my great-grandfather was the municipal council secretary. So there were two or three generations in which the grandfathers spoke Spanish and knew how to write . . . My mother is monolingual and illiterate. I don't know whether they made an agreement to do this, I've never had the curiosity to ask, but my father took charge of us in terms of reading, in [developing] our intellect . . . my mother—whether consciously or unconsciously I'm not sure—was the "guardian of culture"[22] we could call it, in my family. By this I am not saying that this is the case in all families, I am speaking about **my** family. Maya Kaqchikel as a language, spirituality and more material expressions of culture such as weaving, and the explanation of woven designs, care for Mayan culture, these were all given to us by my mother.*

My father helped us to face the outside world which was unlike our Mayan world, that was his emphasis. He sent us to school—we're five, one brother and four sisters, with no difference between male and female siblings; and he would say: "You must act in this manner, as school is somewhat different." For example, we would kiss our grandparents' hand as that is a sign of respect; we learned to never kiss a "ladino's"[23] hand; he taught us that it was different with ladinos, it wasn't a question of not respecting them, but rather a different way of expressing it, saying "good-day" was different . . . In a way, I feel my father took charge of the intercultural part, intercultural education, whereas my mother strengthened our Mayan culture; as I say, I don't know whether this was a conscious decision or agreement or not, but that's the way it was. (Interview, 2003)

But "complementarity" is not only found in women's childhoods. Amalia Velásquez speaks of her courtship and marriage with Mayan movement activist and intellectual Máximo Ba, illustrating the way many intellectual and professional Mayans living in cities are reclaiming culture and living Mayan spirituality:

Complementarity means, well, I will tell you about it from my experience, because that is the way I understand it. When Max and I started our relationship, we first made consultations to see if we were compatible, if Max would be able to understand me, with my weaknesses, my defects and my virtues, and whether I would be able to understand him, as he is, with his negative aspects and his values. We made this consultation with elders, with the great uncles and forefathers . . . I went to Max's house and learned of many things, about what he is, what he has done and not done; his parents were very clear: "You will be going with our son, he has his defects but he also has his virtues." Then one asks: "Do we suit each other or not?" The other thing is to check

*whether our "nawales"[24] are compatible; and if they are not, there is a way of
solving this through ceremonies, giving offerings to the hills, as hills have to
do with resolving this kind of conflict; one can't just go anywhere, as other
places are used in other ways and have different kinds of spirit. As a result, we
embarked on our path as a couple. We even consulted my deceased parents;
we held nine ceremonies to reach them, on the fourth they responded. All of
this is complementarity.*

*So for me, complementarity doesn't just mean that men are breadwinners,
but rather that both of us can do housework, that we are satisfied in our
professional careers, that we give service to the community, and that we also
attend our family. Because I can't conceive of complementarity if a woman
is only in the office and neglects her children, her home, her family. Nor a
man who spends all his time out of the house, in the office . . . So there's a
responsibility for both men and women to keep this equilibrium, this is what
equilibrium means to me.* (Interview, July 2003)

Amalia eloquently conveys the way in which reclaiming culture entails
returning to community practices and at the same time as giving them new
nuances of meaning and significance. Her understanding of complementarity,
duality, and equilibrium is a far cry from a regulatory discourse and pressure
for women to remain in the home, although she also defends the importance
of the home and children. Her vision is forward looking and transformational,
while at once reclaiming community customs and practices of spirituality, as
well as becoming a professional and partaking of modernity.

COMPLEMENTARITY, DUALITY AND EQUILIBRIUM: REGULATORY OR EMANCIPATORY FRAMES?

The above contributions by Mayan women convey the way Mayan values can be a source of inspiration for social transformation. One of the problems is that not everyone who proclaims these principles puts them into
practice in their own lives; nor does everyone conceive of them in the same
way, as many men and even women often have a regulatory set vision about
how women should act, what they should and should not do. Then, too, if
the gap between the ideal vision and reality is too great, the interconnections
between the two and strategies to breach the divide may simply not be apparent. This has led organizations like the Kaqla women's group to state:

*Identity and cosmovision are fundamental issues for the Mayan women of
Kaqla. . . and amongst us we have diverse positions, opinions and feelings
about them. However, many of us have been modifying or clarifying our
respective positions after stopping to reflect upon our daily life experience*

rather than our discourse . . . For most of us, what is said about cosmovision is so utopian that it doesn't help us to ensure a greater quality of life, to relate to people better and to organize. This is why there continues to be inequity between men and women in so many indigenous organizations, because they say we have the same rights, but when it comes down to who manages the money, who decides when and how it will be spent, the answer is always the men. (Kaqla, 2004: 35 and 37)

Others are skeptical. Maya K'iche' Irma Alicia Velásquez Nimatuj considers that the concepts of complementarity, duality, and equilibrium have been appropriated and controlled by men in discourse which naturalizes and invisibilizes unequal power relations between men and women:

In my opinion, it is a discursive concept that remains discourse, it doesn't work in practice. Mayan men in their conferences—not so much now as a few years' back—used to use it as a political banner. They'd talk of the relations between men and women in Mayan communities as complementary, night-and-day, and they would give a series of examples. But in reality, it wasn't so, in reality, "complementarity" meant oppression, it meant that only men could go out, participate politically, speak in public, that is, occupy public spaces, whereas women had to stay in the private sphere and occupy a few economic spaces, but that was it. I'll give you a concrete example. In the case of Quetzaltenango, there are very few K'iche' women who have a national presence, the majority are men. Rather, we find that at a certain age, control is exerted on women to get married, husbands also exert control over women, as do parents-in-law and the community itself, as it is not well regarded that a married woman leaves her home, travels, speaks in public, or enters the public sphere. There are many restrictions. I have heard K'iche' women who have held public office as town councilors tell of their dramatic experiences of repression, in the sense that their ideas are not taken seriously, their proposals looked down upon or simply ignored, jokes made at their expense, their ideas laughed at. I would say it is highly complex, difficult. From the outside, it would appear that complementarity exists and it sounds good as a discourse, but internally, it's not like that.

For me, the concept of complementarity in Guatemala has been used to maintain the oppression of Mayan women. That is how it has been up to now, it's only recently that this oppression is being questioned in the works of Amanda Pop, in the works of Emma Chirix and other (Mayan) women, they have questioned and deconstructed this discourse. Now one rarely hears men talking publicly about complementarity; they are far more measured in what they say; and on the contrary, recently I have heard many more women than men defending the concept of complementarity. We need to understand how women are thinking about it. If it is only the men

*who talk about complementarity, I'd have my serious doubts, but if women
are promoting the concept, it should be taken on board. I would say that
complementarity is something yet to be constructed, in principle I see it as
something negative, but if it's a project in construction I could accept it.
But the problem is that men assume it's a given, and that is simply not the
case. If we see it as something in construction, something which will start
taking place, that's fine, let's create it. And it should be women who say
how they want complementarity to be, and that men put it into practice.
But if men are going to talk about it when women—their partners, their
daughters, their relatives—live in situations of severe oppression, then no.
Or, for example, if a male leader can have (relationships with) six women,
if that's complementarity, then I cannot accept it, I question it.* (Interview,
July 2003)

Appealing discursively to complementarity in order to cover up injus-
tice produces indignation in many.[25] Thus, Mayan women place great emphasis on discerning between the philosophical precepts of cosmovision
and the way it is—or is not—put into practice and lived. Maya Kaqchikel
Emma Chirix questions the way the concept of duality is often invoked in
abstract, ethereal terms, but what do these concepts mean for everyday
life? Emma exemplifies the ways the concept could apply to day-to-day
living:

*For me the word duality implies two: "me with you and you with me" . . .
I am always on about domestic chores. Why is duality not spoken about
when it comes to household tasks? Why do these tend to weigh inordi-
nately on women? Women have so many chores that they are unable to
go out. So if we are talking about duality in terms of gender relations,
I support duality when it comes to household chores, so that both men
and women assume joint responsibility. I say: duality in household chores
and in raising our sons and daughters. Why is duality never mentioned in
this context? Duality usually refers to the very mythical, the very mysti-
cal. Mayan cosmovision has a philosophy, I agree with its philosophy, but
when it comes to practice, that's where I say it's not on. I think the philosophy needs to be reviewed as well. Etymologically, what can we say about
duality? We can decide what duality is going to mean to us women at
this given moment in time . . . I say it's not right that generally it's men,
and particularly leaders, who tell us that "it has to be like this," "it should
be so." I say those dictates are not created by culture, they're an imposition, it's a question of power relations. So let's think about it, let's discuss
it, if we want to build a more democratic culture, let's talk about it . . .
but not on the basis of imposition and on the back of power relations,
I don't agree with that.* (Interview, July 2003)

CRITICIZING SEXISM WITHOUT DISQUALIFYING COSMOVISION

Ixtz'ulu' Elsa Son and Marta Juana López agree with Emma Chirix's criticism of the common gap between men's philosophical discourse and sexist practice. However, the way Mayan culture and cosmovision are often dismissed and disqualified on the grounds of sexism bothers them intensely. Here, it is not a question of divided loyalties, but rather a criticism they make of the way other people—particularly feminists and aid agencies—conflate sexist attitudes with culture, and as such, they feel it sets up a trap that is easy to fall into. In this context, one can understand it when Marta Juana says that *"Mayan men are sexist because they are men, not because they are Mayan."* Ixtz'ulu' Elsa Son argues this point in greater depth:

> So one thing is cosmovision and quite another is putting cosmovision into practice. [Mayan men] shielding themselves by saying that in Mayan cosmovision there is duality and complementarity, thus arguing that machismo doesn't exist, this should not be so and is something I cannot validate ... How can there be complementarity if there is sexism? But then the attack comes, that "Mayan culture is worthless because of men's attitudes, Mayan men are currently sexist, and therefore Mayan culture is worthless" ... I can't share this view, even though sexist positions and attitudes do exist amongst Mayan men. (Interview, July 2003)

In a context where indigenous culture has historically been and continues to be belittled and invisibilized, it is understandable that Mayan women are particularly sensitive to nonindigenous feminist criticism of indigenous culture. Then, too, the feminist tendency to situate gender roles in culture, and to reduce culture to gender relations and expressions, places indigenous women in a double bind, having to opt between gender equity or culture; this is reminiscent of Homa Hoodfar's (1993) grievance of western feminists' attitudes towards Muslim women.[26] This is clearly a false dichotomy, as by resignifying and promoting the concepts of complementarity, duality, and equilibrium, these pioneer Mayan women are reclaiming culture, but also opening up meanings, venues, and strategies to bridge theory and practice, discourse and the daily lives of Mayan women, fostering more equitable relations with men—fathers, husbands, brothers, sons, and colleagues—and also with other women.

It is interesting that most of the Mayan women I interviewed spoke more about complementarity and duality, and less about equilibrium. A notable exception was Ana María Rodríguez, a Maya Mam leader of Madre Tierra, an organization of mainly indigenous women refugees (in the south of Mexico) who returned to Guatemala at the end of the 1990s. Ana María sees equilibrium as the pivotal force between a critique of inequitable power relations between men and women, and her respect for culture, whilst at once recognizing that exile in Mexico had a weakening effect on cultural practices and ties. However, by naming power relations and many men's resistance to change, indigenous women like Ana María receive regulatory pressure not only from men but often women who try to dissuade them from talking about gender equity:[27]

> There are Mayan men "compañeros" who show more integrity and have kept their cultural principles in maintaining respect for women; this is very valuable and it does exist, but it is not the case of the majority of men. I would venture to say that a lot of these values have been lost, for example, amongst the refugee population, both among men and women. There are relations of power, and to change this I have to affect that order to achieve equilibrium. First I have to analyze the imposition of inequality that I am living, to be aware of my condition both as a woman and as being indigenous. If I understand my situation and make my partner understand that his relation of power over us as women is not ideal, is not healthy, that we cannot go on living in these conditions, then this brings his power into question and that's when conflict begins . . . Cosmovision doesn't mean that men should impose (their power) on women, but rather that there should be a balance, there should be complementarity. However, in some practices there is complementarity, but also subordination . . . men doing this and women staying at home, subordinated; here there is no equilibrium, the balance is broken, as is the order established by our values and principles.
>
> . . . I do think that Mayan men still hold our values and our customs, but they are also influenced by sexist culture which is everywhere and permeates all of society. Once a Mayan leader warned us: "Watch out, you are grabbing hold of western values and you're forcing them onto Mayan culture, be careful, because this is going to divide us, and it will destroy families." This is what a Mayan leader said to us when we were speaking about gender; he's from one of the many expressions of the Mayan movement, not everyone thinks like him.
>
> I realized that for this indigenous leader, complementarity meant that women should assume "their role," and if we didn't, we were to blame for family conflict. (According to him), that is why there are so many cases of divorce, so many couples separating, and that we were assaulting family harmony and unity; that is the way a lot of them reason. I also think that a lot of our Mayan male companions don't give much time to analyzing gender, that's the main point for me, because they're so focused on ethnic equity, they only keep to ethnic and cultural struggle, that's where they leave off. So men need to open up and analyze the significance of gender equity. We can't build a (historical) Mayan project without taking into account the gender inequality that currently permeates our people . . . I believe we have to find a focus where women aren't discriminated against, nor men either, that we be equal,

and for there to be balance. We as women are seeking equilibrium, that's what we want. (Interview, July 2003)

Whereas feminists conflate sexism and Mayan culture, Mayan men, like the leader mentioned by Ana María, conflate analysis and criticism of sexist attitudes with western feminism, thus foreclosing the space for Mayan women to criticize subordination and violence against women. Again, Mayan women find themselves in a double bind, as they are often criticized for voicing their criticism, as being disloyal and divisive to indigenous peoples and causes. However, despite these problems, indigenous women are increasingly challenging sexist attitudes, although they frequently choose their spaces to do so, often privileging internal indigenous spaces, but keeping a united front to the outside.

FINAL REFLECTIONS

Through the voices of different Mayan women, it is clear that while the concepts of complementarity, duality, and equilibrium constitute a contested terrain, they also provide an opportunity for indigenous women to at once claim culture and push for gender equity. None of the women I have interviewed or whose publications I have read reject these values per se, but rather are critical of the use they are sometimes given, and the way they can be mobilized to invisibilize or negate gender inequity. Gender analysis tends to raise uncomfortable questions not just about the frequent breach between discourse and practice, or what the discourse can and should mean in practical terms; it also raises issues of power differentials and naturalized oppression; this can be threatening not just to Mayan men, but also to Mayan women. Then, too, cultural difference can also be threatening to nonindigenous people, particularly when ethnocentric or racist assumptions are questioned; and indigenous people tend to close ranks against what they perceive as racist attacks. This puts the issue of positionality at the fore of the debate, as Mayan women with longstanding commitment to gender equity who critique sexism may close ranks with the same men they criticize if they feel that their culture is being dismissed or disqualified, or if they feel an imposition to adopt the other's vision, whether the other is an aid agency, a feminist organization, an academic, a ladino, mestizo, or foreigner.

Thus, many Mayan women tend to close ranks with Mayan men when faced with skepticism from others—particularly, but not only ladinos—who dismiss Mayan culture as being idealized by the Mayan movement, and negate indigenous cosmovision on the grounds that everyone has been "touched" or shaped by modernity. This is countered with an equally dismissive rejection by many Mayans declaring they do not want to be "contaminated" by ladino culture. This highlights the difficulties that abound in a society as highly racialized as the Guatemalan one is; there are few spaces and conditions for serene reflection and debate, as both Mayans and ladinos tend to act defensively. Thus, even though many Mayan women recognize and deplore male sexism, the race/culture cleavages tend to outweigh gender considerations, and in public Mayan women tend to put race and culture first and side with Mayan men.

Another complex issue surrounding complementarity, duality, and equilibrium—apart from the frequent gaps between discourse and practice—is the meaning of the concepts themselves. Epistemologically, these values span very different terrains, from the philosophical and even esoteric domain that Doña Virginia and Don Juan seek to promote and make accessible to Mayan women and men—as well as to nonindigenous people—to more mundane, everyday issues such as gender roles, who looks after the children and who washes the dishes. The working out of strategies to bridge these very different dimensions is an ongoing challenge, particularly as the former is centered more around deepening knowledge and valuing the philosophical dimensions of cosmovision, while the latter resides in the analysis of power and conflict.

This has a parallel in the seemingly unbridgeable gap between academic frames, for example, between Carlos Lenkersdorf's (1999) hemeneutical approach and the more common and academically accepted historical constructionism.[28] However, I consider this to be yet another false dichotomy; researchers working with indigenous peoples and culture need to take on board their worldviews and the epistemological challenges these present to academia (that is, overcome a frequent ethnocentric western bias), whilst power relations, oppression, and subordination in the daily lives of indigenous peoples are also a reality needing to be broached both academically and in daily life. The way in which many Mayan women today in Guatemala are looking to their roots, seeking clues and guidance from their ancestral culture, and resemanticizing these concepts to make them relevant to present day reality constitute powerful means in the reclaiming culture while simultaneously pushing for gender equity. These Mayan women are setting a pathbreaking example conceptually, by decentering western approaches to gender equality and providing innovative strategies for addressing gender issues; they also show immense bravery in standing up to double binds, pressure, and censure from different flanks and multiple others.

Notes

1. For example, a Mayan professional will have a great deal of exposure to modernity, having passed through the entire education system; and by university level, she will be in absolute minority amongst her nonindigenous classmates

and professors. However, if she comes from a municipality and a family where Mayan culture and practices are still strong, and holds a commitment to maintaining and strengthening indigenous culture in the face of assimilation, she will have a stronger sense of and commitment to her cultural identity than, for example, a bonded-laborer whose family has been tied to a large coffee estate or *finca* for generations, and whose immediate interests and pressing needs are focused on basic survival.

2. Cultural reclamation does not mean a "return to an idyllic past," but rather the way in which the knowledge, wisdom, and cultural pride of Mayan civilization is recovered to inform the present and future of today's living Mayans. Cosmovision has a particularly strong appeal in a country like Guatemala, emerging from a 36-year internal armed conflict, in which indigenous people and the cultural difference they represented were the primary targets of extermination and ethnocide.

3. In this article, I situate oppression and asymmetric power relations in **ideology** rather than culture: "*Ideology, according to the latent conception, is a system of representations which conceal and mislead and which, in so doing, serves to sustain relations of domination*" (Thompson, 1990:55). Thus, ideology permeates all spheres of life, including the cultural, social, political, economic, and psychological.

4. See Egla Judith Martínez, 2004, unpublished work.

5. *Building a Future for Our Past: The Rights of the Mayan People and the Peace Process* is the name of a book published by the Council of Mayan Organizations in Guatemala (COMG) in 1995. All translations from Spanish are my own, except when otherwise stated.

6. See Tania Palencia, 1999, and Angela Meentzen, 2000.

7. See Rosalva Aída Hernández Castillo, 2001.

8. See Boaventura de Sousa Santos, 2005.

9. The Mayan movement is not a discrete umbrella organization with registered filiations; rather, I understand it as a loose grouping of heterogeneous NGOs and mass organizations, intellectuals, grassroots community groups, and collective organizing around indigenous claims. The interviews with Mayan women (carried out for my doctorate thesis) do not include indigenous women in *mestiza*-based feminist organizations; all have in common their commitment to equity in gender relations, to equal conditions and opportunities, and the dignifying and empowerment of women, though the way to achieve this, and what it actually means, can differ. I also opted to carry out my research work with what Gramsci calls "organic intellectuals," both professionals and leaders, who are extremely clear and articulate about their ideas and positions.

10. Ruth Bejar explains her role in writing up and publishing the life history of Esperanza, "*As the one who is no longer just expanding her capacities to listen but sitting here snipping and snipping at the* historias *Esperanza told me, only to sew them back into this book as a life history, I fear I am somehow cutting out Esperanza's tongue. Yet when I am done cutting out her tongue, I will patch together*

a new tongue for her, an odd tongue that is neither English nor Spanish, but the language of a translated woman. Esperanza will talk in this book in a way she never talked before" (Bejar, 1993:19).

11. I have opted to keep the authorship of these quotes anonymous, as they are not published documents; my intention in citing them is to highlight the difficulties in pinning down meaning, running the risk of reductionism and/or meaning becoming lost in translation.

12. In the numerous Mayan ceremonies I have attended, I have opted to not situate myself in the role of anthropological participant observer, nor have I tried to intellectually analyze what goes on, as I understand that these are not appropriate means or tools for comprehension. Rather, I intuit that Mayan ceremonies are an invitation to open ourselves to feeling and perceiving, to apprehend the experience of fire and burning of aromatic offerings (candles, sugar, resins, incense, flower petals, alcohol, sesame seeds); and of simply partaking in ceremony together with the spiritual guides and other participants. This evidently makes academic analysis difficult.

13. The book *Complementarity between Men and Women, Gender Relations from an Amerindian Perspective* (in Spanish), edited by the well-known indigenous publishing house Abya-Yala in Ecuador, led many of us to scoop it up, thinking that it promised an innovative insight into the Ecuadorean indigenous movement's take on such issues, rather than European experts' conclusions. This brings into question the issues of representation and who decides what constitutes an Amerindian perspective. This is not to say that nonindigenous people cannot write about indigenous issues, but some level of consultation with—rather than studying of—indigenous people would seem to be not only desirable, but necessary.

14. *Tz'ite'* are usually small red beans used for divination, similar to the sticks or coins used for consulting the I Ching. For a comprehensive study of Mayan divination see Barbara Tedlock's *Time and the Highland Maya* (1982).

15. Rather than a "fixed essence," millenary knowledge communicated through oral tradition imperceptibly changes whilst remaining (*cambiar permaneciendo*), adapting to changing world conditions. On another note, with the spreading of Catholicism, Protestantism to a lesser degree and the subsequent rise of Evangelical sects, spiritual guides had to go underground, as their spiritual practices were and still often are regarded as witchcraft; only in recent years has the practice of Mayan spirituality become more open. The intolerance shown by Christian institutions is bitterly remembered by many spiritual guides and members of the Mayan movement; others have no problem in combining their practice of Catholicism or Evangelism with their Mayan spirituality, whilst still others do so in secret, given their respective churches' reprimands. A spiritual guide I knew, though a member of an Evangelical sect, received the knowledge of the Mayan sacred text "Popol Vuj" through a series of dreams. Dreaming has particular significance in indigenous worldviews, spanning different levels or dimensions of consciousness.

16. Members of the Mayan movement are fascinated with the study of ancient texts—often hieroglyphs sculpted on statues and buildings in sacred sites and scrolls of parchment, as in the Dresden, Madrid, and Paris codices; international epigraphy experts such a Linda Schele, Nikolai Grube, and the Guatemalan Federico Fahsen have supported them in their search to reclaim Mayan history, and Kay Warren, amongst others, in the study of the sacred writings of the Popol Vuj and Annals of the Kaqchikels. See Warren (1996).

17. To illustrate these two different dimensions, my Maya K'iche' teacher Saq Chumil Blanca Estela Alvarado discerns between asking the frequent question "How are you?": "*la utz wach la?*" (literarily, "Is your countenance well?") and the much deeper question: "*Jas kub'ij le k'u'x la?*" "What does your heart say?" That everything—sky, earth, mountains, water-has a heart, soul, or essence expresses the idea that all things are alive (Lenkersdorf, 1999).

18. Through his study of linguistics and many years living amongst Tojolabal Mayans in Chiapas, Mexico, Carlos Lenkersdorf explains that there are no objects in Tojolabal; sentences are constructed through the relationship between subjects, for example, instead of saying "I told you," in Tojolabal one says, "I said, you listened" (1999:25).

19. "***Kulaj*** *is the other I, or the other countenance which brings fulfillment to a human being; this can be referred to as duality.* ***Tz'aqat*** *is completion, nothing is missing. We can refer to this as complementarity.*" Juan Zapil Xivir, e-mail correspondence with the author, June 29, 2007.

20. See Nestor García Canclini, 1989.

21. It seems probable that Mayan women who become professionals have experienced less gender discrimination in the home and more opportunities to study than many other indigenous women.

22. One of the research questions for my thesis was whether Mayan women are—or want to be—"guardians of culture"; Ixtz'ulu' had discussed this before the question on complementarity, hence she is referring back to another part of the interview.

23. "Ladino" is the term usually used in Guatemala to talk about nonindigenous people; it is similar though not interchangeable with the term "mestizo," as it makes no reference to indigenous heritage, whereas the latter explicitly recognizes population of mixed blood (of Spanish, indigenous and/or African descent). It is a contested term, and has not been sufficiently studied, a task pending for identity construction in Guatemala.

24. "Nawal" or "nahual" is like the guardian spirit, usually in the form of an animal or bird, that accompanies a person in once again, a manifestation of duality. One's "nawal" depends on one's day of birth on the *cholq'ij*: the Mayan lunar or spiritual calendar (160 days divided into 20 months of 13 days each).

25. For example, I had the following experience with a Mayan organization. Whilst carrying out an external evaluation, we discovered that male leaders were getting women in their organization pregnant and sending them home without maternity leave. When we raised the issue, a male leader got up and said with

fury that the organization promoted Mayan cosmovision and rejected western feminism. Many Mayan women—and men—reject the way cosmovision is mobilized to cover up sexism and such obvious abuse of power, and the way these attitudes discredit cosmovision in the eyes of others.

26. *"Western feminists, by buying into a racist construction of the veil, and taking part in daily racist incidents force Muslim women to choose between fighting racism or fighting sexism. The question is why should we be forced to choose?"* (Hoodfar 1993:16)

27. A frequent criticism of workshops on gender is that these *create* conflict (rather than bringing out into the open mistreatment of women and gender inequalities). It is one thing to criticize the methodology used in workshops, which can sometimes be confrontational, quite another to state that "everything was fine before" when power relations between men and women were simply naturalized.

28. See Ramón Máiz 2004, José Bengoa, 2000, among others.

REFERENCES

Ajxup Pelicó, Virginia. "Gender and Ethnicity, Cosmovision and Women." In *Faces without Masks, Mayan Women on Identity, Gender and Ethnicity in Guatemala,* ed. Cabrera Pérez-Armiñan and Morna Macleod. Melbourne: Oxfam Community Aid Abroad, [2000] 2003.

Batzibal Tujal, Juana. "Mayan Women: Our Cultural Guides." In *Faces without Masks, Mayan Women on Identity, Gender and Ethnicity in Guatemala,* ed. Cabrera Pérez-Armiñan and Morna Macleod. Melbourne: Oxfam Community Aid Abroad, [2000] 2003.

Bejar, Ruth. *Translated Woman: Crossing the Border with Esperanza's Story.* Boston, MA: Beacon Press, 1993.

Bengoa, José. *La Emergencia Indígena en América Latina.* Santiago: Fondo de Cultura Económica (FCE), 2000.

Consejo de Organizaciones Maya (COMG). *Construyendo un Futuro para Nuestro Pasado: Derechos del Pueblo Maya y el Proceso de Paz.* Guatemala: Editorial Cholsamaj, 1995.

García Canclini, Néstor. *Culturas Híbridas, estrategias para entrar y salir de la modernidad.* México D.F.: Editorial Grijalbo, 1989.

Hernández Castillo, Rosalva Aída. "Entre el Etnocentrismo Feminista y el Esencialismo Étnico, las Mujeres Indígenas y sus Demandas de Género." *Racismo y Mestizaje,* México D.F.: Debate Feminista, año 12, Vol. 24, octubre de 2001.

Hoodfar, Homa. "The Veil in their Minds and on Our Heads: the Persistence of Colonial Images of Muslim Women." *Colonialism, Imperialism and Gender, Resources for Feminist Research* 22, no. 3 and 4 (Fall/Winter 1993).

International Indigenous Women's Forum. "¿Feminismo con Visión Indígena o Visión Indígena Feminista? Definiendo el Feminismo desde la

Perspectiva de Mujeres Indígenas. Desafíos para la Integralidad de la Lucha de las Mujeres." Bangkok, October 2005.

Jocón González, Maria Estela. *Fortalecimiento de la Participación Política de las Mujeres Mayas.* Chimaltenango: Serie Oxlajuj Baqtun, Maya Uk'u'x B'e, 2005.

Grupo de Mujeres Mayas Kaqla. *La Palabra y el sentir de las mujeres mayas de Kaqla.* Ciudad de Guatemala, Kaqla, 2004.

Lenkersdorf, Carlos. *Cosmovisión Maya.* México D.F.: Editorial Ce-Acatl, 1999.

Macleod, Morna. "Historia, Memoria y Representaciones: Encuentros, Desencuentros y Debates entre los Intelectuales Mayas y los Múltiples Otros." *Monografías,* www.globalcult.org.ve, 2006.

Máiz Suárez, Ramón. 2004. "El Indigenismo Político En América Latina." *Revista de estudios políticos,* ISSN 0048-7694, no. 123 (2004): 129–174.

Marcos, Sylvia. "The Borders Within." In *Dialogue and Difference: Feminisms Challenge Globalization,* ed. Marguerite Waller and Sylvia Marcos. New York: Palgrave Press, 2005.

Martínez, Egla Judith. "The Maya Cosmovision as a Site of Resistance." Manuscript, 2004.

Meentzen, Angela. *Estrategias de Desarrollo Culturalmente Adecuados para Mujeres Indígenas.* Washington: Banco Interamericano de Desarrollo (BID), Unidad de Pueblos Indígenas y Desarrollo Comunitario, 2000.

Palencia, Tania (and Hermelinda Magzul, research assistant). *Género y Cosmovisión Maya.* Ciudad de Guatemala: PRODESSA, Editorial Saqil Tzij, 1999.

Perrin, Michel, and Marie Perruchon, editors. *Complementariedad entre hombre y mujer, Relaciones de género desde la perspectiva amerindia.* Colección Abya-Yala No. 43, Quito, Ediciones Abya-Yala, 1997.

Santos, Boaventura de Sousa. *Law and Globalization from Below: Towards a Cosmopolitan Legality,* Cambridge: Cambridge University Press, 2005.

Tedlock, Barbara. *Time and the Highland Maya.* Albuquerque: University of New Mexico Press, 1982.

Thompson, J. B. *Ideology and Modern Culture.* Cambridge, MA: Polity Press, 1990.

Warren, Kay B. "Reading History as Resistance: Maya Public Intellectuals in Guatemala." In *Maya Cultural Activism in Guatemala,* ed. Edward F. Fischer and R. McKenna Brown. Austin: University of Texas Press, 1996.

Willis Paau, Lucía. "Reflections on My Experience as a Woman." In *Faces without Masks, Mayan Women on Identity, Gender and Ethnicity in Guatemala,* ed. Cabrera Pérez-Armiñan and Morna Macleod. Melbourne: Oxfam Community Aid Abroad, [2000] 2003.

Zapil Xivir, Juan. PowerPoint presentations for a cycle of conferences on Mayan cosmovision. Mexico City: University of Mexico City (UACM), July 2006.

CHAPTER 11

Decolonizing our Spirits: Cultural Knowledge and Indigenous Healing

Renee Linklater

Severed roots
fragmented
becoming whole
reconnect
time, energy, resistance, love
re-enforcing twine
roots merge
bone marrow melts
together.

The journey of acquiring knowledge often involves a lifetime of experience, opportunities, and reflective inquiry. My journey as a mixed-blood indigenous woman born on Turtle Island has placed me in a position that inevitably confronts colonization and has inspired my search for an inherent connection to my ancestors' ways of being in the world.[1] This chapter explores my personal journey of decolonizing, seeking Anishinaabe cultural knowledge and bringing these teachings into the contemporary context of healing from colonial trauma.[2]

There is no doubt that colonization has interfered with the transmission of cultural knowledge from generation to generation. My colonial story begins shortly after my birth in 1969. At four months of age, I became part of what is referred to as the "Sixties Scoop," when thousands of indigenous children were removed from their families and placed into foster care or adopted out—largely to nonindigenous families. Fortunately, at six-months old, I was placed with a nurturing and loving Ukrainian family. I was not routed through endless foster homes and institutions, as were many other indigenous children. I grew up in a small village and felt like I was part of the family and community. Nonetheless, I always wondered where my birth family was, and I could never quite comprehend why I was not with them. I grew up distanced from indigenous culture and knowledge. Yet I always knew that some day I would return to my indigenous roots, and to my indigenous teachings. It was a spiritual understanding that was deeply imbedded inside me. My soul grieved for the loss of my family, lands, and ancestors. In 1988, a little more than 18 years after my separation, I returned home. My life had come full circle and I reconnected with my family and began the journey of discovering "who I am" and what had happened to indigenous peoples in Canada.

I found comfort in the cultural knowledge that my family maintained and felt the need to embark on a path that provided the skills and resources that would bring me closer to understanding how my world came to be. I enrolled in an undergraduate university program and completed a degree in Native Studies. This essential opportunity allowed me, alongside my fellow students, to learn about the colonial history that our people had endured. This information was pivotal for my personal development, and I soon realized that the social chaos in our communities was a direct result of being colonized by European nations.

Learning the Colonial Story

The colonization of the indigenous peoples of Turtle Island was first experienced with the immigration of settlers and the creation of colonies under British, French, and Spanish rule. These events brought an onset of missionary activity, which created churches and schools throughout indigenous territory. Initially, indigenous peoples were able to resist cultural breakdown and still engage in relations with the settlers through fur trade, war alliances, and treaty negotiations.

With the creation of Canada in 1867, the signing of the numbered treaties (1871–1921), and the consolidation of Indian policy in 1876, indigenous peoples were systematically displaced from their lands and forced to settle on reserves. Limitations and restrictions under the Indian Act (1876) legislated the mobility of Indians to Indian reserves, outlawed traditional ceremonies, set mandatory attendance at residential schools, replaced traditional clan and leadership systems, and for the most part, reorganized how and where indigenous peoples lived their lives.

My family originates from the territory that is now under the terms of conditions set out in Treaty Number 3. This Treaty covers 55,000 square miles of northwestern Ontario and southeastern Manitoba and was signed between Her Majesty the Queen of Great Britain and Ireland and the Saulteaux Tribe of the Ojibbway Indians in 1873.[3] Despite the adjustments to stationary sites, efforts were made to create communities and utilize the agricultural assistance provided for under the terms of the Treaty. Indigenous peoples continued to cultivate farms and gardens to stimulate growth in the economy and to provide for the community. In 1881, the government passed legislation, which prohibited the purchases of produce from Indians. This had devastating effects on the economy of indigenous peoples. Until that point, they had relied heavily on sales from settlers for the means to trade or to purchase necessary materials or food items. "The penalties and regulations were significant deterrents to Ojibway commerce. During 1883, many chiefs from each Treaty 3 agency complained about the effects of the legislation."[4] This move to limit the economy of "Indians" is an example of the systematic approaches used to violate the rights of indigenous peoples, and more so, encouraged a climate of poverty.

Many indigenous nations quickly began to protest the government's ability to fulfill the terms of the treaties or began to dispute other land and resource issues. In response to this situation, in 1927 Canada amended the Indian Act to make it illegal for Indians to raise money to hire lawyers for land claims. This amendment remained legislation until 1951. In the 1960s, indigenous peoples developed political organizations, with the assistance of federal funding provided by the government of Canada. It was then that a major contemporary political movement emerged; however, Canada maintained a high degree of power over indigenous political expression, as they controlled the funding for these organizations.

Indigenous peoples maintained deep connections to the land, despite hundreds of years of colonial presence in their lives. In writing about the importance of the land for the health of First Nation's Peoples, Wilson writes, "The land represents more than just a physical or symbolic space in which Anishinabek carry out their lives. Individuals have physical, symbolic, and spiritual relationships with the land by putting down tobacco, hunting, trapping, fishing, harvesting food and medicine, and taking part in ceremonies."[5] In recent decades, there has been a resurgence in the practice of indigenous cultural ceremonies, land-based activities, and learning traditional ways of life.

The systematic approach used by the Canadian government thrived off the use of Indian policies as their vehicle for state rule over Indians. Colonization came as a forceful attack on many aspects of indigenous life, including the following: health, autonomy, sovereignty, self-sufficiency and ways of organizing in families, clans, and economic trading systems among nations. And most compelling was the influence of oppression, violence, and religious domination.

Perhaps the most damaging effect on the indigenous spirit was the residential school system, which consisted of church-run, government-funded institutions intended to assimilate, civilize, and Christianize indigenous children. Milloy and Miller documented the extensive spiritual, emotional, psychological, physical, and sexual abuses, and other violations that were experienced by thousands and thousands of indigenous children that attended these residential schools.[6] Quite thoroughly, this school system created communities of intense chaos and crisis. It has become apparent that colonization has caused a displacement in cultural knowledge, as well as violent assaults on and oppression of the spirits of indigenous peoples. Losses of language, traditional ways of living and relating, and sense of life disrupted a very important reference point that Gregory Cajete would describe as a "sense of place."[7]

The residential school system was first launched in the late 1800s and rapidly expanded throughout the 1900s. By 1930, 75 percent of Indian children between the ages of 7 and 15 were enrolled in one of 80 such schools across the country. In the 1940s, attendance was expanded to included Inuit children as well. The schools began closing after the federal government assumed direct control of residential schools by ending church partnerships in 1969. However, there were seven schools in the 1980s, and the last federally run residential school closed in Saskatchewan in 1996.[8]

The abusive and exploitative treatment of indigenous children at residential schools continued to create havoc in various ways. Public light was finally shed on the issues in the early 1990s when survivors publicly disclosed experiences of being sexually and physically abused at residential schools. During this time, the Royal Commission on Aboriginal Peoples was holding hearings across Canada and recorded many testimonies of residential school experiences of abuse, the current conditions in the communities, and the general disruptions that colonization brought to the lives of indigenous peoples.

Apart from the abuse, there was an explicit attitude toward the children that was particularly damaging. Chansonneuve provides examples of degradation at the schools, "There was name-calling and put-downs of kids, parents, culture and language; children were forced to wear dirty or soiled clothes as punishment; sick children were forced to eat their own vomit;

children were hit while eating; children were forced to crawl at the feet of nuns and priests; children were forced to wear diapers for bed wetting; and children were taught that women were below men in all things."[9]

In 1998, the government of Canada issued a statement of reconciliation and announced a healing fund, which essentially established the Aboriginal Healing Foundation. This Foundation published a research series, devised a funding strategy for healing programs, and distributed 3.5 million dollars in funding to support local community initiatives that offered healing services to residential school survivors and their descendants.

Moving Forward into Healing

There have been times during the learning process when I have felt the persistent agony and agitation of continually being reminded that European values, language, and religion have influenced and altered much of the present indigenous world. Even the word "religion" is often met with distressing response, because of the role that organized religion has played within the colonization of indigenous peoples. It wasn't easy to learn how devastated our peoples were by European populations. I remember the responses that we had as undergraduate students learning colonial history, and facing the fact that our families were so damaged as a consequence of Europeans populating our lands. We were at a loss about how to deal with our anger, our resentment, and our multiple unresolved grievances.

I developed an intense revulsion about Catholicism and the church in general, upon learning that my mom and grandparents attended a Catholic-run residential school. I became aware of the abuses and cultural oppression that was experienced at these schools, and felt the personal effects of coming from a family in which two generations had been removed from family, community, and culture. I came to the understanding that my journey into the child welfare system was a direct result of my mother's residential school experience, and her fractured family unit that never learned how to be supportive and nurturing. I also realized that I was part of Canada's systematic approach to colonizing and assimilating indigenous children into dominant society.

In November 2005, the government announced a compensation agreement for all survivors of Canada's residential schools. In a press release issued by the Assembly of First Nations, details of the Agreement in Principle were mentioned: "This includes a national apology; an improved compensation process for victims of sexual and physical abuse; a lump sum payment for former students; and a Truth and Reconciliation Commission with both national and regional processes. The Aboriginal Healing Foundation will also receive additional funding for another five years . . . The Agreement in Principle also calls for an expedited process to resolve the claims of the elderly."[10] This announcement was a well-deserved victory for the indigenous residential school survivors who lobbied the government to compensate each individual for the "common experience" of losses of culture and spirituality. The government had previously held a negotiating position to compensate for only sexual and physical abuse, which did not include abuses committed on a cultural or spiritual basis.

I remember the day in October 2006 when my 90-year-old gramma had traveled on the Greyhound bus for two days to visit her grandchildren and great-grandchildren who lived in southern Ontario. When I arrived at my cousin's apartment to visit her, she called me into the bedroom where she was sitting on a bed in the corner of the room. As always, I was happy to see her. She said, "My girl, come and sit down." I leaned over to kiss her on the cheek and sat beside her as she requested. She looked at me with intense thought, and then counted out five 20-dollar bills—she said, "This is for Blaze" (my son Blaze was 16 years old at that time). She then counted out another five 20-dollar bills, and said, "This is for you." I was puzzled, and said, "We're okay gramma, you don't need to give us any money." She then said, "I got my residential school money and I wanted to share it with my grandchildren." At that moment I burst into tears. The rush of emotion overwhelmed me. All I could think about was how my mom had died in 1985, at the age of 34, and her story of residential school was never told, nor was she part of the compensation that was being offered to survivors. I also felt the deep love that my gramma had for us, and sensed that this was her way of saying sorry for the pain that we had experienced in our family. My gramma passed away the following spring. Although I miss her dearly, I knew that she was tired and ready to return home to the Creator.

DECOLONIZING MYSELF

In graduate school, I learned about the process of decolonization and I was excited to participate in this evaluation of the colonial influences that had contributed to our lives. Wilson and Yellow Bird write: "Decolonization is the intelligent, calculated, and active resistance to the forces of colonialism that perpetuate the subjugation and/or exploitation of our minds, bodies and lands, and it is the ultimate purpose of overturning the colonial structure and realizing Indigenous liberation."[11] I felt that this "academic theory" was going to help significantly in my healing journey and I began to produce academic work that encouraged my expression of the need to address colonial damage.

Over the years, I made extensive efforts to put myself on an indigenous healing and educational path. Many people refer to this as the "Red Road." Through teachings from Elders, cultural knowledge carriers, and healers,

I began to develop an Anishinaabe worldview, from which I was able to understand my connection to my ancestors, and begin to understand indigenous epistemologies. Through ceremonies, social networks, and by attending powwows, I was able to connect with other indigenous peoples who shared the same desire to celebrate indigenous cultures. My spirit continued to grow and my heart began to fill with gratitude and love for the world—the same world that had caused so much injury and pain.

I soon discovered that healing is a bumpy road, full of sharp turns and roadblocks. At times I felt that I had been going in circles, often revisiting troubling circumstances and disturbing places. I accepted the value of these circles when I acknowledged the growth that had occurred as a result of revisiting these experiences—each time discovering another important piece in my story. Eventually I had to face my own disconnect, and accept that I had been operating in survival mode. There was no easy way through the pain, and so I persisted—despite my often-exhausted state of being.

As I continued along this journey I realized that I was developing an identity. To that point I had not put much thought to how important identity formation was in terms of developing a positive and healthy self-image. I began to understand that I lacked an identity, which resulted from the removal of myself as a baby from my indigenous family. I accepted that I had grown up without a cultural foundation. The Ukrainian/Canadian environment of my adoptive family enabled me to develop a deep respect for Ukrainian culture, and through this I learned that culture and language provided for a plentiful life experience. Nonetheless, I did not assume a Ukrainian identity. I was very aware that my blood was of mixed cultures, and I was finally at a place in my personal development where I needed to learn about my Scottish and English ancestors. I had reached a place of facing my own resistance to accepting that part of me that benefited from the devastation of indigenous nations.

For many years I was not interested in identifying with or learning about my British ancestors. Although I initially became warm to the idea of my Scottish roots, because of the Celtic origins, I still felt ashamed of my English blood. Even though I had learned to love my family members, I did not fully process or acknowledge my shame of being part of peoples that have caused so much global damage. Furthermore, my fair skin was a constant reminder of the conflict that existed inside of me. Adding to my personal resistance was the punishing remarks that I endured because of what I represented to other indigenous people. Being a half-breed was not an easy card to play. I continued to pursue the notion of wholeness and began to accept my mixed cultural heritage. I was learning that a major key to healing was forgiveness, and, moreover, that peaceful resolution came with acceptance.

In the summer of 2005, I boarded an airplane and for the first time in my life I flew away from Turtle Island. The next day I landed in London, England. I was excited to finally embrace my painful and shameful history. My spirit came alive as I journeyed through the land, making peace with the church and searching old village graveyards for my ancestors, and, most importantly, coming into contact with beautiful human spirits who I realized held kindness in their hearts and did not deserve the anger and shame that once dominated my view of English people. Letting this anger and shame go and coming to a peaceful resolution provided a sense of relief in my spirit. I could now understand the effects of spiritual unrest on an individual's health and wellness.

As I continued on this journey of decolonizing myself, I made concerted efforts to ensure that my academic work remained rooted in indigenous philosophies, rather than adhering to Western concepts that I felt only entrenched the disregard of indigenous knowledge. I knew in my heart that indigenous philosophies and cultural healing practices were legitimate forms of healing, and I was committed to providing a space for indigenous health care practitioners to participate in research that brought forward this belief. I first prayed for guidance and began by talking to my Elders and teachers. I listened to the people in my communities. I prepared my spirit ceremonially by Fasting, and made offerings to my ancestors and spirit helpers. I knew that if I were to move forward and bring integrity to this work, I couldn't do it alone.

The teachings around conceptualizing our health and wellness motivated my desire to seek out the methods and tools that indigenous peoples were utilizing in the area of learning and healing. Medicine Wheels had become popular symbols in indigenous communities, so I began to seek out these teachings, both through oral history and within the literature. I soon discovered that I was able to make sense of the information that I was learning, and use Medicine Wheels as a way to understand the impact of trauma on a person, and furthermore, draw on Medicine Wheels as a way to talk about wellness. It was the beginning of developing my position that cultural knowledge was essential for indigenous healing.

MEDICINE WHEEL TEACHINGS

Medicine Wheels are contemporary teaching tools that are used to examine and explain concepts, philosophies, and traditional teachings. By nature, they emphasize wholeness and balance. Anishinaabe student Arlene Barry shares that the Medicine Wheel was "originally explained orally with the circle being drawn in the earth and a gradual overlaying of symbols, as meanings were explained by an elder. The elder would usually begin with an explanation of the Four Directions and the center of the wheel which represents the Sacred Mystery."[12] There are extensive teachings that the Medicine Wheels capture, and this tool has proved to be successful in many circles of learners and teachers.

Historically, the concept of Medicine Wheels arose from sacred sites located throughout central North America, specifically Alberta, Saskatchewan, Montana, South Dakota, and Wyoming. There are many variations of Medicine Wheels, with different numbers of "spokes" and stones; however, the wheels are all consistently circular. The English term "Medicine Wheel" was first applied to the Big Horn Medicine Wheel in Wyoming.

The Bighorn Medicine Wheel in Wyoming has been a significant sacred site for the Arapaho, Cheyenne, Plains Cree, Salish-Kootenai, Shoshone, Bannock, Crow, Blackfeet, and Sioux peoples who have traveled from their respective territories and traditional camps to pray, give offerings, fast, and conduct ceremonies. They regard the circle as a piece of religious architecture and an astronomical structure.[13] However, not all indigenous peoples accept the English terminology of the Medicine Wheel. As my late Uncle Gordon Nelson (Anishinaabe) articulated, "These aren't medicine wheels, they tell stories of the universe" (personal communication: March 12, 2006).

Indigenous Elders and cultural teachers began using the ancient symbol of the Medicine Wheel as a contemporary tool, because it had an inherent way of upholding the teachings. It also provided a framework for organizing thought, examining philosophies, and explaining teachings. In 1955, the late Cree traditional teacher Eddy Bellrose (Thunder Child) drew on the Medicine Wheel to provide a teaching model or framework that was rooted in Cree teachings of the pipe. The Elders in the Circle at that time concurred with Bellrose, agreeing that what he was explaining accurately represented the teachings as they understood them (Lloyd Martin [Cree]: personal communication, May 17, 2005). Since then, the Cree Medicine Wheel teachings have been widely used by indigenous practitioners.[14]

In 1982, a historic council of over 100 Elders, cultural leaders and various professionals, representing over 40 nations from North America, was held in Lethbridge, Alberta. This council was convened to discuss the root causes of alcohol and drug abuse within indigenous communities, and inspired the work of the Four Worlds Development Project. This project established philosophy, guiding principles, activities, and strategies for human and community development. This vision was articulated in the *Sacred Tree* (1988), which utilized the Medicine Wheel as a framework for the teachings of the sacred tree. "Just like a mirror can be used to see things not normally seen (like behind us, or around a corner), the medicine wheel can be used to help us see or understand things we can't quite see or understand because they are just ideas and not physical objects . . . All things are interrelated. Everything in the universe is part of a single whole. Everything is connected in some way to everything else. We can understand something only if we can understand how it is connected to everything else."[15]

Medicine Wheels are used by many different indigenous nations. As such, the teachings vary depending on the teachings of the Elder, cultural teacher, or professional practitioner. There is no "correct" or "incorrect" way to use a Medicine Wheel; however, it must be rooted in indigenous episte-mologies and worldviews, which hold values of reverence and reciprocity. For this reason, it is common to see Medicine Wheels that put certain teachings in different quadrants. For example, the Cree Medicine Wheel, as taught by Eddy Bellrose, will have the color red, for *red people,* in the East (Lloyd Martin [Cree] personal communication: May 17, 2005). While Edna Mani-towabi, an Anishinaabe Elder, will put the color yellow in the east to sig-nify the *sunrise,* a teaching she received from her Elder (Anishinaabe), who derived her teachings through dreams (personal communication: June 20, 2005). Herb Nabigon (Anishinaabe Elder) advises people to use the teach-ings of the Medicine Wheel as they have received them (personal communi-cation: April 1, 2005).

ANISHINAABE WELLNESS

Wellness is a model to assist us in living our lives. It is a [w]holistic and integrated approach to health and well-being . . . Wellness is composed of four directions or components: physical wellness, mental wellness, emo-tional wellness, and spiritual wellness. When we travel this [w]holistic path in all directions, we are in balance with ourselves. It is important to acknowledge that the indigenous peoples of Turtle Island have long understood and lived the 'wellness way.'[16]

The wellness movement began in North America during the 1970s and was largely influenced by many movements, particularly that of [w]holistic health, women's rights, consciousness raising, ecology interests, physical fit-ness, futurism and health and/or natural food groups.[17] Wellness character-istics focus on a balanced approach. According to Ardell, the "five commonly employed areas or dimensions of wellness are: self-responsibility, nutritional awareness, stress awareness and management, physical fitness, and envi-ronmental sensitivity."[18] Since then, wellness philosophies have become an important element of health care and community programming.

Conceptualizing wellness within indigenous communities is often rooted in teachings of the Medicine Wheel. The Medicine Wheel, as a model, pro-vides a wholistic framework for understanding balance and harmony. The Medicine Wheel's four quadrants are often used to provide us with an un-derstanding of the areas of the individual: spiritual, emotional, mental, and physical. With this, we are able to understand what balance and imbalance might look like as we move around the Wheel. We can also consider what happens to a person under duress, illness and trauma.

This model is particularly helpful in terms of understanding the healing process and what might constitute a wholistic healing plan. Indigenous perspectives on health and balance would conclude that if even one of the areas of the person was out of balance, other areas would be affected. Further in time, that individual's whole health would be jeopardized.

Conventional medicine and traditional indigenous methods differ greatly in diagnosis and treatment. Where conventional medicine is more likely to treat symptoms with prescription medication, an indigenous healer might bring in ceremony, sacred medicines, bodywork, therapy, and intellectual stimulation through teachings and storytelling as approaches to restoring balance in the person.

Indigenous peoples have their own understanding of how people have been created and, thus, how it is that we "think, perceive, and reason." In a Master's level course, *Anishinaabe Psychology: Ways of Being and Behaviour*, at the Seven Generations Education Institute, Elder Jim Dumont gave teachings on the "Total Anishinaabe Person."[19] Dumont, an Anishinaabe who is Fourth Degree Midewiwin, shared how Anishinaabe philosophy conceptualizes our way of being and behavior.[20]

Dumont's teaching explains the four levels of the person. He begins by acknowledging our life force, the entrance of our spirit into the person. Our spirit (or soul) comes directly from the Spirit World upon inspiration from the Creator, who propels our spirit and gives us life. In our mother's womb we begin the next phase of our development and our hearts begin to beat. From there we are given a mind, and lastly we are given a vessel. This vessel, or body, is connected to all the levels inside us as well as all that is in Creation (course lecture, April 24, 2004). A fundamental Anishinaabe philosophy is that we are connected and related to all of Creation—including the trees, the rocks, the animals, our families, the community, other peoples, the spirits, and all that is alive and part of our universe.

In Dumont's explanation of this teaching, he shares that the spirit—our life force—talks to the heart, the heart talks to the mind, and the mind talks to the vessel. This is how we understand the world. Through the heart we know how to live. The mind has to do with belief, and our life will be according to our beliefs. Belief creates one's reality, reality doesn't create belief, and the belief comes directly from the heart.[21] The vessel is the thick bark around us, which includes our internal and external responses. This vessel protects the mind, the mind protects the heart, and the heart protects the spirit. Dumont also acknowledges that blood memory is at every level (course lecture, April 24, 2004).

Using Dumont's teaching of the Total Anishinaabe Person, I draw on the Medicine Wheel as a way to conceptualize a person, understand how trauma impacts a person, and to understand how to support a person in healing and achieving wellness. The Medicine Wheel quadrants include the Spiritual (soul), Emotional (heart), Mental (mind), and Physical (body), which represent the four levels of the person as conveyed by Dumont's teaching.[22] The Medicine Wheel begins in the east, as this is where our beings are given the first burst of life, and continues clockwise, to explain the creation of the person. This philosophy has serious implications for not only understanding the impact of trauma on Anishinaabe peoples, but also for healing trauma.

The Medicine Wheel provides us with a wholistic concept of viewing personal trauma. At the same time, this teaching inherently connects the person to various aspects of other trauma, which includes historical trauma.[23] Importantly, the Anishinaabe person first experiences the trauma spiritually, as an attack on the spirit; the person then experiences the trauma emotionally, as an impact on the heart; then the person experiences the trauma mentally, as the mind makes sense of the injury; and lastly, the person experiences the trauma physically, and often exhibits bodily/behavioral responses. Trauma that is not resolved at a level that addresses the whole person becomes deeply rooted and manifested in various imbalances. These could play out as spiritual, emotional, mental, and/or physical turmoil. This model of the Medicine Wheel provides a culturally based assessment tool to understand trauma, while at the same time providing a wholistic approach to support individual healing and wellness. Furthermore, this model supports indigenous healing concepts, such as that noted by Duran and Duran, "In Native American healing, the factor that is of importance is intensity, not the passage of time."[24] Taking this into consideration, a healing plan that focuses on the spiritual, emotional, mental, and physical aspects of the being, concurrently, may very well increase a person's ability and likelihood to advance along the wellness path and reach a place of balance and harmony.

CONCLUSION

The journey to wholeness and wellness involves deep personal reflection that can be inspired by processes of decolonization and the desire to heal. Our connections to ourselves, our ancestors, and the universe around us provide a comfort and security that nurtures our spirits and enriches our lives. The path toward reclaiming indigenous knowledge and bringing these teachings into our everyday experiences and practices will support indigenous peoples in our journey to heal from colonial trauma. It is my hope that the sharing of my story will inspires others who are on a journey toward wellness.

NOTES

1. Turtle Island is an indigenous concept that refers to the North American countries of Canada, United States, and Mexico; some teachings include Central and South America. Oral history stories share that a Turtle came to the surface of the water and life began to grow on her.

2. Anishinaabe is the indigenous nation that my mother's family originates from. Depending on geographical location, people of this nation may also be referred to as Ojibwe/Ojibwa/Ojibway, Chippewa, and Saulteaux. The term "Anishinaabe" derives from the Anishinaabe language, and is the preferred term that many individuals use to self-identify.

3. Wayne E. Daugherty, "Treaty Research Report Treaty Three (1873)," (Indian and Northern Affairs Canada, 1986).

4. Leo G. Waisberg and Tim E. Holzkaam, "A Tendency to Discourage Them from Cultivating: Ojibway Agriculture and Indian Affairs Administration," *Ethnohistory* 40, no. 2 (1993).

5. Kathleen Wilson, "Therapeutic Landscapes and First Nations Peoples: An Exploration of Culture, Health and Place," *Health and Place* 9, no. 2 (2003): 91.

6. See J. R. Miller, *Shingwauk's Vision: A History of Native Residential Schools* (Toronto, Ontario, Canada: University of Toronto Press, 1996), John S. Milloy, *A National Crime: The Canadian Government and the Residential School System 1879–1986* (Winnipeg, Manitoba, Canada: University of Manitoba Press, 1999).

7. Gregory Cajete, *Native Science: Natural Laws of Interdependence* (Sante Fe, NM: Clear Light Publishers, 2000).

8. Madeleine Dion Stout and Gregory Kipling, *Aboriginal People, Resilience and the Residential School Legacy* (Ottawa, Ontario, Canada: Aboriginal Healing Foundation, 2003).

9. Deborah Chansonneuve, *Reclaiming Connections: Understanding Residential School Trauma among Aboriginal People* (Ottawa, Ontario, Canada: Aboriginal Healing Foundation, 2005).

10. "Assembly of First Nations National Chief Applauds Historical Reconciliation and Compensation Agreement as a Major Victory for Residential School Survivors," November 23, 2005.

11. Waziyatawin Angela Wilson and Michael Yellow Bird, *For Indigenous Eyes Only* (Sante Fe, NM: School of American Research Press, 2005).

12. Arlene Barry, *Kinoomaadiwinan Anishinaabe Bimaadiziwin (Book of Brochures)* (Sault Ste. Marie, Ontario, Canada: 2001).

13. Jurgita Saltanaviciute, *Native American Sacred Sites: Battle for Protection* (University of Wyoming, 2000).

14. See Herb Nabigon, *The Hollow Tree: Fighting Addictions with Traditional Native Healing* (Montreal, Quebec, Canada and Kingston, Ontario, Canada: McGill-Queens University Press, 2006), Herb Nabigon and Anne-Marie Mawhiney, "Aboriginal Theory: A Cree Medicine Wheel Guide for Healing First

Nation," in *Social Work Treatment: Interlocking Theoretical Approaches,* ed. Francis J. Turner (New York: The Free Press, 1996).

15. Julie Bopp et al., *The Sacred Tree* (Lethbridge, Alberta, Canada: The Four Worlds Development Project, University of Lethbridge, 1988).

16. Billy Rogers, "A Path of Healing and Wellness for Native Families," *American Behavioral Scientist* 44, no. 9 (2001).

17. I spell the word "wholistic" with a "w" at the beginning, rather than the dictionary form "holistic." It was first pointed out to me in 2001 by Alice Olsen Williams of Curve Lake First Nation that I should be not be spelling the word without a "w" as it reminded her of the word "holy" which referenced masculine, a male god and the Bible—with further implications of patriarchal power and force. She further noted that the word described an empty space. After much thought, I decided that there were many good reasons to spell the word using a "w," particularly because I felt that the word conveyed different meanings when spelt with or without the "w." In the context that I was using it, I felt that wholistic needed to convey wholeness, and describe an all encompassing perspective. Spelling it as "holistic" seemed to limit the notion of wholism. I have since learned that many indigenous peoples, including writers and Elders, prefer that we use the spelling with the "w."

18. Donald B. Ardell, *The History and Future of Wellness* (Dubuque, IA: Kendal/Hunt Publishing Company, 1985).

19. Seven Generations Education Institute is Indigenous Institute located on Coochiching First Nation in northwestern Ontario.

20. Midewiwin is a Medicine Society, which is traditionally for Anishinaabe peoples that had been initiated into the Lodge through ceremony.

21. In precolonial times, Anishinaabe belief systems were developed through their life experiences, which were consistently cultural in context. Colonization brought an onset of foreign beliefs that shifted the Anishinaabe belief system and created complex realities in which foreign beliefs now became part of the complex systems of those colonized.

22. Many indigenous peoples use the Medicine Wheel to discuss the spiritual, emotional, mental, and physical aspects of an individual. However, each educator/practitioner may position the aspects in different locations, which will represent their teachings. I have located the aspects of the being in specific quadrants, which reflects Dumont's teaching of the "Total Anishnaabe Person."

23. See Eduardo Duran et al., "Healing the American Indian Soul Wound," in *International Handbook of Multigenerational Legacies of Trauma,* ed. Yael Danieli, *The Plenum Series on Stress and Coping* (New York: Plenum Press, 1998); also Maria Yellow Horse Brave Heart-Jordan, "The Return to the Sacred Path: Healing from Historical Trauma and Historical Unresolved Grief among the Lakota" (Smith College of Social Work, 1995).

24. Bonnie Duran and Eduardo Duran, "Applied Postcolonial Clinical and Research Strategies," in *Reclaiming Indigenous Voice and Vision,* ed. Marie

Battiste (Vancouver, British Columbia, Canada: University of British Columbia Press, 2000).

REFERENCES

Ardell, Donald B. *The History and Future of Wellness*. Dubuque, IA: Kendal/ Hunt Publishing Company, 1985.

Assembly of First Nations. "Announcements: Assembly of First Nations National Chief Applauds Historical Reconciliation and Compensation Agreement as a Major Victory for Residential School Survivors" (2005): http://www.afn.ca/article.asp?id=1935.

Barry, Arlene. "Kinoomaadiwinan Anishinaabe Bimaadiziwin." In *Book of Brochures,* edited by Arlene Barry. Sault Ste. Marie, Ontario: manuscript, 2001.

Bopp, Julie, Michael Bopp, Lee Brown, and Phil Lane. *The Sacred Tree*. Lethbridge, Alberta: The Four Worlds Development Project, University of Lethbridge, 1988.

Cajete, Gregory. *Native Science: Natural Laws of Interdependence*. Santa Fe, NM: Clear Light Publishers, 2000.

Chansonneuve, Deborah. *Reclaiming Connections: Understanding Residential School Trauma among Aboriginal People*. Ottawa, Ontario: Aboriginal Healing Foundation, 2005.

Daugherty, Wayne E. "Treaty Research Report Treaty Three (1873)." Indian and Northern Affairs Canada, 1986.

Duran, Bonnie, and Eduardo Duran. "Applied Postcolonial Clinical and Research Strategies." In *Reclaiming Indigenous Voice and Vision,* edited by Marie Battiste, 86–100. Vancouver, BC: University of British Columbia Press, 2000.

Duran, Eduardo, Bonnie Duran, Maria Yellow Horse Brave Heart, and Susan Yellow Horse-Davis. "Healing the American Indian Soul Wound." In *International Handbook of Multigenerational Legacies of Trauma,* edited by Yael Danieli, 341–54. New York, NY: Plenum Press, 1998.

Heart-Jordan, Maria Yellow Horse Brave. *The Return to the Sacred Path: Healing from Historical Trauma and Historical Unresolved Grief among the Lakota*. Northampton, MA: Smith College of Social Work, doctoral dissertation,1995.

Miller, J. R. *Shingwauk's Vision: A History of Native Residential Schools*. Toronto, Ontario: University of Toronto Press, 1996.

Milloy, John S. *A National Crime: The Canadian Government and the Residential School System 1879–1986*. Winnipeg, Manitoba: University of Manitoba Press, 1999.

Nabigon, Herb. *The Hollow Tree: Fighting Addictions with Traditional Native Healing*. Montreal: McGill-Queens University Press, 2006.

Nabigon, Herb, and Anne-Marie Mawhiney. "Aboriginal Theory: A Cree Medicine Wheel Guide for Healing First Nation." In *Social Work Treatment: Interlocking Theoretical Approaches*, edited by Francis J. Turner, 19–38. New York: The Free Press, 1996.

Rogers, Billy. "A Path of Healing and Wellness for Native Families." *American Behavioral Scientist* 44, no. 9 (2001): 1512–14.

Saltanaviciute, Jurgita. *Native American Sacred Sites: Battle for Protection*. Laramie, Wyoming: University of Wyoming, master's thesis, 2000.

Stout, Madeleine Dion, and Gregory Kipling. *Aboriginal People, Resilience and the Residential School Legacy*. Ottawa, Ontario: Aboriginal Healing Foundation, 2003.

Waisberg, Leo G., and Tim E. Holzkaam. "A Tendency to Discourage Them from Cultivating: Ojibway Agriculture and Indian Affairs Administration." *Ethnohistory* 40, no. 2 (1993): 175–211.

Wilson, Kathleen. "Therapeutic Landscapes and First Nations Peoples: An Exploration of Culture, Health and Place." *Health and Place* 9, no. 2 (2003): 83–93.

Wilson, Waziyatawin Angela Yellow Bird, and Michael Yellow Bird. *For Indigenous Eyes Only*. Sante Fe, NM: School of American Research Press, 2005.

Suggested Reading

Álvarez, Sonia E. "Latín American Feminisms 'Go Global': Trends of the 1990s and Challenges for the New Millennium." In *Culture of Politics Politics of Culture,* ed. Sonia E. Alvarez, Evelina Dagnino, and Arturo Escobar, pp. 293–352 (chapter 12). Boulder, CO: Westview Press, 1998.

Apffel-Marglin, Frédérique. "Andean Concepts of Nature." Presentation at the Conference on *Orality, Gender and Indigenous Religions,* Claremont School of Religion, May 2001.

Apffel-Marglin, Frédérique, ed. *The Spirit of Regeneration. Andean Culture Confronting Western Notions of Development.* London and New York: Zed Books, 1998.

Bell, Diane. *Daughters of the Dreaming.* Melbourne: McPhee Gribble Publishers, 1983.

Bell, Diane. *Ngarrindjeri Wurruwarrin: A World That Is, Was and Will Be.* Melbourne: Spinifex Press, 1998.

Benjamin, Walter. *Illuminations,* edited by Hannah Arendt, translated by Harry Zohn. New York: Schocken Books, 1968.

Bissio, Robert Remo, ed. *The World.* Montevideo and Oxford: Instituto del Tercer Mundo/Oxfam.

Bonfil, Paloma, "Oficios, conocimientos y padecimientos: la salud como práctica política en el mundo indígena femenino," *La mujer en el medio rural, Cuadernos Agrarios,* no. 13 (1996).

Bourdieu, P. *Outline of a Theory of Practice.* Cambridge: Cambridge University Press, 1995.

Burckhart, Louise. *The Slippery Earth: Nahua Christian Moral Dialogue in Sixteenth Century Mexico.* Tucson: University of Arizona Press, 1989.

Carlsen, Laura. "Autonomía indígena y usos y costumbres: la innovación de la tradición," *Chiapas 7* ERA, Mexico city, (1999): 45–70.

Cazés, Daniel. "Consulta o distensión." In *Las Alzadas,* ed. Sara Lovera and Nellys Palomo, pp. 310–312. Mexico city: CIMAC—*La Jornada,* 1999 (2nd edition).

Ceceña, Ana Esther. "El mundo del nosotros: entrevista con Carlos Lenkersdorf" *Chiapas* 7 (1999): 191–205.

Chabram-Dernersesian, Angie. "I Throw Punches for my Race, but I don't Want to Be a Man: Writing us—chica-nos (girl, us)—into the Movement Script." In *Cultural Studies,* ed. Lawrence Grossberg, Cary Nelson, and Paula Treichler, pp. 81–95. London: Routledge, 1992, pp. 88 ss.

Cox, James L. "Characteristics of African Indigenous Religions in Contemporary Zimbabwe." In *Indigenous Religions,* ed. Graham Harvey, pp. 230–242. London and New York: Cassell, 2000.

Del Valle, Sonia. "Representantes de 26 pueblos indios conformaron la Coordinadora Nacional de Mujeres Indígenas." In *Las Alzadas,* ed. Sara Lovera and Nellys Palomo, pp. 408–411. México city: CIMAC—*La Jornada,* 1999 (2nd edition).

Esther, Comandante. "Queremos ser indígenas y mexicanos." Perfil de *la Jornada,* March 29, 2000, 4, 7, pp. 2–4.

Esther, Comandante, and Maria de Jesús Patricio. "La ley actual, no la de la CO-COPA, discrimina a las mujeres." *La Triple Jornada,* no. 32, April 2, 2001.

Estrada, Alvaro, ed. *Maria Sabina, Her Life and Chants.* Santa Barbara, CA: Ross Erickson Publishers, 1981.

Favret-Saada, Jeanne. *Les mots, la mort, les sorts.* Paris: Gallimard, 1977.

Gargallo, F. "La voz de las mujeres en el Tercer Congreso Nacional Indígena." *La Triple Jornada,* no. 32, April 2, 2001, p. 3.

Garza, Mercedes, de la. *Libro de Chilam Balam de Chumayel.* Mexico: SEP, 1985.

Geertz, Armin W., and Russell T. McCutcheon, eds. *Perspectives on Method and Theory in the Study of Religion.* Adjunct Proceedings of the XVIIth Congress of the International Association for the History of Religions, Mexico City, 1995. Leiden, Boston, Köln, 2000.

Gil Olmos: see Le Bot and Touraine.

Gil Olmos, José. "México en riesgo de caer en caos y caciquismo: Touraine." *La Jornada,* November 6, 2000, p. 7.

Gil Olmos, José. "Moderno y creativo el movimiento de indígenas en América Latina." Interview with Yvon Le Bot, in *La Jornada,* March 26, 2000, p. 3.

Goody, Jack. *Literacy in Traditional Societies.* Cambridge: Cambridge University Press, 1968.

Gossen, Gary. "Mesoamerican Ideas as a Foundation for Regional Synthesis." In *Symbol and Meaning Beyond the Closed Community,* ed. Gary Gossen. Albany, NY: The University of Albany, SUNY, 1986.

Gossen, Gary H. *Telling Maya Tales. Tzotzil Identities in Modern Mexico.* New York and London: Routledge, 1999.

Gossen, Gary, and Miguel Leon Portilla. *South and Mesoamerican Native Spirituality,* Vol. 4 of *World Spirituality: An Encyclopedic History of the Religious Quest.* New York: Crossroad, 1993.

Graham Harvey, ed. *Indigenous Religions*. London and New York: Cassell, 2000, pp. 190–203.

Grewal, Inderpal, and Caren Kaplan, eds. *Scattered Hegemonies. Postmodernity and Transnational Feminist Practices*. Minneapolis: University of Minnesota Press, 1997 (1994).

Griffin-Pierce, Trudy. *Earth is my Mother, Sky is My Father. Space, Time, and Astronomy in Navajo Sandpainting*. Albuquerque: University of New Mexico Press, 1992. With a foreword by N. Scott Momaday.

Grim, John A. "Indigenous Traditions and Ecology." *News, Bulletin of the Harvard University Center for the Study of World Religions* 5, no. 1 (Fall 1997): 1, 4–5.

Guiteras-Holmes, Calixta. *Perils of the Soul, the Worldview of a Tzotzil Indian*. New York: The Free Press of Glencoe Inc., 1961.

Harvey, Graham, ed. *Indigenous Religions*. London and New York: Cassell, 2000.

Harvey, Graham, ed. "Introduction." In *Indigenous Religions*, pp. 1–19. London, New York: Cassell, 2000.

Harvey, N. *La Rebelión de Chiapas*. Mexico, ERA, 2000.

Hernández, Rosalva Aída. "Building a Utopia: The Hopes and Challenges of the Women of Chiapas." In *The Other Word. Women and Violence in Chiapas Before and After Acteal*, ed. Rosalva Aída Hernández. Copenhagen, Denmark: International Working Group for Indigenous Affairs, 2001.

Hernández, Rosalva Aída. "From Community to Women's State Convention— The Chiapas Campesinos and Their Gender Demands." In *The Explosion of Communities in Chiapas*, Copenhague, ed. June Nash et al., pp. 53–63. Copenhagen, Denmark: International Working Group for Indigenous Affairs, 1995.

hooks, bell. *Feminist Theory: From Margin to Center*. Boston, MA: South End Press, 1984.

Humm, Maggie. *The Dictionary of Feminist Theory*. London: Prentice Hall / Harvester Wheatsheaf, 1995.

Jaggar, Alison M. ed. *Living with Contradictions*. Oxford: Westview Press, 1994.

Jaidopulu, M. "Las mujeres indígenas como sujetos políticos." In *Chiapas 9*, Mexico: Era—Instituto de Investigaciones Económicas de la UNAM, 2000, pp. 39 ss.

Jaimes Guerrero, M. A. "Native Womanism: Exemplars of Indigenism in Sacred Traditions of Kinship." In *Indigenous Religions*, ed. Graham Harvey, pp. 37–54. London and New York: Cassell, 2000.

Johansson, Patrick. *La palabra de los Aztecas*. Mexico: Editorial Trillas, 1993. With a foreword by Miguel León-Portilla.

Joyce, Rosemary A. *Gender and Power in Prehispanic Mesoamerica*. Austin: University of Texas Press, 2000.

Karttunen, Frances. "In Their Own Voices: Mesoamerican Indigenous Women Then and Now." English manuscript for an article in Finís, 1983.

Katzenberger, Elaine, ed. *First World, HaHaHa! The Zapatista Challenge.* San Francisco, CA: City Lights Books, 1995.

Kellogg, Susan. "Aztec Women in Early Colonial Courts: Structure and Strategies in a Legal Context." In *Five Centuries of Law and Politics in Central Mexico,* ed. Ronald Spores and Ross Hassig, pp. 25–38. Nashville, TN: Vanderbilt University Publications in Anthropology, no. 30, 1984.

Kellogg, Susan. "Cognatic Kinship and Religion: Women in Aztec Society." In *Mesoamerican Studies in Memory of Thelma D. Sullivan,* ed. J. Kathryn Josserand and Karen Dakin. BAR International Series 402, 1988.

Klein, Cecilia. *Gender in Pre-Hispanic America.* Washington, DC: Dumbarton Oaks, 2001.

Klor de Alva, Jorge."Contar vidas: La autobiografía confesional y la reconstrucción del ser Nahua." *Arbor* 515–516, Madrid, 1988.

Lagarde, Marcela. "La belleza y la paz: democracia, género y etnicidad." In *Convergencia Socialista* 3, no. 13 (March–April 2001).

Lamas, M., A. Martínez, M. L. Torres, E. Tuñón. "Encuentros y Desencuentros: el Movimiento amplio de mujeres en México, (1970–1993)." June 1994. ms.

Lawson, Jonathan. "At This Moment in Time It Is Sacred." Report of a conference by Trudy Griffin Pierce. *News,* Bulletin of the Harvard University Center for the Study of World Religions 4, no. 2 (Spring 1997): 7.

Le Bot, Yvon: see Gil Olmos, José.

Le Bot, Yvon. *La guerra en tierras mayas: Comunidad, violencia y modernidad en Guatemala (1970–1992).* Mexico: Fondo de Cultura Económica, 1995.

Le Bot, Yvon. "La Política según Marcos. ¿Que zapatismo después del Zapatismo?" *La Jornada,* March 15, 2001, p. 19.

Lenkersdorf, Carlos. *Los hombres verdaderos. Voces y testimonios tojolabales.* Mexico: Siglo XXI, 1999 (1996).

León-Portilla, Miguel. *El destino de la palabra. De la oralidad y los códices mesoamericanos a la escritura alfabética.* Mexico: Fondo de Cultura Económica, 1996.

León Portilla, Miguel L. *Literaturas de Mesoamérica.* Mexico: SEP-Cultura, Cien de México: 1984.

Lockhart, James. "Y la Ana lloró: cesión de un sitio para casa, San Miguel Tociulan." *Tlalocan* 8 (1980): 22–33.

López Austin, Alfredo. "Cosmovisión y salud entre los Mexicas." In *Historia General de la Medicina en México,* Vol. I. Mexico: UNAM, 1984.

López Austin, Alfredo. *Cuerpo Humano e Ideología.* Mexico: UNAM, 1984.

López Austin, Alfredo. "Los acuerdos de San Andrés entre la paz y la guerra." *Chiapas* 6 (1998): 206.

Lovera, Sara. "Introducción." In *Las Alzadas,* ed. Sara Lovera and Nellys Palomo. Mexico: CIMAC—*La Jornada,* 1999 (2nd edition), p. 16.

Lovera, Sara and Nellys Palomo. *Las Alzadas*. Mexico: CIMAC—*La Jornada*, 1999 (2nd edition), pp. 322–326.

Lugo, Carmen. "Pioneers and Promoters of Women." *Sisterhood is Global*, ed. Robin Morgan, pp. 444–456, esp. p. 445. Harmondsworth: Penguin, 1985.

Marcos, Subcomandante. "La cuarta guerra mundial," *Ideas* 1, no. 3 (December 2001): 18–30.

Marcos, Subcomandante. "Testimonios de lucha Zapatista (EZLN): El 'Primer Alzamiento', marzo de 1993." In *Las Alzadas*, ed. Sara Lovera and Nellys Palomo, op. cit., pp. 60–61.

Marcos, Sylvia. "Beyond Binary Categories: Mesoamerican Religious Sexuality." In *Religión and Sexuality in Cross-cultural Perspective*, ed. S. Ellingson and M. C. Green. New York: Routledge, 2002.

Marcos, Sylvia. "Embodied Religious Thought: Gender Categories in Mesoamérica." *Religión* 28, no. 4 (October 1998).

Marcos, Sylvia. "Gender, Bodies and Cosmos in Mesoamerica." In *Feminist Post-Development Thought,* ed. K. Saunders. London: Zed Books, 2002.

Marcos, Sylvia. "Gender and Moral Precepts in Ancient Mexico: Sahagun's Texts." In *Concilium*, ed. Anne Carr and Elizabeth Schlüssler Fiorenza. No. 6 (December 1991).

Marcos, Sylvia. "Género y reivindicaciones indígenas." *La Doble Jornada*, December 5, 1994, pp. 1, 4.

Marcos, Sylvia. "Mesoamerican Religions." *Encyclopedia of Women in World Religion*. New York: Macmillan Reference, 1999.

Marcos, Sylvia. "Mujeres, cosmovisión y medicina: las curanderas mexicanas." In *Trabajo, poder y sexualidad*, ed. Orlandina de Oliviera. Mexico: El Colegio de México, 1992 (1989).

Marcos, Sylvia. "Mujeres indígenas: notas sobre un feminismo naciente." *Cuadernos Feministas* 1 no. 2 (1997): 14–16.

Marcos, Sylvia. "Pensamiento Mesoamericano y categorías de género: Un reto epistemológico." In *La Palabra y el Hombre*. No. 6. Xalapa: Universidad Veracruzana, 1995.

Marcos, Sylvia. "Religion y Genero." *Enciclopedia Iberoamericana de Religiones*. Vol. 3. Madrid: Trotta, 2004.

Marcos, Sylvia. "Sacred Earth: Mesoamerican Perspectives." In *Concilium*, ed. Leonardo Boff and Virgil Elizondo. No. 5 (October 1995).

Marcos, Sylvia. *Taken from the Lips: Gender and Eros in Mesoamerican Religions*. Leiden: Brill, 2006.

Marcos, Sylvia. "Twenty-Five Years of Mexican Feminisms." *Women's Studies International Forum* 22, no. 4 (1999): 431–433.

Marcos, Sylvia, and Marguerite Waller. *Dialogue and Difference: Feminisms Challenge Globalization*. New York: Palgrave, 2005.

Mataira, Peter J. "*Mana* and *Tapu*: Sacred Knowledge, Sacred Boundaries." In *Indigenous Religions*, ed. Graham Harvey, pp. 99–112. London and New

York: Cassell, 2000. McCutcheon, Russell T. "Taming Ethnocentrism and Trans-Cultural Understandings." In *Perspectives on Method and Theory in the Study of Religion*, ed. Armin W. Geertz, Russell T. McCutcheon. Adjunct Proceedings of the 17th Congress of the International Association for the History of Religions, Mexico City, 1995. Leiden, Boston, Köln, 2000.

Memoria. "Hablan las mujeres Zapatistas: 8 de Marzo, Día Internacional de la Mujer." *Memoria* 146 (April 2001): 39.

Menchu Tum, Rigoberta. *Memoria: Primera Cumbre de Mujeres Indígenas de América*. Mexico: Fundación Rigoberta Menchu, 2003.

Millán, Margara. "En otras palabras, otros mundos: la modernidad occidental puesta en cuestión." *Chiapas* 6. Mexico: Era, 1998, pp. 213–220.

Miller, Robert Ryal. *Mexico: A History*. Norman: University of Oklahoma Press, 1986.

Mohanty, Chandra. "Under Western Eyes: Feminist Scholarship and Colonial Discourses." In *Third World Women and the Politics of Feminism*, ed. Chandra Mohanty, A. Russo, L. Torres. Bloomington: Indiana University Press, 1991.

Mohawk, John. "A Native View of Nature." Interview with Charlene Spretnak, in *Resurgence* 178 (September–October 1996): 10–11.

Momsen, Janett Henshall. *Women and Development in the Third World*. London: Routledge, 1991, pp. 40, 101.

Montemayor, Carlos. *Arte y composición en los rezos sacerdotales mayas*. Merida: Facultad de Ciencias Antopológicas de la Universidad de Yucatán, 1995.

Montemayor, Carlos. *Arte y trama en el cuento indígena*. Mexico: Fondo de Cultura Económica, 1998.

Moore, Henrietta L. *Feminism and Anthropology*. Minneapolis: University of Minnesota Press, 1988.

Morgan, Robin, ed. *Sisterhood is Global*. Harmondsworth: Penguin, 1985, p. 443.

Morrison, Kenneth M. "The Cosmos as Intersubjective: Native American Other-Than-Human Persons." In *Indigenous Religions*, ed. Graham Harvey, pp. 23–36. London and New York: Cassell, 2000.

Nash, June. *Mayan Visions: The Quest For Autonomy in an Age of Globalization*. New York and London: Routledge, 2001.

Olivera, M. "La consulta por los derechos de las mujeres en Chiapas." *Memoria* 139 (September 2000): 23–27.

Olson, David R., and Nancy Torrance, eds. *Cultura escrita y oralidad*. Translated by Gloria Vitale. Barcelona: Gedisa, 1998. Original title: *Literacy and Orality*. Cambridge: Cambridge University Press, 1991.

Olupona, Jakob K. (ed.). *Beyond Privitivism: Indigenous Religious Traditions and Modernity*. New York and London: Routledge, 2004.

Olupona, Jakob K. "Report on the Conference Beyond Privitivism: Indigenous Religious Traditions and Modernity." Davis, CA, March 1996, ms.

Ong, Walter J. *Orality and Literacy: The Technologizing of the Word.* London and New York: Routledge, 1982.

Oyewumi, Oyeronke. *The Invention of Women.* Minneapolis and London: University of Minnesota Press, 2003 (1997).

Palomo, N. "San Andrés Sacamchen. Si caminamos parejo, nuestros corazones estarán contentos." In *Las Alzadas,* op. cit., p. 450.

Pérez Cardona, Antonio. "La Ley Bartlett detiene la lucha por el reconocimiento indígena." *La Jornada* September 1, 2001, p. 17.

Perfil de *la Jornada,* February 17, 2001.

Perfil de *la Jornada,* March 29, 2001.

Pitarch, Pedro, Shannon Speed, and Xochitl Leyva. *Human Rights in the Maya Region.* London and Durham, NC: Duke University Press, 2008.

Prabhu, Joseph. "Raimon Panikkar on Colonialism and Interculturalism." *News,* Bulletin of the Harvard University Center for the Study of World Religions 2, no. 1 (Fall 1994): 1, 4–5.

Pratt, Mary Louise. *Imperial Eyes: Travel Writing and Transculturation.* London and New York: Routledge, 1992.

Primera Cumbre de Mujeres Indígenas de las Américas. "Gender from the Indigenous Women's Perspective." *Background Papers.* Oaxaca: First Indigenous Women Summit of America, December 2002, pp. 27–38.

Primera Cumbre de Mujeres Indígenas de las Américas. "Género desde la visión de las mujeres indígenas." First draft, Universidad de las Regiones Autónomas de la Costa Caribe Nicaraguense (URACCAN), *Primera Cumbre de Mujeres Indígenas de las Américas,* Oaxaca, December 2002, Working document.

Primera Cumbre de Mujeres Indígenas de las Américas. "Mensaje de las mujeres indígenas mexicanas a los Monseñores de la Comisión Episcopal de Indígenas." *Delegación de Mexico firmada por 39 mujeres asistentes a la Primera Cumbre de Mujeres Indígenas de las Américas,* Oaxaca, December 2002, ms.

Ramona, Comandanta. 1995. "Mensaje de Ramona." In *Las Alzadas,* op. cit., p. 303.

Reyes Heroles, Federico. TV talk, Channel 11, March 22, 2001.

Robles, Sofía and Regino, Adelfo. "Floriberto Díaz y el renacimiento indígena." *La Jornada Semanal,* no. 314, Mexico, March 2001.

Rojas, Rosa. "Agenda." *La Jornada,* Mexico, March 15, 2001.

Sánchez, Martha. "Ya las mujeres quieren todo." *Cuadernos Feministas* 3, no. 15 (2001): 31.

Scheindlin, Dahlia. "Inés Talamantez Speaks on Religious Studies." *News,* Bulletin of the Harvard University Center for the Study of World Religions 3, no. 2 (Spring 1996): 3.

Schroeder, Susan, Stephanie Wood, Robert Haskett. *Indian Women of Early Mexico.* Norman and London: University of Oklahoma Press, 1997.

Smith, Jonathan Z. "Religion, Religions, Religious." In *Critical Terms for Religious Studies*, ed. Mark C. Taylor. Chicago and London: University of Chicago Press, 1998.

Speed, Shannon. *Rights in Rebellion: Indigenous Struggle and Human Rights in Chiapas*. Stanford, CA: Stanford University Press, 2008.

Speed, Shannon, Aida Hernandez, and Lynn M. Stephen. *Dissident Women: Gender and Cultural Politics in Chiapas*. Austin: University of Texas Press, 2006.

Spivak, Gayatri Chakravorty. *A Critique of Postcolonial Reason*. Cambridge, MA: Harvard University Press, 1999.

Stephen, Lynn. *Women and Social Movements in Latin America: Power From Below*. Austin: University of Texas Press, 1997.

Sullivan, Lawrence E. "Foreword to Johannes Wilbert's *Mindful of Famine: Religious Climatology of the Warao Indians*." *News*, Bulletin of the Harvard University Center for the Study of World Religions 4, no. 2 (Spring 1997): 4–5.

Taylor, Mark C., ed. *Critical Terms for Religious Studies*. Chicago and London: University of Chicago Press, 1998.

Tedlock, Barbara. *Time and the Highland Maya*. Albuquerque: University of New Mexico Press, 1982.

Tedlock, Barbara, ed. *Dreaming. Anthropological and Psychological Interpretations*. Santa Fe, NM: School of American Research Press, 1992.

Tedlock, Dennis. *The Spoken Word and the Work of Interpretation*. Philadelphia: University of Pennsylvania Press, 1983.

Thompson, Charles D., Jr. "The Unwieldly Promise of Ceremonies: The Case of the Jakalteco Maya's Dance of the Conquest." In *Indigenous Religions*. London and New York: Cassel, 2000.

Tong, Rosemarie. *Feminist Thought*. London: Routledge, 1993.

Touraine: see Gil Olmos, José.

Vera, Ramón. "Autonomía no es independencia, es reconciliación." *La Jornada*, March 27, 2001, p. 6.

Viqueira, Juan Pedro. "El discurso usocostumbrista." *Letras Libres*. Mexico, March 2001.

Vogt, Evon Z. *Zinacantán. A Mayan Community in the Highlands of Chiapas*. Cambridge, MA: The Belknap Press of Harvard University, 1969.

Yolanda, Comandanta. "El viaje de la palabra." Perfil de *la Jornada*, February 17, 2001, p. 4.

Yuval Davis, N., and D. Stasiulis, eds. *Unsettling Settler Societies: Articulations of Gender, Race, Ethnicity and Class*. London: Sage Publications (Sage Series on Race and Ethnic Relations), 1995.

Zapatista Women. "Ley Revolucionaria de Mujeres." In *Las Alzadas*, ed. Sara Lovera and Nellys. pp. 59–60. Palomo. Mexico: CIMAC—*La Jornada*, 1999 (2nd edition).

About the Editor and Contributors

Frédérique Apffel-Marglin is Professor Emerita, department of Anthropology, Smith College, Massachusetts, and Director of the nonprofit Centro Sachamama in the Peruvian High Amazon. Her latest book is *Rhythms of Life: Enacting the World with the Goddesses of Orissa*. She is finishing a book based on her experiences in Peru entitled *Subversive Spiritualities and Science: Beyond Anthropocentrism*.

Ana Mariella Bacigalupo is Associate Professor of Anthropology at SUNY Buffalo. She researches Mapuche shamans in Chile. Her books include *Shamans of the Foye Tree: Gender, Power and Healing Among the Chilean Mapuche* (2007) and *The Voice of the Drum in Modernity: Tradition and Change in the Practice of Seven Mapuche Shamans* (2001).

Nuvia Balderrama Vara is a Nahua indigenous woman working with CIDAHL AC on women's rights and citizenship issues. She is also a dancer and has been committed to revitalizing the indigenous identity of her native town, Tepoztlan and to foster environmental care. She has contributed to the academic domain with writings and analysis in research collaboration with CRIM (CentroRegional de Investigaciones Multidisciplinares) of UNAM, Universidad Nacional Autonoma de Mexico.

Diane Bell is a feminist anthropologist who, over the past two decades, has written with passion and courage about the rights of indigenous women (with a particular focus on the Aboriginal people of Australia), indigenous land rights, human rights, indigenous religions, violence against women, and the writing of feminist ethnography. Her books include *Daughters of the Dreaming* (1983/93), *Generations: Grandmothers, Mothers, and Daughters* (1987), *Law: The Old and the New* (1980); *Religion in Aboriginal Australia* (co-edited 1984), *Radically Speaking: Feminism Reclaimed* (co-edited 1996), *Ngarrindjeri Wurruwarrin: A World That Is, Was, and Will Be* (1998), *Evil: A Novel* (2005), and *Kungun Ngarrindjeri Miminar Yunnan: Listen to Ngarrindjeri Women Speaking* (2008).

Janet Chawla holds an MA in Theology and directs MATRIKA, a nongovernmental organization advocating traditional midwifery and noninvasive birth methods. Based in New Delhi, she researches, lectures, and writes on the religiocultural and ethnomedical traditions of dais. Her edited work, *Birth and Birthgivers: The Power behind the Shame*, explores Indian women's birth culture.

Laurel Kendall is Curator of Asian Ethnographic Collections at the American Museum of Natural History and Adjunct (full) Professor at Columbia University. Among her publications are *Shamans, Housewives and Other Restless Spirits: Women In Korean Ritual Life* (1985), *The Life and Hard Times of a Korean Shaman* (1988), *Getting Married in Korea: Of Gender, Morality, and Modernity* (1996), and *Shamans, Nostalgias, and the IMF: South Korean Popular Religion in Motion* (2009).

Renee Linklater is a PhD candidate at OISE/University of Toronto. Her research is entitled *Decolonising Trauma Work: Indigenous Practitioners Share Stories and Strategies*. She is the author of *Weaving the Web of Families: My Journey through Adoption* (2003), *Journey of Our Spirits: Challenges for Adult Indigenous Learners* (2002), and *Aboriginal Women and Community Development* (1998).

Morna Macleod is a freelance researcher and development consultant based in Mexico City, currently working on a book based on her doctoral thesis: *Culture and Politics and the Struggle for Mayan Self-Representation in Guatemala, 1970–2005*. She has written widely on local power and indigenous women and indigenous movements in Guatemala.

Sylvia Marcos researches and writes on gender and women's issues in ancient and contemporary Mexico. She has taught at Harvard University, Union Theological Seminary, and Drew Theological Seminary, among others. At

Claremont Graduate University, School of Religion, she has been Visiting Professor since 1996 of Gender in Mesoamerican Religions. She is the author or editor of several books and many articles on the history of psychiatry, religion, and women's popular culture in pre-Hispanic and contemporary Mexico. Among them are: *Religion y Genero, Volume III, Encyclopedia Iberoamericana de Religiones,* (Madrid: Trotta, 2004), *Dialogue and Difference: Feminisms Challenge Globalization* (coeditor, 2005), *Gender/Bodies/Religions* (editor, 2000), and *Taken from the Lips: Gender and Eros in Mesoamerican Religions* (2006). Dr. Marcos has conducted extensive ethnohistorical research on the construction of gender and sexuality in both indigenous and colonial religious culture. She is a member of the editorial board of *RELIGION,* International Editor of *Gender and Society,* International Editor of *Journal of Feminist Studies in Religion* (JFSR), and International Editorial Advisor for the journal *ALTER/NATIVE.* She is founding member of the International Connections Committee of the AAR (American Academy of Religion) and a member of the permanent Board of Directors of ALER (Asociacion Latioamericana para el Estudio de las Religiones). In Mexico Dr. Marcos is a founding senior member of the Permanent Seminar on Gender and Anthropology with the IIA (Instituto de Investigaciones Antropologicas) at UNAM (Universidad Nacional Autonoma de Mexico). She teaches seminars at Colegio de Mexico's PIEM (Programa Interdisciplinario de Estudios de la Mujer) and at CEIICH (Centro de Investigaciones Interdisciplinares en Ciencias y Humanidades) of UNAM.

Ana María Salazar Peralta is Anthropologist at the Research Institute in Anthropology of the Universidad Nacional Autónoma de México; Professor of Graduate Studies in Anthropology, Philosophy School, UNAM; and founder of the Permanent Seminar on Anthropology and Gender (1991). Among her recent studies is *Ethnopolitical Movements in the Community of Original Towns of Tepoztlán* (2009).

Darilyn Syiem is a teacher and women's rights activist. She is currently with the Shillong Polytechnic, the North East Network and People's Learning Center in Shillong, Meghalaya. Her concerns are bridging social communication gaps, gender sensitivity, and natural resource management.

Hien Thi Nguyen got her bachelor of literature and Russian in Russia in 1987, and master's (1999) and PhD (2002) in folklore with a minor in religious studies at Indiana University. She worked as a postdoctoral fellow at American Museum of Natural History in New York (2003) and at the University of California, Los Angeles (2004). She is currently a researcher at Vietnam Institute of Culture and Arts Studies, Ministry of Culture, Sports and Tourism. Her recent interest and work focus on transnational rituals will be incorporated into a book coauthored with Karen Fjelstad, San Jose State University. Her newest coedited book is *Possessed by the Spirits: Mediumship in Contemporary Vietnamese Communities* (Cornell Southeast Asia Program, 2006).

Index

Machi Abel, 164
Aboriginal and Torres Strait Islander Heritage Protection Act, 5, 13
Aboriginal Healing Foundation, 221–22
Advaita philosophy, 134
Aging ideology, 79–80
Agreement in Principle, 221–22
Agriculture: affinity with nature and, 28–29; Andean rituals for, 23–27; calendar/cycle for, 55, 75; rain-invoking rituals and, 69–71, 77–86; of Tepoztlán peoples, 72, 82–84
Agronomy, 23–26
Ajxup, Doña Virginia, 198–99, 200
Alexandrina Council, 15
Altepehuitl festival, 189–90
Altered state of consciousness (ASC), 146, 148–49, 155–56, 158–66
Alterity of spirits, 102, 109
Amelia Park, Goolwa, 14
American Baptists, 115
Machi Ana, 155, 157
Ancestors/ancestral traditions: cosmo-vision and, 72, 75; following, 116, 186, 195, 199; gender duality and, 57; indigenous spirituality and, 46, 51, 58, 61–64; manifesting, 98, 106, 107; Mayan, 199; mother (*Ka Iawbei*), 116–17, 123; relationship with, 84, 99–101, 120, 217–18, 223–24; wisdom from, 48, 124, 160–61, 164, 210.

See also Costumes; Religion/religious practices; Ritual(s)
Andean culture, 22–27, 35–41. *See also* Yarqa Aspiy festival
Angas, George French, 9
Animals: caring for, 28, 32, 136; cattle festivals, 32; gender equity and, 56, 59, 61; horses/horsemanship, 32, 146–48, 153–57, 159, 162; husbandry, 26, 35; kinship with, 75, 147–50, 164, 165–66, 200; in rituals, 32, 146–47, 155–56; souls of, 153–58; as spirits, 40, 153–58; wisdom from, 6, 10, 23, 27
Anishinaabe wellness, 223–28
Anunciación, Fray Domingo de la, 186
Apology to Australia's Indigenous People, 13
Apprentice/apprenticeship, 98, 100, 107
Asociacion Bartolome Aripaylla (ABA), 26–27, 28–29, 39
Assembly of First Nations, 221
Association of Women in Development's (AWID), 196–97
Austin, Alfredo López, 55, 80
Authorities for rituals, 31–34
Axis mundi, 71–72
Aymara indigenous women, 61
Ayurveda, 132, 134, 135

Bacigalupo, Ana Mariella, 102–3
Ba dong. See Vietnamese shamans

Balzer, Marjorie Mandelstam, 102–3
Basket weaving, 3–4, 7–10, 203
Batzibal, Juana, 200
Becerril, Alicia María Júarez, 79
Bellrose, Eddy, 225
Bemata deity/goddess, 129, 136
Berndt, Ronald and Catherine, 8
Bighorn Medicine Wheel, Wyoming, 225
Big toe ritual, 134, 135
Bihar workshop, 135
Birth Grandmother spirit, 107
Birth traditions, 95–96, 120, 130–32. See
    also Dais (midwife) birth imagery
Black magic, 37
Blood (molfuñ), 148–49
Body-governing God (momju taesin),
    101–2
Body-mind complex, 128
Bonney Reserve, 12
Boundary Bluff, 12
Bourguignon, Erika, 164
Boy attendant spirits, 109
Breath-sharing kinship, 149–50
Broda, Johanna, 74
Brodie, Aunty Veronica, 5–6, 15
Brown, Nanna Ellen, 8
Buddha's Birthday, 100, 107
Buddhist Sage spirit, 107
Burma, 95, 116
Bush tucker, 4, 5, 12
Butler, Judith, 53, 95

Cabalas, Christian, 37
Cajete, Gregory, 220
Camp Coorong, 5, 6–10
Canadian indigenous populations. See
    Colonization
Caste, in birth traditions, 130–32
Catholic religion: abuse from, 221;
    Andean spirituality and, 27; conflict
    over, 37–39; cosmo-vision and, 70;
    ecofeminist theology vs., 61; in India,
    115; indigenous spirituality and, 45–46,
    79; in Latin America, 47–48; Mapuche
    sacred numerology and, 155; Mexican
    bishops, 51–53; rituals and, 34–35, 83;
    social roles in, 71

Cattle festivals, 32
Cave rituals, 76–82
Centro de Estudios e Información de la
    Mujer Multiétnica (CEIMM), 46
Chachahuate (ceremonial meal), 181
Chacra (cultivated field), 23–24, 27
Chatterbox Mansin, 102
Chau van music, 100, 107, 108
Chauveau, Jean Dubernard, 186
Chicha (fermented corn water), 28, 34
Chief/chieftans, 117, 120, 121, 124–25,
    178
Childbearing: agrarian life and, 83;
    Catholic religion and, 51; fertility
    rituals for, 72–73, 75; gender roles and,
    127, 138–39; geomysticism and, 138;
    mapping and, 129; power through, 71,
    73, 83, 187–88; shamans and, 152–53.
    See also Reproduction/reproductive
    rights
Child/children: basket weaving and,
    8; bond with, 132; burial site of, 16;
    care of, 4, 32, 98, 128, 131, 204, 210;
    complementarity and, 203; education
    of, 8, 23–24; environment and, 9–10;
    foster care and, 218, 221; gender roles
    and, 201; marriage prospects of, 96;
    religion and, 220–21; rituals and, 31,
    106–7, 179–80; stories and, 17
Child Spirits, 102, 107
Chilean shamans. See Mapuche shamans
Chimalacatepec cave, 76–77
Chinelo jump, 183
Chinese statecraft, 103
Chirix, Emma, 205–6
Christians/Christianity: ancestral spirits
    and, 161; Andean spirituality and, 27;
    in Canada, 220; "classical theism"
    and, 61; Eve in, 128; as faith healers,
    121–22; in India, 115–16, 121;
    indigenous spirituality and, 40, 45–46,
    50, 54–55; shamans and, 36, 38, 96.
    See also Catholic religion
Chueca sticks, 155
Cisnero, Modesto, 27–28
Clan (kur), 116–17
Cleanliness concept, 131

Climate change, 82, 86
Clothing. *See* Costumes
Cockles, 12
Co-gender identities, 146
Collectivity: Andean spirituality and,
36; as collective memory, 80, 82;
indigenous spirituality and, 51–52,
62–64, 84, 86, 178; political, 48
Colonialism, 48, 64, 65, 222
Colonization: Anishinaabe wellness and,
223–28; decolonization and, 222–24;
healing from, 221–22; history of,
218–21; Medicine Wheel teachings
and, 224–28; overview, 217–18
Comandanta Esther, 63
Comision Episcopal de Indígenas, 51
Community (*comunera*), 24, 27, 29, 31,
39, 71, 133, 189
Complementarity: as controversial, 63;
gender equity and, 85; in Mayan's
women's lives, 201–4; principle of,
52, 57–58, 195–201; regulatory or
emancipatory frames in, 204–6
Confucian marriage bond, 101
Consciousness: altered states of, 146,
148, 149, 155–56, 158–66; community,
189; magic, use of, 22; *zuam* as, 160
Cord-cutting traditions, 132–33
Cosmology/cosmo-vision: ancestral
traditions and, 72, 75; cultural
practices and, 70–71, 75; defeat of,
38; ethnic-territorial identity and,
75; Mayan gendered spirituality and,
197–201; Mesoamerican, 74, 75, 85;
modernity and, 21; overview, 209–10;
principles of, 46–48, 50, 56–64;
sexism and, 207–9; of Tepoztlán
peoples, 72
Costumes: Korean shamans and, 93–95,
97, 100, 102–5; *kut* and, 93–95,
97, 100, 105–6; magic and, 94; for
mediums, 104–5; in rituals, 76, 93–95,
189; Vietnamese shamans and, 93–95,
97, 100
COTESU (Swiss development project),
23, 29
"Countenance" concept, 199

Courtesan, 96
Cree teachings, 225, 226
Crianza (language of nurturance), 36
Criar (nurturing), 29
Cultural affirmation/roots: colonization
and, 217–28; community (*comunera*),
24, 27, 29, 31, 39, 71, 133, 189;
gender and, 58; of geography, 73–74;
of indigenous women, 48–49; in
rain-inducing rituals, 71; shamanism
and, 97–98; sociocultural dynamics,
69–70; stories and, 3–5, 10, 17. *See
also* Ancestors/ancestral traditions;
Elders; Old People; Ritual(s)
Cunningham, Myrna, 46

Daahatun (healing ritual), 152, 162
Dais (midwife) birth imagery: caste and,
130–32; cosmic/earthly connections,
136–38; gender poetics, 138–39;
maternal connections, 132–34; *narak*
and, 136–38, 139–40; overview,
124–29; during postpartum, 137–38;
relational body in, 134–36
Damsel spirits, 108–9
Dancing, 12, 96, 104, 182–84
Dao Mau. See Mother Goddess Religion
de Alarcón, Hernando Ruíz, 77
Decolonization, 53–54, 222–24
Deities: Bemata deity, 129, 136; Catholic
religion and, 27; gender roles of, 102;
geomysticism and, 136; inert material
and, 21–22; Matri Masaan deity, 136;
Ngünechen deity, 146, 161, 162–63;
personification of, 61, 70, 146;
possession by, 165, 166; protection by,
101, 157, 162; relations among, 59,
101; rituals for, 84, 121–23, 160–61;
seduction of, 153; shamans and, 93,
95, 107–8, 155; of Tepozteca's, 73, 75,
83–84; water as, 30, 33, 40; *yeyecatl-
yeyecame*, 72. *See also* Spirit(s)
Descartes, René, 37–38
Destiny, 95, 97, 102, 160
"Divinity of Duality," 55
Divorce, 31, 97, 208
Dodd, Aunty Margaret, 4

Domination, 146–47, 154, 166, 195, 220, 224. *See also* Patriarchy/patriarchal domination
Dong thay (master mediums), 98–99
Duality principle: gender and, 56–59; in Mayan's women's lives, 201–4; overview, 54–56; principle of, 197–201; regulatory or emancipatory frames in, 204–6
Dube, Leila, 128
Dumont, Jim, 227–28
Dungumachife (translator), 149
Duran, Bonnie and Eduardo, 228

Earth (*narak*), 136–38
Ecofeminist theology, 45, 61–62
Ecstasy state. *See* Altered state of consciousness
Education: of children, 8, 23–24; environment and, 119; lack of, 131, 202; in Latin America, 47; modern, 23–26, 39; residential schools and, 219, 220–22; tradition knowledge and, 51, 222
"Effeminate" men, 93, 102
Ehecatl culture, 70, 74–77
Elders: authorities for rituals, 31–34; health warnings by, 120–21; as inner spirit, 7; Medicine Wheels teaching by, 222–28; oral traditions and, 56; respect for, 4. *See also* Old People
Machi Elena, 147–50
Eliade, Mircea, 159
Emancipatory strategies, 196–97, 204–6
Embodiment, 62, 130, 147, 156–57
Ensoulment, 147
Environmental concerns, 8–10, 13, 60, 119, 139, 200, 226
Episcopal Commission for the Indigenous, 51
Epistemology, 53–55, 210
Equilibrium principle, 58–60, 197–206
Erotic spirituality, 151
Estamos parejos (we are all even), 63
Esther, Comandanta, 48–49
Ethnography, 70, 158
Eurasian shamanisms, 103
Evangelical religion, 27, 28, 35, 39, 51

Faith healers, 121–22
Families, 54–55, 72–73, 75. *See also* Child/children; Motherhood
Fatherhood, 54–55
Feminine/femininity: feminine-masculine dolls, 81, 83; ignorance by, 131; "manly" females, 102; masculine/feminine duality, 54–56, 59, 63, 71; meanings of, 71; pain assumption by, 128; in rituals, 94, 109; by spirits, 107, 151. *See also* Gender/gender issues
Feminism: complimentarity and, 196, 200–201; cosmo-vision and, 195–97; duality and, 58–59, 196, 200; ecofeminist theology, 45, 61–62; future of, 53–54; nonindigenous criticism of, 207; subordination and, 195–96
Fertility rituals, 72–73, 75
Machi *fileu*, 160–64
First Nation's Peoples, 219
"Five Cleans," 131
Fludd, Robert, 37
Fluid duality, 55–56
Foerster, Rolf, 163
Folklore tradition, 85, 97
Food(s), 103, 106, 148–49, 179
Four Worlds Development Project, 225
Freedom of religion, 27, 35, 52
Machi Fresia, 164

Gabriel, Calixta, 46
Galindo, Alfonso, 31
Gates of speech (*malmun*), 98
Gay subculture, 94
Gender/gender issues: co-gender identities, 146; cosmo-vision and, 196–97; cultural construction of, 70–71; duality and, 56–59; equilibrium and, 59–60; of God, 117–18; of Khasi tribe, 123–24; male-centric unconscious and, 71; performance of, 105–9; poetics of, 138–39; spirit gender, 101–2; in Tepoztlán spirituality, 177–79. *See also* Mapuche shamans; Masculine/masculinity; Mayan gendered spirituality; Patriarchy/patriarchal domination

Gender-opposite rituals, 93–95
General spirits, 106
Gente de razón (capacity of reason), 52
Geographic space, 72–74, 77–78, 85–86, 116, 219, 220
Geomysticism, 136, 138, 139
Gevara, Ivone, 61
Ghandi, Mahatma, 130
Giménez, Gilberto, 71
Girija, P., 132
Globalization, 46, 69, 70, 131
Glockner, Julio, 84
God(s)/Goddess(es): *ba dong* and, 94; Bemata goddess, 129, 136; Body-governing, 101–2; brides of, 151–52; Child God, 107; in Christianity, 36, 40, 54, 61, 122, 161, 178; gender issues with, 117–18; invoking, 33, 129, 164, 168; Mountain, 106; Ometéotl, 55; pre-Hispanic, 186, 188; relationship to, 61–62, 117–18; reverence for, 81–82, 117; rituals to, 138; Tepoztecatl, 72, 73, 180, 185; Tepozteco, 187; Tlaloc, 75; Tlalticpaque, 77; *U Blei*, 117–18, 120; wind gods, 73. *See also* Deities; Mother Goddess Religion; Spirit(s)
Gollan, Neville, 10, 14
Goolwa wharf, 16
Granny Koomi, 5–6
Great shaman (*k'un mansin*), 98
Great Spirit Grandmother, 107
Guatemalian Mayans. *See* Mayan gendered spirituality

Hair/hairdo rituals, 96, 151, 179–81, 182
Hamayon, Robert, 101
Harmony principle, 58–59
Hartman, Vicki, 10
Healing. *See* Medicine/healing
Health/health care: among Khasis, 118–19, 123; of cattle, 32; community and, 29, 31, 133; for Elders, 4; gender roles and, 146; holistic, 137; land importance and, 219, 220; rituals and, 149; spirits and, 98–99, 107, 118, 224; *Syiem Sad* and, 119–21; wellness and, 226–28. *See also* Medicine/healing

"Heart" concept, 199
Heavenly Abode (*Ka Dwar U Blei*), 119
Hemming, Steve, 8
Hill worship, 74, 77–78, 85–86
Hindmarsh Island Bridge Act, 14
Hinduism, 136–37
Holistic health, 137
Hoodfar, Homa, 207
Horses/horsemanship, 32, 146–48, 153–57, 159, 162
Huntsman spider totem, 11
Husband(s), 29, 31–32, 107, 122, 135, 152, 166

Immanence, spirituality of, 60–62
Indian Act, 218–19
Indian sacred medicines/healers. *See Dais* (midwife) birth imagery; Khasi tribe
Indigenous spirituality, 46, 50, 51, 56, 58, 61–64
Indigenous women. *See Dais* (midwife) birth imagery; Feminine/femininity; Indigenous Women's Summit of the Americas; Khasi tribe; Korean shamans; Mapuche shamans; Mayan gendered spirituality; Ngarrindjeri people; Tepoztlán peoples, spirituality; Vietnamese shamans; Women's issues
Indigenous Women's Summit of the Americas: decolonizing epistemology, 53–54; duality and, 54–59; embodied religious thought, 62; equilibrium and, 59–60; gender issues and, 56–59; indigenous spirituality and, 50; Mexican bishop's response to, 50–53; modernization of spirituality, 47–50; overview, 45–47; resolutions proposed by, 49–50; spirituality of collectivity, 62–64; spirituality of immanence, 60–62
Individualism, 28
Initiation(s): hairdo rituals and, 179; possession and, 159; religious identity during, 93, 95–99; as shamans, 101–5; spiritual kinship and, 146–50, 152–56, 160, 166
Inner spirit (*Ka Rngiew*), 118–19

Insanity, 96
Inspired speech, 100
In Tepoztlán spirituality: gender/gender issues, 177–79
International Indigenous Women's Forum, 196–97
Invisiones antics, 34–35
Irrigation rituals, 21–22, 27–31
Ixpocatl ritual, 182

Machi Jacinto, 162
Jacobs, Aunty Maggie, 5–7
Jaintia tribe, 116
Machi Javiera, 147–50
Jee (life force), 132
Jiménez, Doña Jovita, 78–82
Jocón, María Estela, 57, 200–201
Machi José, 145

Ka Iawbei (ancestral mother), 116–17, 123
Kaqla women's group, 204–5
Ka Rngiew (inner spirit), 118–19
Karpany, Louisa, 8–9
Kartinyeri, Aunty Doreen (née Gollan), 8, 13–15
Kendall, Laurel, 102
Khasi tribe, Indian indigenous healers: belief system of, 117–18; gender analysis of, 123–24; geography of, 116; health among, 118–19, 123; lineage of, 116–17; medical treatment by, 119–20; other women healers of, 121–22; sacred-secret knowledge of, 122–23. *See also Dais* (midwife) birth imagery
Kinship: animal, 147–50; breath-sharing, 149–50; spiritual, 146, 147–50, 152–56, 158, 160, 166
Konpapüllu (spiritual state), 162
Kopiwe flowers, 147, 150–52
Korean shamans (*mansin*): becoming, 95–97; costume rituals and, 93–95, 97, 100; gender performances by, 105–9; inspired speech by, 100; performing spirits' work, 97–99; rituals and cash, 99–100; robes/costumes for, 102–5; spirit gender and, 101–2

Lord Krishna, 128
Kumarangk (Hindmarsh Island), 5, 7, 13–16
Kungun Ngarrindjeri Yunnan agreement, 16
K'un mansin (great shaman), 98
Kur (clan), 116–17
Kurewen (couple), 149, 151
Kut (costumed rituals), 93–95, 97, 100, 105–6
Küymi (altered state of consciousness), 162

Land (geographic space), 72–74, 77–78, 85–86, 116, 219, 220
Latin America, 45–48, 196. *See also* Indigenous Women's Summit of the Americas
Lee, Diana, 102
Leeches, 7, 12
Len dong (costumed rituals), 93–95, 97, 100
Lenkersdorf, Carlos, 210
Llankalawen leaves, 147, 150, 151
Lopez, Alma, 57–58
López, Marta Juana, 201–2, 207
Lower castes, 130–31
Lyngdoh (Khasi priest), 117

Machaca, Marcela, 21–31, 39–40
Machi: brides, 153; *kutran* (illness), 148, 149; *machiluwün* (machi initiation), 148; Mounted Warrior, 153–58. *See also* Mapuche shamans
Mack, Margaret "Pinkie," 8
Madness, 96
Magic: beings, 4; black, 37; consciousness and, 22; costumes for, 94; flight and, 155, 159; in foods, 148; witch hunts and, 36, 37–38
Maldonado, Druzo, 74
Male-centric unconscious, 71
Malmun (gates of speech), 98
Mandarin spirits, 108
Manitowabi, Edna, 226
"Manly" females, 102
Mansin. See Korean shamans

Mapuche shamans (*machi*): altered states of consciousness and, 158–66; animal kinship and, 147–50; animal souls and, 153–58; gendered relationships and, 158; overview, 145–47; sacred numerology and, 155; seducing a spirit, 150–53
Mapudungun language, 152, 161
Marcos, Sylvia, 199
María, Doña Juana, 84–85
María Cecilia's initiation, 147–50, 156
Machi María Cristina, 156
Marriage: Confucian marriage bond, 101; divorce and, 31, 97, 208; *kurewen* (couple), 149, 151; pregnancy and, 135–36; prospects, 96; shamanism and, 97–98; spiritual, 161, 188
Martin, Lloyd, 226
Masculine/masculinity: altered states of consciousness and, 160, 162, 165–66; co-gender identities and, 146; "manly" females, 102; masculine/feminine duality, 54–56, 59, 63, 71; in rituals, 93–95, 167, 183, 200; by spirits, 101–3, 106–7, 109, 154–55. *See also* Gender/gender issues; Patriarchy/patriarchal domination
Master mediums (*dong thay*), 98–100
Matawayta flowers, 32–33
Maternal body, 127, 134
Mathews, Jane, 14
Matri Masaan deity, 136
Mayahuel culture, 72
Maya K'iche' spirituality, 198, 199, 205
Mayan gendered spirituality: complimentary and, 201–4; cosmogenic principles, 197–201; duality and, 201–4; equilibrium and, 201–4; overview, 195–97, 209–10; regulatory or emancipatory frames in, 204–6; sexism and, 207–9. *See also* Indigenous Women's Summit of the Americas
Mayo, Katherine, 130–31
Mayordomías (traditional community leadership), 84
McHughes, Aunty Eileen, 4, 10–12, 17

McLachlan, Ian, 13
Mechanistic dualistic philosophy, 37–38
Medicine/healing: Ayurveda, 132, 134, 135; colonization and, 221–22; *daahatun* (healing ritual), 152, 162; Elder warnings and, 120–21; faith healers, 121–22. *See also* Health/health care; Khasi tribe
Medicine man (*nongduwai*), 120
Medicine Wheel teachings, 224–28
Meditation, 7, 128
Mediums: Body-governing God and, 102; female, 159–60; spirit costumes of, 104–5; spirit possessions by, 106–9. *See also* Shamans/shamanism
Menchú, Rigoberta, 46, 50, 60
Mendieta, Gualberto Machaca, 25–27, 35
Meningie, 8, 10, 12
Menstrual rhythms, 139
Mersenne, Marin, 37
Mesa (altar), 33
Mesoamerican millenarianism, 85
Mesoamerican spiritual traditions. *See* Indigenous Women's Summit of the Americas; Tepoztlán peoples, spirituality
Mexican bishops, 50–53
Mexican spiritual traditions. *See* Indigenous Women's Summit of the Americas; Mayan gendered spirituality; Tepoztlán peoples, spirituality
Milera, Roslyn, 6
Miller, J. R., 220
Milloy, John S., 220
Miminar (women), 4, 9, 12, 13, 17
Mingka bird (messenger of death), 10–11
Miscarriage prevention, 136
Miwi (inner spirit), 4, 7
Mixcoton Pipiltzín ritual, 179–81
Modal states of being, 135
Modernization: cultural geography and, 74; of education, 23–26, 39; globalization and, 70; of spirituality, 47–50, 82–83
Molfuñ (blood), 148–49
Moloj Mayib', 54
Momju taesin (Body-governing God), 101

Morales, Mario Roberto, 201
Mother Earth, 85
Mother Goddess Religion (*Dao Mau*), 95, 97, 104–5, 108
Motherhood, 54–55, 127, 131, 132–34. *See also* Reproduction/reproductive rights
Motherhood and Traditional Research, Information, Knowledge and Action (MATRIKA), 127, 131–32, 137
Mountain Gods, 106
Mounted warriors, 147, 153–58, 166
Mudang. *See* Korean shamans
Mulyawongk hole, 10
Murray-Darling system, 7
Murray Magpie, 11
Murray Mouth areas, 13
Murrunggung (Brinkley), 7–9
Music/musicians: Reto al Tepozteco and, 188; during rituals, 34, 94, 99–100, 105, 108, 164; shamans and, 98, 104, 182, 183. *See also* Songs/singing

Nabigon, Herb, 226
Narak (earth), 136–38, 139–40
National Aboriginal and Islander Day Observance Committee (NAIDOC), 12
Nativist followers, 79–80
Natural resources, 21, 22, 36–37
Nelson, Gordon, 225
New Community Movement, 96
Newen (strength, power), 148, 161
Newton, Isaac, 38
New Zealand, 46
Neyen (horse's breath), 148
Ngarlung, 6
Ngarrindjeri people: Kumarangk and, 5, 7, 13–16; McHughes, Aunty Eileen and, 4, 10–12, 17; practical reconciliation for, 16–17; Rankine, Aunty Leila and, 5–7, 15; stories and, 3–5, 17; Trevorrow, Aunty Ellen and, 3, 7–10, 17; weaving by, 3–4, 7–10
Ngarrindjeri Regional Authority (NRA), 15–16
Ngatji (totems), 4, 5, 11–12, 15, 17
Ngori (pelican) totem, 5–7

Nguillatun rituals, 155–56
Ngünechen deity, 146, 161, 162–63
Nicaragua, 46
Nimatuj, Irma Alicia Velásquez, 205–6
Nonbelievers, 70, 86
Nongduwai (medicine man), 120
Nonreligious certainty, 37–40
Numerology, 155
Nuñez, Julian, 30
Nunez, Lorenzo, 28, 33
Nünkün (emotion), 160

Occult philosophy, 38
Oehmichen, Cristina, 71
Offerings: benedictions with, 185–86; at Bighorn Medicine Wheel, 225; failure in making, 107; food as, 103, 106, 179; funding, 78; *pago,* 33; preparing, 188, 224; in rituals, 27–28, 60, 76–84, 98–101, 108, 186–87; in shrines, 97; spirits and, 150, 152, 161; during Yarqa Aspiy festival, 32–34
Official spirits, 106–7
Ojibway Indians, 219
Old People: burial sites of, 16–17; *mingka* bird and, 11; pelicans and, 6; spirits of, 15; stories of, 4, 13; weaving and, 8. *See also* Elders
Ometéotl, 55
Ometochtli culture, 74, 186
One Indivisible Truth, 37
One Mile Camp, 10, 12
Ong dong. *See* Vietnamese shamans
Otherness, 72, 102, 155
Other-than-human world: Catholic religion and, 38–39; communal space and, 72; sacredness of, 36; "subaltern," 56; supernatural entities, 73–74; Yarqa Aspiy festival and, 21–22. *See also* Deities; Spirit(s)
Oyo-Yoruba Shango priests, 153

Pago (the offering), 33
Paksu mudang. *See* Korean shamans
Machi Pamela, 152, 156–57, 163–64
Panamenian Kuna chanters, 163
Parikh, N. N., 130

Park Chung-hee regime, 96
Paternalism, 51
Patriarchy/patriarchal domination: male-centric unconscious, 71; of Mapuche, 150, 153; matrilineal tradition and, 124; in school, 202; socio-political power and, 153; transgression to, 80; women's role in, 85–86, 187–88
Pelican totem, 5–7
Performance of gender, 105–9
Personhood. *See* Mapuche shamans
Peru, 23–27. *See also* Andean culture
Petecatl culture, 72
Pinto, Sara, 133–34
Placenta traditions, 132–34
Pondi (Murray Cods), 7
Popular beliefs, 74
Porosity principle, 63
Possession state. *See* Altered state of consciousness
Postpartum imagery, 137–38
Poverty, 53, 96, 99, 129–31, 139, 219
Prakriti (field matter), 127–28
Prayers: Catholic-based, 36; for fertility, 106; for marriage, 152; for remembering, 84; during rituals, 77, 80–82, 120–21, 124, 149; shamans and, 164, 169; for welfare, 118, 122, 157, 161
Pregnancy rituals. *See* Dais (midwife) birth imagery
Princes Hogu spirit, 107
Prince spirits, 107–9
Principia Matematica (Newton), 38
Prophecy, 96, 122
Protestant religion, 37, 38
Puberty, 137
Machi *püllu*, 160–63
Purush (consciousness), 127–28

Quetzalcoatl culture, 70, 72, 74–77
Quispillacta, 23–28. *See also* Yarqa Aspiy festival

Rain-invoking rituals, 69–71, 77–86
Rakiduam (thoughts), 160

Rankine, Aunty Leila, 5–7, 15
Raukkan, 5
Redness of women, 138–39
"Red Road," 222–23
The Reformation, 36–37
Relational body rituals, 134–36
Religion of the Four Palaces (*Tu Phu*), 95
Religion/religious practices: American Baptists, 115; Andean spirituality, 22–27, 35–41; embodied thought, 62; Evangelical sects, 27, 28, 35, 39, 51; freedom of, 27, 35, 52; nonbelievers and, 70, 86; nonreligious certainty *vs.*, 37–40; power structure of, 70; Protestants, 37, 38; syncretism in, 83. *See also* Catholic religion; Christians/Christianity; Ngatji; Prayers; Ritual(s); Shamans/shamanism; Spirituality; Tepoztlán peoples, spirituality; Yarqa Aspiy festival
Remembering, 22–23, 35–37, 84
The Renaissance, 36–37, 38
Reproduction/reproductive rights: Catholic church and, 51; cosmo-vision and, 83; fertility and, 138; gendered poetics of, 138–39; mapping of, 127; patriarchy and, 187–88; shamans and, 152–53; spiritual *vs.* material body and, 127; water and, 73
Residential schools, 219, 220–22
Respect system, 4, 11–12, 40–41
Reto al Tepozteco event, 177–79, 184–85, 188–89
Rewe, 145, 147–49, 155
Rigney, Lizzie, 5
Rimpoche, Khentse, 139
Ritual gendered relationships. *See* Mapuche shamans
Ritual(s): Andean spirituality and, 35–37; animals in, 32, 146–47, 155–56; cash and, 99–101; in caves, 76–82; children and, 31, 106–7, 179–80; dancing at, 12, 96, 104, 182–84; for fertility, 72–73, 75; geography and, 73–74; hairdo, 96, 151, 179–81, 182; for irrigation, 27–29; logic of, 86; Mayan spirituality and, 60; in Mesoamerican

region, 55; object representation in,
82–83; prayers during, 77, 80–82,
120–21, 124, 149; during pregnancy,
134–38; rain-invoking, 69–71, 77–86;
sacrificial, 75; for sustenance, 75; of
Tepoztlán peoples, 69–70, 72. See
also Costumes; Initiation(s); Magic;
Mapuche shamans; Music/musicians;
Offerings; Yarqa Aspiy festival
Machi Rocío, 155, 156, 161
Rodríguez, Ana María, 207–9
The Royal Commission, 13–14, 15
Royal Commission on Aboriginal Peoples,
220
Rudd, Kevin, 13
Runas (humans), 30
Rushes (for weaving), 8–9
Ruwi (country), 4, 7, 12, 15

Sabios (sages), 78
Sacred places, 5, 13, 15, 38, 71, 85
Sacred-secret knowledge, 122–23
Sacred Tree teachings, 225
Sacrificial rituals, 75
Sahumerio (incense), 181
Samuel, Geoffrey, 129
San Andrés de la Cal, 77–78, 80, 82, 84
Sankhya philosophical system, 127
Saunders, Cheryl, 13
Scientific process, 23, 39
"Secret women's business," 13, 15
Seduction, 109, 146, 150–54, 157,
166–67
Selby, Martha Ann, 138–39
Seven Generations Education Institute,
227
Seven Stars spirit, 107
Sexism, 207–9, 210
Sexuality and ritual. See Gender/gender
issues; Tepoztlán peoples, spirituality
Shamans/shamanism: becoming, 95–99;
Body-governing God and, 101–2;
childbearing and, 152–53; Christianity
and, 36, 38, 96; cultural affirmation/
roots, 97–98; dancing and, 12, 96, 104,
182–84; deities and, 93, 95, 107–8,
155; Eurasian, 103; great shaman

(k'un mansin), 98; initiation as, 101–5;
Mapuche, 146; marriage and, 97–98;
music/musicians and, 98, 104, 182,
183; of Northeast Asia, 93–95; poorly
trained, 98; prayers and, 164, 169;
songs/singing by, 96, 107, 148; spirit
possession by, 106–9; suffering and,
95–96. See also Korean shamans;
Mapuche shamans; Mediums;
Ritual(s); Vietnamese shamans
Shining Path, 29, 35
Signs, 24–25, 27
Singh, Anuradha, 134
Sinomoni (spirit mother), 98
Sister Nga, 99
"Sixties Scoop," 218
Snake symbols, 76
Social justice, 46, 49, 53, 197
Sociocultural dynamics, 69–70
Sociopolitical practices, 50
Son, Ixtz'ulu' Elsa, 202–3, 207
Songs/singing: during burial rites, 6; in
rituals, 30, 33, 35, 182; by shamans,
96, 107, 148. See also Music/musicians
South Australia, 8–9
South Australian Museum, 8
South Korea. See Korean shamans
Spirit(s): alterity of, 102, 109; animals
as, 40, 153–58; Birth Grandmother,
107; Boy attendant, 109; Buddhist
Sage, 107; Child Spirits, 102, 107;
Christianity and, 161; Damsel,
108–9; Elders as, 7; feminine, 107,
151; foods for, 148–49; gender and,
101–2; General spirits, 106; Great
Spirit Grandmother, 107; health care
and, 98–99, 107, 118, 224; horses/
horsemanship, 147–48, 153–57,
159, 162; inner spirit (Ka Rngiew),
118–19; Ka Rngiew (inner spirit),
118–19; konpapüllu (spiritual state),
162; Mandarin spirits, 108; masculine/
masculinity, 101–3, 106–7, 109,
154–55; mediums and, 104–9; miwi
(inner spirit), 4, 7; mother (sinomoni),
98; Official, 106–7; of Old People, 15;
possession by, 106–9; Prince, 107–9;

seducing, 150–53; Seven Stars, 107; supernatural entities, 73–74, 96–97; Warrior, 106–7. *See also* Deities; Korean shamans; Mapuche shamans; Other-than-human world; Vietnamese shamans; Water spirit

Spirituality: in Andean culture, 22–27, 35–41; authority and, 177–78; Catholicism and, 46, 79; of collectivity, 62–64; erotic, 151; family life *vs.*, 153; freedom of, 52; gender and, 56–59; of immanence, 60–62; indigenous, 46, 50, 51, 56, 58, 61–64; kinship and, 146, 147–50, 152–56, 158, 160, 166; *machi* and, 146–50, 153; marriage to, 161, 188; Maya K'iche', 198, 199, 205; modernization of, 47–50; multiplicity in, 55; respect system in, 40–41; sacredness of, 61; theme of, 46–47. *See also* Indigenous Women's Summit of the Americas; Mayan gendered spirituality; Religion/religious practices; Tepoztlán peoples, spirituality

Spivak, Gayatri, 54

Stories, 3–5, 10, 17

Strength, power (*newen*), 148, 161

Sturt, Charles, 9

Subordination, 195–96

Subtle body. *See Dais* (midwife) birth imagery

Suffering, 95–96

Sumner, Adeline, 10

Supernatural entities, 73–74, 96–97

Sustenance rituals, 75

Syiem Sad (Chief's female relative), 117, 120, 121, 123–24

Syncretism, 83

Tantric male rites, 134

Taplin, George, 9

Teciuhtlazque (rainmakers), 84

Tedlock, Barbara, 102–3

Tepeilhuitl (hill festival), 76

Tepepulco la Corona, 80–82

Tepoztlán peoples, spirituality: agriculture and, 72, 82–84; *Altepehuitl* festival, 189–90; cultural geography and,

73–74; gender and, 177–79, 185–88; initiation ceremonies, 179–85; overview, 69–73; rain-invoking rituals, 69–71, 77–86; religious pantheon of, 74–77; Reto al Tepozteco event, 177–79, 184–85, 188–89; rituals of, 69–70, 72

Thirty Years War, 37

Three Mile Camp, 10, 11, 12

Three worlds (*triloka*), 136–37

Tickner, Robert, 13

Tiger snake totem, 11

Time-duality, 55

Tiongia, Pauline, 46

Tlaloc culture, 70, 74–77

Tlamazcaqui (priest), 78–80, 84, 86

Tokens of gratitude, 99–100, 123

Total Anishinaabe Person, 228

Toulmin, Stephen, 37, 38

Traditional birth attendants (TBAs), 131–32

Trance state, 98, 123, 162

Trevorrow, Aunty Ellen, 3, 7–10, 14, 17

Trevorrow, Tom, 6, 7, 8, 10, 12

Trevorrow, Uncle George, 6

Triloka (three worlds), 136–37

Truth and Reconciliation Commission, 221

Tu Phu (Religion of the Four Palaces), 95

Turtle eggs, 12

Turtle Island colonization. *See* Colonization

U Blei (God), 117–18, 120

Umbilical cord traditions, 132–33

United Nations (UN), 46

Universidad de las Regiones autonomas de la Costa Caribe Nicaraguense (URACCAN), 46

Upanishads, 134

Usos y costumbres (custom and usage), 177

Valladolid, Julio, 25

Varayoqs (authorities for rituals), 31–34

Veintiuno, Siglo, 201

Velásquez, Amalia, 203–4

Vietnamese shamans (*ong dong/ba dong*): becoming, 95–97; costumed rituals and, 93–95, 97, 100; gender performances by, 105–9; harassment of, 96–97; performing spirits' work, 97–99; rituals and cash, 99–100; robes/costumes for, 102–5; spirit gender and, 101–2
Virgin ritual, 181–82
von Doussa, John, 14–15
Voodoo priests, 153, 164

Wamanis (sacred ones), 28
Warnung (Hack's Point), 12
Warren, Kay, 48
Warrior spirits, 106–7
Water spirit: irrigation rituals, 27–29; modern education and, 23–26; natural resources *vs.*, 21–22; remembering and, 22–23. *See also* Yarqa Aspiy festival
Watson, Ethel Wympie, 9
Weaving, 3–4, 7–10, 203
Wellness teachings, 226–28
Welsh Calvinist Methodists, 115, 120
Wenu Mapu (the Mapuche sky), 147, 148, 156, 157, 164, 168–69
Whiteness of men, 138–39
Willis, Lucía, 202
Wilson, Ellie, 12
Wilson, Victor, 14
Wind gods, 73
Witch hunts, 36, 37–38

Women priestess. *See* Tepoztlán peoples, spirituality
Women's issues: becoming a shaman, 95–99; divorce, 31, 97, 208; ecofeminist liberation theology, 45; female ignorance, 131; husbands, 29, 31–32, 107, 122, 135, 152, 166; motherhood, 54–55, 131, 132–34; rain-invoking rituals and, 84; "secret women's business," 13, 15; spiritual authority, 177–78; urban *vs.* indigenous, 47; witch hunts and, 36, 37–38. *See also* Child/children; Costumes; *Dais* (midwife) birth imagery; Feminism; Indigenous Women's Summit of the Americas; Khasi tribe; Marriage; Miminar; Patriarchy/patriarchal domination; Reproduction/reproductive rights; Weaving

Xochipizahuatl dance, 184

Yarqa Aspiy festival: *invisiones* antics, 34–35; as irrigation ritual, 21, 22, 28, 29–31; offerings/asking permission, 32–34
Yates, Frances, 37
Yeyecatl-yeyecame (lords of weather), 83, 85

Zapil, Juan, 198
Zuam (consciousness), 160